Switchback

Switchback

Matthew Klein

W F HOWES LTD

This large print edition published in 2007 by
W F Howes Ltd
Unit 4, Rearsby Business Park, Gaddesby Lane,
Rearsby, Leicester LE7 4YH

1   3   5   7   9   10   8   6   4   2

First published in the United Kingdom in 2006
by Orion Books

A CIP catalogue record for this book is available
from the British Library

ISBN 978 1 84632 132 0

Typeset by Palimpsest Book Production Limited,
Grangemouth, Stirlingshire
Printed and bound in Great Britain
by Antony Rowe Ltd, Chippenham, Wilts.

For Laura

PROLOGUE

Later, standing over the dead girl's body, the detective decided it made perfect sense. The case wrapped itself up neatly – in a bow, he would explain, to anyone who cared to ask. It was a simple story: about a rich man who had everything, but wanted more; a story about what happens to people who try to break the rules.

The dead girl lay in the kitchen of the rich man's house, her skull crushed by a marble sculpture. Blood had drained from her corpse and gathered in a weird pool near her head, shaped like a cartoon dialog bubble emanating from her mouth, as if she was saying something big and important and red. But her eyes were vacant, and she was dead, and the detective concluded it was unlikely she would say anything important again.

A uniformed cop joined the detective and looked down at the girl.

'Pretty,' the uniform said. The girl was wearing a black cocktail dress, and even though a patch of skull was visible behind her ear, she was still obviously beautiful.

'Anything?' the detective asked.

'Three wine glasses in the sink. Three sets of dishes. They ate steak, and what's that stuff called? The green leaf that people eat?'

'Lettuce.'

'*Arugula*,' the uniform said, as if he had known the answer all along. 'Steak with arugula leaves. That's what they ate.'

The detective stared at the bloody footprints on the floor – a single set, a man's. Near the girl's body a swab of red looked like a knee-print. The detective tried to make sense of it. Maybe the rich man killed her in a fit of passion, and then regretted it, so kneeled down next to her to whisper that he was sorry. Not an easy conversation, probably.

The detective's suit jacket began to play Tchaikovsky's 1812 overture. He reached inside, pulled out his cell phone and flipped it open.

'You find him?' the detective asked.

The voice on the other end was tinny, washed in static, barely audible.

'Only his car,' the voice said. 'Black BMW, right?'

'Where are you?'

'Wells. Mule Canyon.'

'Same cliff as his wife?'

'Yes.'

'And him?'

'Still looking.'

'I'll come down. Give me a couple hours.'

2

The detective closed the phone and dropped it into his pocket. He turned to the uniform. 'They found his BMW. His body can't be far.'

The uniform nodded. 'Then that's two.' He paused, waited for the detective to respond. When he didn't, the uniform said: 'Three sets of dishes. Three wine glasses. Him and the girl—' He indicated the dead woman in the cocktail dress. 'That makes two.'

'Yes,' the detective said. He thought about it. But he didn't have an answer yet. So he walked away to explore the rest of the house.

CHAPTER 1

At half past nine on a Thursday morning, Timothy Van Bender learned that he had lost twenty-four million dollars.

The way he discovered the news was this: while he pried the plastic lid from his coffee cup, holding it over his desk to protect his pants from stains, he looked up and saw the Kid standing in his doorway.

'Timothy,' the Kid said, looking pale. 'Where have you been?'

It was not an accusation. It was a plea for help. The Kid dripped with sweat. Wet cotton bunched under his arms, ruining what was once a crisp white button-down.

Timothy sipped his coffee and put down the cup. He looked at his watch. 'I just got in. The line at the coffee place . . .' He shook his head. For fifteen years his morning ritual had been to visit University Cafe, arriving there at 9.10 a.m. – exactly ten minutes after the rest of the world was required to start work. For fifteen years this ritual had been a success, allowing Timothy to whisk in, buy a bagel and coffee, and glide into his own office. But recently Northern California had changed: every twenty-two-year-old software programmer with long hair and questionable hygiene was now a paper millionaire, and everyone who worked in a cubicle with shoulder-high partitions had somehow become a white-collar employee who set his own hours. This meant that the 8.55 a.m. morning rush at the cafe had somehow turned into a 9.25 a.m. rush, with disastrous consequences for actual millionaires like Timothy, whose wealth pre-dated the Internet by decades, and whose assets were stored not in the ephemeral stock of some surely soon-to-be-worthless Internet shoe retailer, but in cold fungible cash.

Timothy thought about explaining all this to the Kid – that something needed to be done about the line at the coffee place, or the number of paper millionaires in Palo Alto, or the age at which people should be allowed to set their own work-place hours. But then Timothy noticed the sheen on the Kid's face, and the perfectly formed sweat droplet hanging from the Kid's chin. It clung there for a long moment and then fell to the hardwood floor. Timothy decided to say nothing.

The Kid looked over his shoulder, then closed the door. He stepped into Timothy's office. 'We have a problem.'

Timothy pulled the bagel from his brown paper bag. He unwrapped the wax paper, smoothed it over his desk like a table-cloth, and cut his bagel neatly in half with a plastic knife.

'What kind of problem?' Timothy said.

'The yen,' the Kid said. 'Haven't you heard?'

The way the Kid said it, Timothy probably should have heard. But he hadn't. Timothy lived ten blocks away, in a Palo Alto home close to work. His commute consisted of a ninety-second car ride, and then a quick descent into the parking garage under his office building. No time for radio. No time for news.

'Tell me,' Timothy said, neither admitting nor denying that he had heard.

'It's shooting up. It hasn't risen like this in . . .' The Kid shook his head, shrugged. It had never risen like that. Not for as long as the twenty-five-year-old, with three years of finance experience, could remember.

'Where's it at?'

'I don't know. Seventy-five when I last checked. But it's not stopping. The BOJ announced they might buy their own bonds. They're going to try to reflate. It's a new policy. The finance minister held a surprise press conference, and he . . . Jesus, I don't even know where to begin.'

Timothy was a little confused himself. Deflate, reflate . . . buy bonds, sell bonds. It was a bit murky how these actions – or merely the talk of these actions, announced in the bowels of some ministry building in crowded Tokyo, six thousand miles away – could possibly affect his own life in sunny Palo Alto.

Timothy ran his hedge fund without worrying

too much about what those inscrutable Japanese – or anyone else, for that matter – said they were going to do. He had a simple philosophy that made him money year in and year out: he bought things when they were moving up, and sold them when they were moving down. It was easy. And it worked nine times out of ten. There was no other way to beat the market. So many people worked so hard, poring over computer printouts, studying charts, examining the cryptic comments of foreign government officials like so many bird entrails. No, making money was easy if you didn't think too much and didn't work too hard. As the old saw said: The trend is your friend. And: Don't fight the tape.

'Listen, Kid,' Timothy said. He corrected himself. 'Jay. Listen to me. Don't fight the tape. Remember, the trend is your friend . . .' He let his voice trail off. This was a valuable lesson for the Kid, who needed a little seasoning. Timothy had hired him straight out of Stanford Business School. Jay Strauss was a bright Jewish kid, dark and swarthy. But he dressed well, in tailored suits and gold cufflinks, and apparently he had a good head on his shoulders. He had a Harvard degree in economics, and had worked at Salomon Smith Barney in New York after college.

Which is where Smith Calhoun was president. Smith was an old Yale classmate of Timothy, a great guy – not to mention an early investor in Timothy's hedge fund. And so one thing led to another, and one day over drinks in the Four Seasons, Smith said: You ought to meet this Jewish kid; he's graduating Stanford – I'd want him myself, but with the way things are going here at Salomon, it wouldn't be right. Soon enough Timothy had his second full-time employee.

The Kid did all the leg work. He called himself the 'Quant', while Timothy was the 'Face' – the man who raised the money and presented himself to investors, family offices, wealthy people. Timothy would come up with an idea – like, for instance, shorting the Japanese yen – and then the Kid would figure out how to do it, what quantity to short, which brokers to call, where to set the limit price, how much margin would be required. It was a good division of labor, Timothy often thought, because it allowed each person to do what he was good at: the Kid dealt with numbers, Timothy with human beings.

Timothy looked up at the Kid, to see if his words about not fighting the tape had soothed him. The Kid seemed even more pale, and Timothy noticed he was trembling.

'How much did we lose?' Timothy asked.

'Twenty-four.'

'Thousand?'

'Million,' the Kid said. And then, to be clear: 'Dollars. Not yen.'

'I see,' Timothy said. He felt light-headed. The room closed on him like a drawstring sack.

The Osiris Fund II, the fund Timothy managed

and which employed the Kid, had started the year with around a hundred million dollars. Which meant that between the time Timothy went out to dinner the preceding night, and the time he opened his coffee lid this morning, the fund had lost a quarter of its value. Which further meant, for example, that Pinky Dewer, the earliest and largest investor in Osiris, had lost nearly eight million dollars while Timothy was eating tuna tartar and soft shell crabs at Tamarine. And which meant that Timothy himself, who had invested five million of his Van Bender dollars in the fund, had lost over a million dollars before dessert.

'Twenty-four million?' Timothy said again.

'You wanted to make a big bet,' the Kid said, suddenly defensive. 'You said, "Make a big bet." Right?' He stopped, pulled back. More gingerly now: 'Didn't you say that?'

Timothy nodded. 'I did.'

The Kid stared at him, waiting for some kind of instruction, some kind of order. In his life, Timothy had seen that look a thousand times before.

For as long as Timothy could remember, people looked to him as a leader. Some of this came from his deportment – thanks to Father's constant needling, Timothy carried himself rigidly, never slouched, never crumpled under stress. Some of it came from genetic luck: Timothy had been born handsome, with a pleasant face and an easy smile, and people gravitated to men like that.

9

But part of it came from effort. Long ago, Timothy had decided that you could go farther in the world by being willing to say something, even if you were unsure about whether or not your words were right. It is the secret that all successful people eventually learn, but seldom want to share: the mere act of making a decision, of speaking, of taking a chance, is enough. Most people are frozen by fear of failure, but men like Timothy understand that failure, when it comes, is never a permanent state – you can always try again, after all.

When had he first realized this? Maybe he had always known it vaguely, subconsciously. But it had crystallized thirty years earlier, at Exeter. One night, Headmaster Tillinghast – with his buttery jowls, owl glasses and tiny slits for eyes – marched imperiously into the freshman dorm. He announced that everyone in the dorm would be punished equally, and severely, for a horrendous crime. Mickey the janitor, while doing electrical work in the dorm's common room, had discovered an ounce of pot in the space above the drop-ceiling. Only by coming forward and admitting guilt could the culprit save his classmates from what would surely be a life-altering punishment.

That night, hours before Tillinghast was to mete out his sentence, the boys debated. Some wanted to turn in the actual pot-smoking culprit – the sad-faced, gangly Martin Adams – rather than face expulsion. Some boys cried, terrified of wrecked academic careers, parental disappointment, family shame. Expulsion was no idle threat: Tillinghast had done it to poor Chaz Dominick just a month earlier, for showing up to Latin with alcohol on his breath. Other boys – the minority – wanted to fight, to resign from the school en masse, to protest at the barbarous collective punishment.

Then the debate stopped and they turned to Timothy who, even at fifteen, always seemed to have an answer, and who understood the value of presenting it with confidence. 'I'll tell you what we need to do,' he said, without knowing the words that would follow. 'What we need to do is this.' And then, magically, the words were there, and he explained it all clearly and forcefully: they would send a group of three boys into Tillinghast's dark, oak-paneled office the next morning, and they would stand at attention, with their blue blazers and regimental ties, and they would admit, ruefully, that yes, they knew who had placed pot in the ceiling, and they regretted that they had to report such a thing about a former classmate, but their duty to the school required it, and so, they were turning in . . . Chaz Dominick, who had hidden the pot some months earlier.

It hardly mattered that the plan was little more than a hastily concocted scheme, or that it was neither honorable nor true, or that it pinned a crime on an innocent boy who was not present to defend himself – but, rather, what mattered was that it was a plan, a course of action, and

Timothy had proposed it with great confidence and vigor.

Yes, Timothy had seen the look of the Kid many times before – that look of helplessness, of longing to know an answer, any answer. Timothy's life had been a living proof that confidence alone is the answer. Ninety percent of all doubts can be soothed by self-assurance. A solid handshake and a nice suit take care of the other ten.

This was how it had been at Yale, too, where Timothy never worked more than an hour at night – not when there were so many other pleasant distractions: cocktails, parties, time well spent with friends. But Timothy did not fail, or even do poorly; his special talent, as he came to understand it, was the ability to do well by doing the absolute minimum required.

Like all talents, this too required a fine judgment, an aesthetic sense, like that of a painter who knows to use the smallest dab of watercolor to great effect. Sometimes Timothy received good grades in a course by being a vocal participant in the classroom, raising his hand often, drawing tenuous links between Hamlet and, say, Thomas Jefferson – all without having read a page of the course work. In another class, the opposite approach was required: a Tantric stillness, a blending into the background and hardly breathing. In other classes, a well-timed bottle of Macallan twelve given to a Latin professor did the trick, or the purchase of dinner at Mory's. The success Timothy continuously enjoyed – first at Exeter, then at Yale, then in New York, and finally at the helm of Osiris – was not the result of tricking people, or of buying them off. His success came from giving them exactly what they wanted: answers.

And so the Kid, having just witnessed Timothy lose twenty-four million dollars, and worried perhaps about his own young career, about the lead-lined suit he would be forced to wear as a reputation, stood there sweating, the circles under his armpits spreading, his dark complexion strangely sallow, his knees bent, weak, and near collapse. He too wanted an answer from Timothy.

Timothy calmly sipped his coffee. He took great care to keep his hand steady. He put down the cup, recapped it, and then refolded the wax paper over the uneaten half of his bagel.

'I have a plan,' Timothy said, as he waited for it to arrive. 'Here's what we are going to do.'

And then he laid out the plan for the Kid, who lapped it up eagerly, like a bulldog at a rain puddle, and agreed that it was a good plan, and was thankful to be given a task – any task – by a man who could still smile after losing twenty-four million dollars.

CHAPTER 2

The plan, if one could call it that, was simply this: double up the bet and try again.

The yen had briefly risen to seventy-five – that is, one dollar could buy seventy-five of them – but this was an unsustainable price, Timothy explained. The yen, after all, had been falling for over three years. It had plummeted from a hundred and fifteen, down through the psychological barrier of a hundred, and then on down through ninety, through eighty, through seventy, without pause.

Everyone agreed the yen would continue to fall until it reached fifty, its natural level. That's why Osiris had shorted the yen at sixty-nine; that is, it had bet that it would fall even lower than sixty-nine. Osiris sold three thousand futures contracts on the Chicago Mercantile Exchange. Which meant that when the yen fell to fifty, Osiris would make a profit of seventy-one million dollars.

But the original wager had not exactly worked out. Almost the day after Osiris placed the trade, the yen had jumped back to seventy-five. Still, Timothy had explained to the Kid, this was not

14

something to fear. This was typical, and moments like these separated men from boys. Indeed, this was a profit opportunity. So while everyone else was running for the exits, liquidating positions, calling in collateral, Osiris would be able to take advantage of the irrational market. It would double its bet, gambling now with six thousand contracts instead of three thousand, and would be able to make back all its losses, and then some.

So these were the instructions Timothy gave to the Kid. He ticked them off quietly and quickly, like a general to his adjutant under the hail of cannon. First, liquidate all stock positions in order to free up margin. Next, get Refco, Bear Stearns, Barclays, Citigroup on the line. Split the trade across four brokers. No front running.

'And one more thing,' Timothy added.

Jay had already turned to leave. He stopped at the door, his hand perched on the knob. He was eager to get moving, to place the trade, to start making money again.

'We can't alarm our investors,' Timothy said.

The Kid removed his hand from the door. 'Okay,' he said. But he frowned.

'We don't want to tell them about this setback,' Timothy explained, 'not yet. We need to recoup the losses first. When the yen falls back down and we've broken even, then we'll tip our hand.'

'But Timothy,' the Kid said, 'we need to report our results. We send August statements to investors in two weeks.'

'Yes,' Timothy said. 'But two weeks is a long time. Practically forever. You know what can happen in two weeks? Anything. So we'll report then. No use alarming people about details.'

'Okay,' said Jay.

'The thing is,' Timothy continued, 'if our investors find out that Osiris lost twenty-four million dollars, some of them might get antsy. They might pull their money out. And if they pull their money out, then we won't have enough cash to sell six thousand contracts. You see what I'm saying?'

'I think I do,' Jay said.

'What I'm saying,' Timothy continued, 'is that we won't be able to make back the money for the other investors. So, really, it's a question of fairness.'

The Kid said, 'I see.'

'Fairness for all the other investors,' Timothy said again. This was an important point.

'Okay,' Jay said.

'So let's not talk to our investors now. No phone calls. No meetings. Just . . .' He brushed a finger to his lips and let it float away, like ragweed. 'Quiet.'

'Okay, Timothy.'

Timothy smiled and winked. 'See now,' Timothy said, 'this is a great learning experience. Now you'll see how the world really works.'

The Kid nodded. He left the room – in too much of a hurry, Timothy thought – and got to work.

CHAPTER 3

When he finished the remaining half-bagel, Timothy shuffled from his office to the reception area. At work for less than thirty minutes, he had already had a long day.

Osiris was on the twenty-third floor of the Bank of America building, the only tall building in Palo Alto. On a clear day like this one, when everyone else in San Mateo County was twenty floors below him, Timothy could observe his entire world without moving. He could see his own house, ten blocks north: an old Tudor surrounded by ornamental grasses and apricot trees. To the east he could see the Stanford campus, its red Spanish roofs and sun-colored brick, where hundreds of computer scientists scurried into classrooms and wrote the software he used to make money. To the south he could see Sand Hill Road, with its lawyers and venture capitalists and sloshing pools of cash, where investors sat in low-slung office buildings, sipping lattes and smiling at Timothy's perfect money-raising pitches. He could see as far as the San Mateo Bridge and SFO, his portal to Manhattan, where a first-class ticket set him back

17

eight hundred dollars but bought him as much decent cabernet as he could drink in five hours and dropped him thirty minutes from the Four Seasons.

He leaned against the wall of windows, his breath fogging his view of the Bay. Further out, the San Mateo Bridge, an ugly barrel of concrete, was shrouded in its own Bay fog.

'It's a beautiful day,' said Tricia Fountain. Tricia was Osiris' receptionist. She sat at the reception desk, in front of a wall that said in simple brass letters 'Osiris LP'.

Timothy had hired Tricia six months ago, after interviewing a handful of other candidates. Those candidates included a middle-aged black woman with two kids, a Chinese man from Stanford who Timothy suspected was gay, and two fat women whose resumes Timothy failed to read.

No other candidate had Tricia's qualifications. First, she was twenty-three. Second, she had bright blue eyes, dark hair, clear skin, and chiseled cheeks. Third, she dressed well. Today it was navy blazer over cashmere sweater, tight and blue, which displayed her body in a thoughtful, understated way. The way Tiffany's displays engagement rings, Timothy had thought the first time he looked at her breasts. No point being gaudy about them. They speak for themselves.

'Beautiful?' Timothy said.

She was born in Orange County, and – beneath the Ralph Lauren blazer and stylish librarian

18

glasses and fashionable bob in her hair – Timothy found that proud stupidity so common in people from the south of the state. For instance, the way she said, 'Awesome,' when discussing a matter that clearly wasn't awesome in any way. Or the way she once admitted that she had no idea exactly what Timothy and Osiris actually did, and didn't want to. Or the way Timothy often caught her looking at herself in the reflective brass letters that spelled OSIRIS on the wall behind her desk, without embarrassment.

He supposed none of this was surprising, since she had originally wanted to be an actress. That was a profession that Father had always warned him about. The story of how she came to Silicon Valley, fresh from UCLA, was never clear to Timothy. There's a certain decorum required when a forty-seven-year-old man interviews a girl half his age. He can't seem too interested – especially when an EEOC lawsuit might drop from the sky like a vengeful Thor's hammer. Which was a shame, because the few details he did extract from her seemed interesting. Something about her father dying when she was twelve, an acting career that didn't pan out, a spur-of-the-moment road trip north with a drug-addled boyfriend – who now apparently had disappeared into the Bay fog – and then, finally, an afternoon spent at the Stanford Coffee House, where the Kid had met her and suggested she come in to Osiris for an interview.

But however she got to Osiris, the important thing, as far as Timothy was concerned, was that Tricia was very pretty, and very unencumbered, and the sharp prickles of sexual energy he felt when seeing her each morning made the drive to the office exciting, and enlivened otherwise dull days.

Timothy turned to her.

She held up a pink phone message pad. 'There were a few calls while you were in your meeting,' Tricia said. She tore off the top sheets. 'Tran called. He's not coming in today. He's running behind at another client, so he'll come on Monday.' Tran was their part-time computer consultant. He came in once a week to spend a few hours fixing all of the damage Timothy had managed to create in the preceding seven days.

'Good,' Timothy said.

'Pinky Dewer called,' she continued. 'He said it was nothing important; just checking in.'

'Great,' Timothy said. As Pinky was the largest investor in Osiris – and now the largest money-loser – it was vital that Timothy have no contact with him until Osiris could fix the yen situation. He didn't want to have to lie about how things were going. So that meant he would need to accidentally misplace Pinky's message, perhaps under a pile of papers on his desk. Or maybe straight into the trash.

'I'll take that message.' He reached across her desk and tried to snatch the papers from her hand.

She held tight. His fingers grasped hers. She raised an eyebrow.

'And,' she said, 'one more. Your wife called.'

Timothy lowered his hand. He tried to keep his voice neutral. 'Oh?'

'She reminded you about Friday. About Big Sur.'

He and Katherine had been planning a long weekend at the Ventana Inn to celebrate their twentieth wedding anniversary. Originally she had wanted to spend two weeks in Hawaii, but somehow, with a wink and a smile and just the right soothing words, he had managed to talk her down to just three days a mere ninety miles away.

If yesterday Timothy was ambivalent about the trip, today he was dreading it. Certainly, he loved Katherine. He couldn't imagine being without her. But just because you love someone doesn't mean you want to be locked in a rustic cabin with them for three days. When had anniversary celebrations become misdemeanor sentences?

He already knew how the trip would play out: three days of hurt looks and quiet barbs, of forced smiles and trying to be the husband he knew he ought to be, but couldn't. And now, on top of it, there was the small detail that his hedge fund was tottering on the verge of ruin, that his entire reputation and career depended on whether a gaggle of Oriental men in Tokyo woke up in a good mood.

Tricia said: 'She said don't forget to bring your

21

work home tonight. You're leaving tomorrow.' They would be driving down to Big Sur on Friday, and then Timothy would take a three-day weekend.

'Okay,' Timothy said.

'You don't sound very excited,' Tricia said.

'I am excited,' he said dully.

'I wish someone would take me to Big Sur,' Tricia said. She peered at him over the top of her glasses, pushed a strand of hair behind her ear.

'I would offer,' Timothy said. 'But then what would my wife say?'

'Would she have to know?'

They had flirted like this before. It was harmless, Timothy assured himself. Just a distraction, to keep the workplace interesting.

'Something to think about,' he said. He snatched the phone messages from her hand – this time she didn't resist – and turned to go back to his office and stare at the price of the yen.

CHAPTER 4

When he arrived home at four o'clock in the afternoon, the yen thankfully had fallen to seventy-four, and Katherine was having a glass of chardonnay on the back patio. Each of these facts encouraged Timothy equally. With the yen moving in the right direction, perhaps he could enjoy his long weekend with Katherine after all. And that she was having a drink on her own instead of waiting for him at home like a cat anticipating a piece of string, was also a sign that she might be in a good mood, and that their weekend might turn out pleasant.

He slid open the glass door to the patio and walked up behind her. She didn't turn. 'You're home late,' she said. She reached across the table and took a sip of wine.

Timothy followed his wife's gaze into the back yard, to figure out what she was staring at. Whatever it was, it was more fascinating than her husband, because nearly a half-minute passed, and Katherine still hadn't turned around. Alas, he saw only: an apricot tree, still fruitless and barren after many summers; a sixty-dollar clump of ornamental grass from the Arestradero Nursery; and a rock garden studded with bits of moss their landscape designer had assured them was 'interesting.'

He sighed. He put down his briefcase on the slate patio. He leaned over and kissed her neck. 'Happy anniversary,' he said.

She turned around, finally, and looked up at him. 'You remembered.'

'Well,' he said, 'you did call my office to remind me.'

'But that was hours ago,' she said. Her tone was bright, her smile warm, as if she really might be delighted.

'I didn't get any flowers,' he said, figuring preemption now was safer than disappointment later. 'And your gift – I'll give it to you this weekend, at Big Sur.'

'How spontaneous,' she said. Not quite an accusation, and not quite angry. Just disappointed. That would be a fitting epitaph on her tombstone, he thought:

> *Katherine Van Bender*
> *1958–*
> *Disappointed*

Things had been different once. They had met when Timothy was at Yale and Katherine at Smith. Timothy's was the first co-ed class in New Haven, but after an early rush of giddiness about the possibilities co-education would bring, Timothy

24

and his friends were soon disenchanted. The women that ventured into the Ivy League those early years were selected, disappointingly, for their academic records and intellectual prowess, not for their beauty or accommodation. The girls at nearby Smith, in contrast, with their stylish looks, sunny dispositions, and tradition of snaring Yale men, were more eager to please. And so, over the years, Timothy and his friends ventured regularly to Smith – sometimes once or twice a month – to enjoy a party, or to test a particularly promising double- or triple-date.

That was how he had met Katherine. He and his roommate, Chauncey, made the ninety-minute drive to Northampton one weekend because a friend promised an off-campus Smith party that would be remembered for years to come. And while the weekend was remembered, it wasn't for the party. That night it rained, curtains of water, breaking previous New England records. When Timothy's Olds blew a tire on Route 10, he insisted Chauncey stay dry in the car. 'No point in both of us getting wet,' he volunteered, secretly hoping that perhaps Chauncey might feel the same way, and might be quicker to grab the door handle.

But the roommate proved slow on the draw. So, hunched over a jack, on the side of a dark road in Massachusetts, Timothy's blazer soaked, his hair dripping, he stolidly replaced the tire with a spare. Thirty minutes later, with water in his shoes and his shirt clinging coldly against his chest, he and Chauncey found the party. Within a half-hour, Timothy decided he was miserable. He was cold and wet, and his shoes squished like sponges when he walked.

He quietly left the party and drove to a diner, where he would warm himself with hot coffee before returning for Chauncey and the ride home. It was there that he saw her. She was sitting next to him – one table over, alone – sipping a hot chocolate while she read a book (*Rebecca* by Daphne du Maurier). She was clearly a Smith girl: her clothes (peasant skirt, v-necked blouse) said rebellion, but the peaceful, good-taste, moneyed kind, as if the sans culottes had stormed the Bastille merely to install new, less fussy flatware. She was blonde, freckled, fresh-scrubbed, carefully manicured, with her hair parted neatly in the center and loose strands gathered by a barrette.

How she differed from the other Smith girls Timothy had met was this: instead of glancing down shyly at her book, she looked up and stared at Timothy directly, tilting her head, as if considering something important. Then, without breaking eye contact, she said: 'You look absolutely miserable.'

'I was miserable,' Timothy said, and then unleashed his practiced Melt-the-Smith-Girl's-Defenses smile. 'Until about thirty seconds ago.'

'My goodness,' she said, and returned a smile of her own. 'That has got to be the most incompetent line I've ever heard.'

That first encounter summed up Katherine perfectly: direct, clever, outwardly friendly, but with strong bones of anger under her skin – and the ability to slap him into place without warning.

That night she took him back to her apartment (which was rather forward, he thought, as he followed her car), and offered him a dry sweat-shirt and pants that belonged to a man (the name of the original owner he never learned). He expected something else – at least a kiss, maybe more – but she ended that fantasy quickly by saying, as she handed him the dry clothes: 'These will remain on for the rest of the night.'

But she said it with a smile, and that was all it took. Perhaps it was this moment when Timothy decided that this woman enchanted him. She was a mystery, with nothing at all easy about her, in any sense of the word. Every aspect of her was slightly peculiar, from her diction (she enunciated every syllable and sounded like a cross between Kate Hepburn and Queen Elizabeth) to her features (overall quite pretty, but feature-by-feature odd: a nose too aquiline, a chin too promi-nent, so that when she walked she looked like the prow of a ship). Even her socioeconomic class was an enigma – and these things mattered to a man like Timothy – she dressed, and spoke, and carried herself as if she had money; but every now and then, by accident, she stumbled, and it was as if, for a moment, the beautiful heiress at the black-tie ball bent over to reveal a dowdy tattered slip.

Timothy still remembered one of those incidents. It happened early in their courtship, during an afternoon date at New York's Metropolitan Museum of Art. Hand in hand they strolled through the gallery of French pastellists, and they stopped at Ducreux's portrait of the Count of Bougainville. Katherine read aloud the placard beside the painting, but instead of pronouncing it correctly ('*boo*-gin-ville'), her French was all wrong; she said, '*bow*-gin-villa,' like a tacky restaurant in Little Italy with red and white table cloths.

And the oddest thing of all, which Timothy still recalled even twenty years later, was not that her French was wrong, or that perhaps she had read more of the language than she had opportunity to speak aloud – but that he insisted on correcting her, there in the museum, in public – with other museum-goers beside them, listening.

'It's Bougainville,' he said, with the French tripping off his tongue; and though he smiled as he said it, he immediately regretted it, because they both knew it was an attack, a subtle way to put her back in her place. Later he would wonder what prompted his correction. He decided that it was her fault, really; that she typically offered up so little of herself – she was like one of those sheer-faced mountains that affords climbers no purchase, no place to grab hold – that he felt the need to dig in when the rare chance came.

And also: it was an opportunity to remind her that while she might be a charming enigma, a pretty girl with a quick wit and a steely reserve, who dressed well and carried herself gracefully, he was still a Van Bender, and he had come from a family where class had been passed down over generations and not simply learned at some women's college in Massachusetts, in dollops of thirty-two credits per year.

That day in the museum, when he said, 'It's Bougainville,' she pressed her lips together and made a face that might, to the other museum patrons, anyway, resemble a grateful smile, but Timothy knew he had gravely wounded her. She was quiet for the rest of the afternoon.

Could that have been the first sign? Should he have recognized then that their marriage would not be an easy one?

Later there were other signs, too. The night before their wedding, their first serious fight arrived, at approximately the same time as the out-of-town wedding guests. They were in Menlo Park, in Father's house, upstairs in the study. Their two families were below, taking seats at the dinner table. Her family had arrived from Boston that afternoon: her mother and father, her sister, even her grandmother – then almost ninety – and dozens of out-of-town guests. In the back yard, two white and green canvas tents had been raised for the next day's party.

There in the upstairs room, Timothy asked her to sign a prenuptial agreement.

The agreement, he explained, would preserve his

family's assets in the unlikely event of their marriage ending in divorce. It was something Father wanted, not himself, and certainly she could understand?

But of course she could not.

From downstairs came the sound of sudden activity before dinner was served: of chairs scraping the floor, of ice clinking into glasses, of clattering plates, of sudden laughter and raised voices. In the background a television set droned a summer baseball game.

Upstairs, Katherine stared at the one-page prenuptial agreement. She turned the page over to look at the empty back of the sheet.

'It's only one page, Katherine,' he told her.

'I don't care how long it is,' she said. 'I'm not Simon and Schuster. That's not the point.'

It took him fifteen minutes to calm her, and then she signed the agreement with her thin freckled lips pressed together so hard that they were white. After that, neither of them spoke about the agreement again, for twenty years.

Sometimes it surprised Timothy that they had managed to stay married for so long. Over the years she seemed sad so often that he wondered why she didn't drive away one afternoon when he was at work, without leaving a note or saying goodbye. He could imagine the scene: his wandering through the house, carrying his briefcase from room to room, calling her name, wondering – did she go to the grocery store? Did she visit Anne Beatty down the street? At what point would he realize that she never was to return? Would he realize that first night she was gone? The first sunrise without her?

Timothy understood the secret that it takes newlyweds years to learn: the way to insure a long marriage is to fantasize about its being over. Timothy had tried, often, to imagine life without Katherine. Sometimes the thoughts came when he heard about yet another divorce of an old friend, information always imparted by a colleague who clucked about it in jealous tones. Sometimes the thoughts came when Timothy sat at his desk, and his mind drifted, and he realized that Tricia Fountain, with her twenty-three-year-old body, was mere feet away, and so available. He toyed with the scenarios: what would he do when single? Would he date many other women? Would he sell his Palo Alto house and move into a more manage-able apartment, a bachelor pad, maybe something closer to the Stanford campus, with its bounty of sun-buffed co-eds? Would he date Tricia? What about the lithe, tall Asian hostess at Tamarine, who always smiled at him when Katherine's back was turned?

How long would he have to wait before it would be decent to be seen with another woman? Could he bring a new girlfriend to the Circus Club? Would he be able to play golf every Saturday, and go sailing every Sunday, without guilt?

But the fantasies, initially so appealing, quickly grew dreary. He tried picturing spending time with Tricia. After the sex, what would they do? What would they talk about? What woman, besides Katherine, would he enjoy a conversation with? Who would verbally spar with him? Who would keep him humble, would remind him to tithe to the church with a single dead-pan comment like: 'Where would any of us be without the Father?'

Whom would he spend time with? Who would put up with – and then tease him about – his flaws, his arrogance, his egotism? Who would make fun of the limp in his left leg, teasing him in front of friends about his 'war wound from 'Nam' when in fact the injury happened thirty years ago on a Yale squash court. ('Come, on, Gimpy,' she would stage whisper at a dinner party, using her pet name for him. 'Tell them what happened to your leg that night in the rice paddies.')

Who would remind him what he liked to eat when they ordered in a restaurant? Who would talk to him about work, would advise him about how to treat a prickly investor, would reflate him after Father knocked him down? Who would pack for him the night before he traveled? And with whom would he lie in bed and talk to in the dark about nothing in particular – about the latest neighborhood gossip, about the couple moving into the house down the street, about who had been refused a zoning variance, about whose kid had turned into a pot-head at Wesleyan, about who had totaled their car on Highway 101 but really wasn't hurt?

The fantasies about being single, far from

weakening his will, always ended the same way: they made him more committed to their marriage, and reminded him that despite her bitterness and sadness, he loved Katherine more than any other woman, and that – after twenty years – he knew there would be no other woman, not ever, and that, chances were, he would die before she did, still married to her, and still very much in love.

And now, standing behind her on their patio, with his arms on the back of her chair, he said, 'It's hard to be spontaneous after twenty years. Twenty years is a long time.'

'Are you tired of me?' she asked.

'A little,' he admitted. 'But that's the point, isn't it? You're supposed to grow tired of each other. That means you've succeeded at staying married. Excitement is for young kids.'

'Timothy,' she said. She looked up at him, squinted into the sun behind his shoulder. 'I don't know if that's the nicest thing or the meanest thing you've ever told me.'

'The nicest,' he said simply. 'You're my wife, and I love you more than any woman in the world, and we're going to spend the rest of our days together.'

'Oh my,' she said. For the first time she had no brassy come-back, and the words sounded choked in her throat. He thought – but couldn't be certain – that tears welled in her eyes. 'What's gotten into you?'

'Since when is it illegal to be in love with your wife?'

'It's not illegal,' she said. 'Just not customary.'

'I don't know what part of the world you're from,' Timothy said. 'But in my neck of the woods, marriage means forever.'

'In sickness and in health?' she asked.

'That's right.'

'Good times and bad?'

'Yes.'

'For richer and for poorer?'

'Let's not get carried away.'

She smiled.

She reached up for his hands, pressed them hard into her shoulders. It felt good to be held by her, to be a good husband, if only for a minute or two, and he thought maybe this weekend would turn out all right after all.

CHAPTER 5

Big Sur is a ribbon of coastline ninety miles long, running from Carmel to San Simeon. The earliest Spanish settlers in Monterey called the swathe of unexplored land straddling the Pacific Ocean the 'Big South' because everything about the land was vast and dramatic – the surf that pummeled the rock-cragged cliffs, the miles of undulating dunes and marsh, the dark forests where hundred-year-old redwoods sliced sunlight into horizontal shafts.

The drive took two and a half hours. Katherine and Timothy rode their black BMW two-door, first east across the Santa Cruz mountains on hairpin Route 17, then south on 85. Timothy drove, and for long stretches Katherine slept.

They stopped for lunch in Carmel at Grasing's. While Katherine headed to the table, Timothy excused himself. 'I'm going to call work,' he said.

He passed the maitre d', who nodded to him, and walked out the front door. Out on the street, he used his cell phone to call the Kid. The yen was down again, now at seventy-three. Osiris had made a paper profit of a million dollars in less than a day. Only twenty-three million to go, Timothy thought.

The Kid said, 'And I keep getting calls from Pinky Dewer.'

'Oh?' Timothy said. He stood on Mission Street, outside the restaurant. With the cell phone pressed to his ear, he began walking west on the cobblestones, toward San Carlos Street.

'I did what you said,' the Kid said. 'I didn't take his call. But he's tried three times. It's hard to keep pretending I'm in meetings. He knows I'm not that important.'

'You're important to me,' Timothy said. He crossed San Carlos and walked west on Sixth, toward Dolores. He passed art galleries and bistros. It was a sunny Friday afternoon during peak August tourist season, and Carmel was crowded with window-shoppers and sidewalk cafe tables. To Timothy it seemed that there were more bottles of Perrier on this single street than all of France.

Down the block Timothy saw what he was looking for. A small, understated sign said: 'Michael Sherman Jewelry Design.'

'All right, Kid,' Timothy said, 'I have to go. Call if something happens. I'll see you Monday morning.'

'Have a good weekend, Timothy.'

Timothy snapped his cell phone shut and dropped it into his blazer pocket. He entered the store. The air conditioning was cool and the store dark. Small halogen spotlights illuminated glass counters filled with diamond and platinum rings.

A petite woman in her fifties appeared behind the counter. She had dark hair, an olive complexion, and tiny features. Her skin was pulled tight across her face – too many facelifts.

She approached slowly. 'Hello,' she said, and smiled.

Timothy had no time for the soft sell. 'Okay,' he said quickly. 'Let's cut to the chase. My wife is waiting for me in a restaurant up the hill, and by now she's mad as hell that I left her alone. It's our twentieth wedding anniversary, and I don't have a gift. I need something big and expensive, something that will make up for all the terrible mistakes I've made, and all the mistakes I don't even know about. You're a woman. Tell me what to buy.' He pulled his wallet from his back pocket. He removed his Black American Express Card and placed it on the glass counter in front of him. 'I have fifteen thousand dollars to spend. And about sixty seconds to spend it.'

The woman smiled and raised an eyebrow. 'That's twenty seconds more than you'll need,' she said. She took his charge card before he could change his mind, and led him to another glass counter. She leaned over, pulled a key from her pocket, and unlocked the case. She removed a necklace, mounted on black felt, and placed it on the counter before him. Diamonds were mounted along its entire length, gradually increasing in size toward the bottom, where a pendant – sapphire and diamond and gold – dangled. It glittered electrically, blue and white, under the point spotlight.

'Eighteen carat white gold,' she said. 'One hundred and five near-colorless diamonds. The pendant is one carat diamond and one carat sapphire. Total diamond weight is nine point five carats. And, luckily, it's fifteen thousand dollars exactly.'

'What a coincidence,' Timothy said. 'I'll take it.'

She smiled, flicked his charge card through the magnetic reader mounted on the wall behind her and keyed in a number. From the speaker came the brief sound of computerized phone dialing, and then silence. After a moment, the display said 'APPROVED.' What a country! Timothy thought. The entire annual GDP of some godforsaken province in Bangladesh has just changed hands between two strangers, and no one saw coin or cash.

'I assume you don't have time for gift wrapping,' the woman said. 'So here's a pretty box.'

Back at the restaurant, Katherine had ordered a glass of wine, and had finished half of it. He sat down across from her.

'You're sweating,' she said. 'Are you hot?'

'I was hurrying to get back.'

'Is everything okay at work?'

'Everything is fine,' Timothy said. 'Jay says hello.'

'And what does Tricia say?'

'She says hello, too.' Timothy kept his voice neutral.

'I'm a little jealous of her,' Katherine admitted.

Timothy was surprised. 'Have you even met her?'

'No,' Katherine said quickly. 'Which is why I'm jealous. I've talked to her on the phone quite a few times. What does she look like?'

'She's very plain,' Timothy said.

'Is she younger than me?'

'Yes.'

Timothy looked at Katherine's arms, exposed in her sleeveless blouse, as she leaned forward with her elbows on the table. The skin below her triceps was losing its firmness. This was new, something he hadn't noticed before, and it brought a small rush of tenderness.

'Prettier?' she asked.

'No.'

'Liar.' But she smiled.

Timothy said: 'Is it your intention to sabotage our anniversary weekend?'

'No,' she said.

In their twenty years of marriage, Timothy had cheated on Katherine three times, but Katherine knew about only one incident with certainty. Timothy treated his affairs the way he treated his business relationships, and the way he treated the pool boy at the club: at all times he tried to be a gentleman.

So: he confined his cheating to one-night flings

in far-away cities with women he did not know. He never revealed his real name to the women, and he always insisted on using a condom – he was careful to leave nothing behind: no identity, no paternity, nothing for a woman to latch onto.

In twenty years, he had made only one mistake. It happened at his last affair. Seventeen years into the marriage, he was visiting Palm Beach for two days, raising money for Osiris Fund IV. He had looked up an old Exeter friend, Mack Gladwell. Gladwell, who had inexplicably transformed himself from clench-jawed scion of the Gladwell family fortune to drug-addled record producer, had no liquid cash to invest in Osiris, but he offered something almost as good: he insisted on taking Timothy out for a night on the town in Palm Beach, 'Gladwell Style,' as he described it.

They visited three bars that night. Timothy drank more than usual, and got sloppy. He wound up going home with a pretty cocktail waitress. He did not remember much of the night, only that he was careful not to use his real name, and to tell the waitress absolutely nothing about himself.

It was not until the next morning when, hungover, he tried to board his plane back to SFO, that he realized he had left his wallet in the waitress's apartment. The wallet had his driver's license, his business cards – his identity. Which meant that the waitress could find him.

And of course she did. She called their house in Palo Alto when Timothy was on the flight home.

Katherine answered. The waitress – angry, drunk – asked to speak to her 'boyfriend' Timothy. She described in great detail his body, the mole on the back of his thigh, and the positions in which he enjoyed having sex.

When Timothy returned home that night, he thought Katherine was going to leave him. She had packed a bag for him, and calmly told him to take it to Hyatt Rickey's. She made him stay there for a week, refusing his phone calls. When he showed up at the house and rang the doorbell, she declined to open the front door, yelling instead through the wood that he should leave before she called the police.

After forcing him to live in the hotel for seven days, she suddenly – and to him, surprisingly – relented. Just when he thought he had lost her, that divorce was imminent, she drove to the Hyatt, knocked on his door, and said, 'Come home.'

He returned to the house, and they never spoke about the affair again.

Now – sitting with Katherine in the restaurant in Carmel, and discussing whether Timothy's secretary was in fact attractive – the incident with Mack Gladwell and the cocktail waitress lurked just below the surface of their conversation like a stingray. He tried always to head off discussions before they approached dangerous waters. Avoid all talk about other women, about jealousy, and, above all, about Palm Beach. And always tell her you love her.

'I love you,' he said.

'I know you do.' She opened her menu and started reading. After a moment, she peered at him over the top. 'They have braised short ribs,' she said. 'You like that.'

'I like it when you remind me what kind of food to order.'

'Well, after twenty years,' she said to her menu, and sighed, and Timothy knew exactly what she meant.

Over dessert, Katherine said, 'There's something I want to ask you.'

The waiter, a little lithe man with a shock of dyed blond hair and the body of a dancer, pranced behind her and laid two coffees on the table. Timothy's was black; hers had cream and sugar. She always ordered it the same way: light and sweet.

Katherine waited for the server to leave. He made a little plié, bending at the knees, and scurried off.

'It's a bit uncomfortable,' she said.

Timothy frowned. They had held many uncomfortable conversations in the past, but never had she pre-announced that one would be uncomfortable. What every uncomfortable conversation had in common was that it was a surprise, that it began with an innocuous comment or a flip remark, that it arrived like the monsoon, sudden and violent.

'I'm very interested,' he said.

'I need a project,' she said. 'Something to do. While you're at work.'

'Okay,' he said. It sounded unobjectionable so far.

'I think about why I get sad sometimes, and I think it's because . . . because I have too much time, too much time to think, too much time to stew. I always stir things around in my mind. While you're at work, I'm alone at the house, and maybe that makes me a little crazy. So if I had something to do . . .'

'Like what?'

'Well, I don't know. It hardly even matters. But I need a project. Something to occupy my time.'

'Okay,' he said. But it was clear she already had something in mind.

'I was thinking about redecorating the house. You know, updating the look a little. Making it a little more . . .' She searched for the word. 'Contemporary.'

'Okay.'

'I would hire a decorator. You know, and work with him. And that would give me something to do.'

'That sounds fine,' he said.

'But, Timothy, I want this to be my project. I don't want to keep asking you permission, asking for money, getting you to sign checks. I think I need to be, you know, in control of something.'

'What are we talking about, exactly?' Somehow,

life always came down to money. One person extracting money from someone else.

'Don't worry. We would agree on a budget up front. Nothing extravagant. But once we agreed, I would ask you to trust me, to let me manage everything.'

'Give me a number.'

'Two hundred thousand dollars,' she said.

'To decorate? That's crazy.'

'Well, maybe it's a little much. But that's the worst-case scenario. I'd try to spend less. But there's so much we could do. The house is full of dead space – the living room, the dining room. We could make it so much warmer.'

'You're saying I should just put two hundred thousand dollars in your checking account, and let you spend it however you see fit.'

'That would make me happy,' she said.

'I would like to make you happy,' he said. 'But Katherine.'

'Please, Timothy.' She reached across the table and took his hand. 'It would mean so much to me.'

He looked into her eyes. They were still the pretty blue eyes he had first looked into more than twenty years ago, but now there were crow's feet at the corners, and fine dry lines etched around her mouth. Maybe what she said was true, that she needed a project, something to keep her busy, something to call her own. She had been cooped up in the house for so long, while Timothy was able to enjoy his life, to come and go as he pleased, to travel, to work. And two hundred thousand dollars was a lot of money to most people, but to him it was one month's worth of management fees for his fund. It was one good trade.

'What the hell. Don't spend it like a drunken sailor.'

She smiled. 'Thank you, Timothy. I think this will really help us.'

'I'll take care of it at work on Monday. The money, I mean.'

'I love you.'

'While we're on the subject of love and money,' he said, 'I have something for you.' He removed the jewelry box from his blazer and held it out between his fingers, as if offering a cigar. 'Happy anniversary,' he said.

She touched her hand to her mouth. Her hand shook nervously. She opened the case and stared at the necklace. The diamonds and sapphire glittered in the sunlight. 'Oh God,' she said.

'If I had known about the whole house redecorating plan . . .' he said.

She ignored him. 'Timothy, this is beautiful.'

'Well, after twenty years,' he said, 'you're more beautiful than ever, and you deserve something equally beautiful.' Timothy looked around the room for the waiter. He needed more coffee. 'I hope you enjoy it,' he said. He made eye contact with the ballerina waiter, gestured to his coffee cup. 'I think this is going to be a great year – a great year for us,' he said, hoping. 'Our best year yet.'

And then something strange happened, something Timothy was not expecting. Katherine began to cry. A younger couple at an adjacent table looked up at her and then down again, quickly, embarrassed.

'Katherine,' he said. He leaned over the table and grabbed her forearm. 'Katherine, what's the matter?'

She shook her head, wiping the tears from her face. Other patrons in the restaurant turned to look. She sniffled, stopped crying. She dabbed at her eyes with her napkin. The waiter arrived with the coffee decanter, saw her eyes, and walked away without pouring.

'Katherine,' he said again, 'what's wrong?'

She shook her head. Timothy chalked it up to female emotion: the pretty restaurant, the anniversary weekend, his agreeing to her decorating scheme, the necklace. It was not until later that he realized it was something else, something he could never imagine. But for now he sat quietly, and wondered if he would ever be able to get that second cup of coffee.

CHAPTER 6

Despite his initial dread, Timothy enjoyed the anniversary weekend. Outside the house, alone with her husband, away from the familiar landmarks that reminded her of her own unhappiness, Katherine was a different woman – or, rather, she was the woman that she used to be, before the years had worn her down. The weekend reminded Timothy of what he loved about her: her cool, reptilian insight – the way she could size up other couples from across the room and tell Timothy their story. 'Look at them,' she said, sitting in the Ventana Inn restaurant, during Saturday's dinner. 'He hates her. You can see it the way he won't look at her. He's embarrassed by her.' Or: 'You see that couple? Third marriage. She's too young to be the first, and he's ignoring her too much to be the second.'

He liked the way Katherine's plain, fresh-scrubbed looks made her look more wholesome than the other older wives at the Ventana Inn, and the fact that, away for the weekend, she didn't bother covering up the freckles on her cheeks. He liked her sarcasm, the way she mocked the New

Age pretentiousness of the resort, with its 'Spa Menu' that included a Sea Enzyme Organic Mask ('Seagull poop,' she said to Timothy through clenched lips, as the masseuse plopped it on her face) and 'Astrology Readings' and 'Color Energy Analysis,' whatever that was.

On Saturday they hiked through Point Lobos Park. They parked their car in a small lot and walked a quarter-mile to the beach. ('Come on, Gimpy,' she called over her shoulder to him. 'Don't let that war wound slow you down.') At the beach, they removed their sneakers and flats and padded through the sand, weaving a path of wet footprints through seaweed and stranded jelly-fish. It was low tide: it smelled of sulfur and salt. They were the only people on the shore.

The beach ended at a rocky promontory, a solid wall of stones a hundred feet high, which jutted into the sea. A sign indicated the beginning of a trailhead. It said 'Use Caution,' and stressed the point with an illustration of a stick-figure man leaning precariously over the edge of a cliff.

Katherine's gaze followed the trail up into the rocks. 'Can you make it to the top?'

He wasn't sure if she was teasing or genuinely concerned. Either way, that forced his hand. 'Of course.'

They followed the trail away from the water and up onto the wall of rocks. The trail started off steeply and then pitched even steeper. At times it was not even a trail at all but rather a set of tiny steps carved out of the rock, a WPA project from back when chiseling sandstone by hand was a good day's work and shoes only reached size six.

By the tenth step, Timothy's knee hurt. He looked down and saw that he had managed to climb only twenty feet. Only another hundred to go.

The stairs ended and deposited them on a dirt path, which weaved back and forth, a long vertiginous switchback, with a heavy chain running along the ocean side of the path to keep hikers from falling down the cliffs.

After ten minutes they reached the top, a plateau on the crag. They looked down. One hundred feet below, beyond the switchback trail, the ocean pounded against the jagged seawall, throwing foam whitecaps into the air.

They stood there for five minutes, silently, at the edge of the cliff. Timothy held Katherine tightly from behind, his hands locked around her ribs. They watched the ocean crash and ebb. 'It's beautiful,' she said, loudly, so he could hear her over the waves.

She took his hands and guided them down to her belly. She pushed them into her flesh. 'Empty,' she said.

He understood what the word meant. The word represented the greatest source of sadness for her, that they could never have children. It was one more strange thing about Katherine: every time she saw something beautiful, instead of being happy, she felt sad, as if she couldn't allow herself a moment of peace, and needed instead to remember the awful parts of her life.

They had tried several times to have children. She had first miscarried when they had been married for three months. They waited to try again. A year and a half later, she had her second miscarriage, this time at four months. She was devastated. All the women around her – at church, at her college reunion, in the supermarket – were having children. Some of her peers had already had a second, and dinner parties suddenly became new parents' forums, where the talk revolved around issues about which Katherine had no idea: teething, first steps, nursery school, doctors' visits, sibling rivalry.

Another year passed and Timothy convinced her to try again. This time, when she reached six months of pregnancy and she was showing, they thought she would make it. They decided what to name the child: if it was a boy, Connor, after her grandfather; if a girl, Lisa, after her grandmother.

At the end of the sixth month she knew it would be a boy, could feel it in her bones, and she and Timothy talked about Connor, imagined what he would look like, pictured him as a schoolchild, then as a teenager. The miscarriage came a day before she started her seventh month. The child was stillborn.

Katherine stayed in the house for the next

month, refusing visitors, turning away company. Timothy cared for her as best he could, but didn't know what to say, whether to commiserate with her or to downplay the tragedy, to be sad or to be strong. So he did nothing, and instead just waited for her sadness to pass.

It did, eventually. When Timothy concluded they would never have children, he was disappointed at first, but the feeling passed. He realized that he was secretly relieved: relieved that the problem wasn't his fault, relieved that he could continue to enjoy his life – going to the office, putting in six-hour days, flying to New York to meet with investors, playing tennis at the Circus Club on the weekend, traveling to St Bart's once each year – without the burden of children.

At first there was some talk of fertility specialists, or of adoption, but Katherine dropped these ideas and stopped speaking about the subject of children altogether. Soon the entire matter was put away, never to be spoken of, just one more item in that cluttered attic that held their marriage's disappointments.

'It is beautiful,' Timothy agreed, as they stared at the ocean below, crashing against the rocks. 'And I love you.' Which was the only thing he could say when confronted with her sadness.

That evening, back in the hotel room, they had a few unscripted hours before their dinner reservation. Katherine suggested that Timothy have a massage in the Ventana's spa – to 'work on those soldier's knees' she said. Timothy said that they should go together, but she insisted on staying behind, alone, in the room.

'I could use some quiet time,' she said.

He didn't complain. A couple hours of separateness were welcome. As he strolled across the Ventana grounds, following the signs for the spa, he tried to conjure a picture of his masseuse. He decided she should be a young Swedish girl – tall, with strong hands. A firm grasp of English was of secondary importance.

So he was disappointed when the matron at the spa's front desk informed him that only one masseuse was available on such short notice, and that he was a 'gentleman' named Tony.

He may indeed have been a gentleman, Timothy decided as he lay naked under Tony's pounding fists – but only if the Crips of Compton made a habit of opening car doors for their ladies. Tony was a large black man, handsome and muscular. Although he was clean cut, he had a raised scar carved along his jaw line, like a long lyrical paragraph written in Braille. Timothy decided it was probably not a massage-related injury.

But, after some initial discomfort at being naked and rubbed by another man – and one who had possibly been at the receiving end of a filet knife – Timothy soon relaxed, and was surprised to be awakened from sleep fifty minutes later at the end of the session.

'I hope you enjoyed that, Mr Van Bender,' Tony said.

'I certainly did,' Timothy said. 'Those are some powerful hands.' He realized that last remark could be construed as homosexual, so he added: 'Much better than my wife.'

Tony smiled. His look said: Don't flatter yourself. 'Take your time getting dressed.' He left the room.

Timothy put on his clothes, returned to the front desk and put the bill on his room tab. He left Tony a fifty-dollar bill in a small envelope.

Then he headed back to his room.

He started back across the Ventana grounds, whistling a Puccini aria and windmilling his arms, savoring the feeling of relaxed muscles and loose joints. He came to his room. He turned the key in the lock and pushed open his door. Katherine sat cross-legged on the bed, with her back to him. She was leaning over, writing in her diary, a thick, leather-bound journal with gold leaf pages. She continued writing, and studiously ignored him.

Katherine was a prodigious diarist. For as long as he had known her, she had carried out her strange daily ritual: scrupulously recording each day's events, her feelings, her longings, in a tightly wound script that practically required a magnifying glass to read. Sometimes, after fighting with Timothy, she would retreat to her bedroom like a sullen teenage girl, and write. Once, two years into their marriage, when Katherine had left the house, Timothy skulked into her closet and stared at the neat stack of journals, the identical leather-bound volumes piled in obsessive rows, between old sweaters and purses – and he couldn't resist. He carefully removed the top volume, flipped to a random page, and read.

It was a strange experience: first, the sheer tediousness of it, the obsessive detail – what she ate ('for breakfast: muesli and skim milk; one half grapefruit; one piece wheat toast; jam'), what she wore ('blue floral Ralph Lauren sun dress; straw hat'), where she went, whom she saw on the street ('saw Betty inside Gristede's; later, said hello to Nancy Stanton in the parking lot'). Interspersed in the monotonous catalog were startling, mean-spirited observations, which flashed and lit the dreary page like lightning on a moonless night. He remembered one passage in particular, about an incident that occurred when they drove to the opera in San Francisco: 'When the police officer pulled us over, Timothy smiled at him and tried to bribe him. He did it in his usual charming way, so that it hardly seemed like a bribe. It was, of course, typical of him. Why does he feel that he is above all rules, that he can get away with anything, that the laws of the universe do not apply to him? I suppose it gives the people who work for him a kind of comfort – that this man is so clearly in charge, and able to navigate the world without impediment. But, truthfully, it disgusts me.' She underlined the word 'disgusts' twice, hard enough that the pen indented the vellum.

When he read that passage, he felt dazed. He remembered the incident, when he had managed to extract himself from a speeding fine. It surprised him that he recalled it as a small achievement, as a victory of his panache and calmness under pressure. That his own wife had a different view – a hateful one – was shocking. He closed the diary and replaced it on the shelf. He was careful to replace it exactly as he had found it: the corner askew, out of alignment with the rest of the pile, a yellow sweater arm resting carelessly on the edge of the leather binding.

How had she figured out that he had read the journal? He was never sure, but somehow, she did. When she arrived home that day, she was surprised to see Timothy in the kitchen. She ascended to the bedroom, but returned a moment later, paprika red, the vein in her forehead bulging. 'How dare you! This is the most despicable thing you have ever done.' She spat out the words. Then she added in a low, menacing voice: 'And I know you have done many despicable things!'

Timothy refused to admit that he had read the book. She was testing him, wanting him to plead guilty, but he knew that – as angry as she was at that moment – any admission, any hesitation, would make things worse. He was unrelenting: he had no idea why she was accusing him.

Finally, she shook her head. 'Typical,' she said,

as if she knew the exact page of the diary he had read. 'So typical.'

She stormed off and hardly spoke to him for days. He continued to pretend to be hurt and outraged – how could she falsely accuse him of something so low? – but his protests were wan and thin. He just wanted the incident to blow over.

It did, eventually. But he never read her diaries again. He was afraid: afraid that she had some kind of secret system for protecting the books, semiotics involving minute hair follicles, or traces of talcum powder, or ultraviolet light. More than that, he was afraid of what he might read, that perhaps the paragraph was just the beginning, the overture in a much grander symphony. Sometimes, he realized, it's best not to know the truth.

Now, back in the hotel room in Big Sur, he walked up behind her. Clearly she heard him enter, but made a show of continuing to write in her journal, unhurried, not threatened by his presence. When she had finished her thought, she underlined a word on the page and pressed down an emphatic period. She recapped her pen and closed the book gently. She pushed it a few inches away from herself on the bed. She turned around, finally, and looked at him over her shoulder.

'How was your massage?'

'All right,' he said.

'Was she beautiful?'

'Who?'

'The masseuse.'

Timothy said: 'Yes, she was beautiful.'

Katherine nodded. She had expected as much.

He sat down on the bed beside her. His weight pressed an indentation into the mattress, and the leather diary slid down into the gravity well and bumped against his thigh. Gingerly, he pushed it away, careful not to disturb it, like a loaded weapon.

'But I love you more, Katherine. I love you more than my beautiful Swedish masseuse. I love you more than my hot young secretary. I love you more than anyone. I love you.'

'Timothy,' she said. She looked at him with a strange expression. He couldn't place it. For an instant, it seemed like sorrow. Then he realized it was something else – regret, perhaps? But no. Timothy decided: it was love. Funny, he thought, after twenty years, love is so fleeting, you can't recognize it in your own wife's eyes.

'Come on,' Timothy said. 'Let's get dressed for dinner.'

In addition to massages and hiking, they visited small art galleries – more his speed, he explained, since it involved less walking – where they bought a wind-chime and two abstract acrylic paintings that Timothy didn't care for, but which Katherine thought would go well with the soon-to-be-remodeled living room. They ate in out-of-the-way roadside restaurants, where

Timothy enjoyed deep-fried oysters in cornmeal ('You can't find that in Palo Alto,' he said) and where she ordered greasy cheeseburgers, always bloody and rare.

On Sunday, the final day of their vacation, they decided to check out from the hotel and then visit a few more art galleries on Route 1 before continuing north back to Palo Alto. At the Crabbe Gallery, Katherine found a piece of sculpture she liked, and Timothy offered to buy it for her. It was another abstract, piece, two interlocking marble U shapes. 'Perfect for the foyer,' she explained to Timothy, who figured that five hundred and ninety-five dollars was a small price to pay to end the trip in a haze of pleasantness.

As they stood beside the cash register and the gallery proprietor wrapped their sculpture in tissue paper for the trip home, Katherine began to search the inside of her purse.

'Damn it,' she said.

'What's wrong?' He was signing the charge card receipt and didn't look up at her.

'My sunglasses. I must have left them in the room.'

Timothy tried to keep his face still, continued looking down at the credit card receipt. Now they would have to double-back and drive south another fifteen minutes before returning home. She had added thirty minutes to the trip because of her own carelessness.

'It's no problem,' he said pleasantly. 'We'll just drive back and take a look.

He handed the clerk his signed receipt, and the clerk handed Timothy the heavy bundle of tissue paper.

He and Katherine left the store and started toward the BMW.

She stopped, touched his elbow.

'What?' he said.

She smiled. 'It's still our anniversary weekend, right?'

'Sure,' he said.

'You've been so kind to me this whole trip.'

He thought she was apologizing for leaving her sunglasses behind in the inn. 'It's no problem, Katherine,' he said.

'So can I ask you for one more thing?' She pointed across the parking lot to a second art gallery. 'Can I browse in there?'

'But we need to go back to the hotel.' Then he understood what she wanted. He was to drive back to the Ventana Inn by himself and locate her sunglasses, while she continued shopping at the second gallery. Then he would return and pick her up for the drive home. 'Oh, I see,' he said. The August sun was beating on his scalp, and the tissue-paper-wrapped sculpture was heavy in his hands. He felt the first prickles of sweat on his neck, and realized he needed to urinate. He felt like saying, 'You must be kidding.' Instead, he said: 'Absolutely, no problem,' and smiled. This was typical of her, he thought to himself, as he continued to the car. He put the sculpture in the back seat. She always wanted to push him, to test his limits, to see whether she could turn a nice weekend – which he had actually enjoyed – into a fight. But he decided not to take her bait. 'I'll be right back,' he said. He circled the car and climbed into the passenger seat.

'Timothy,' she said.

'What?'

'Your American Express. Can I have it? I won't go crazy, I promise.'

He reached a sweaty hand into his back pocket and pulled out his wallet. 'Of course,' he said. He handed her the charge card.

'I love you, Gimpy,' she said.

'And I you,' he said. He climbed into the car and drove off.

Twenty minutes later, back at the Ventana Inn, Timothy pulled into the front reception area under the veranda, where a sign said, 'For Guests Checking In.' The bellboy, a pleasant-looking boy with a Midwestern moon face, hopped to the car and chirped, 'Welcome to the Ventana Inn! Checking in?'

Timothy got out of the car and shook his head wearily. What he needed to do, more than anything else, was take a piss. 'Not exactly,' he told the bellboy. 'My wife and I just checked out.'

The bellboy looked in the passenger seat of the BMW to see if he should help Timothy's wife from the car. It was empty. 'No, she's not . . .' Timothy let his voice trail off. 'She sent me back here because she forgot something in the room, and she'd rather keep shopping than drive with me.' He rolled his eyes, as if to say, 'You know how hard it can be to be married, right?' But the Midwestern bellboy just stared at him. Marriage was remote and hypothetical to him, like some novel academic theory that he had heard of, vaguely, but never spent much time dwelling on.

'Okay,' Timothy said. He opened his wallet, pulled out a twenty-dollar bill and handed it to the bellboy. 'I'm going to the bathroom, then I'll talk to the front desk. Just leave the car here for a second, all right?'

'Yes, sir!' the bellboy said. He didn't understand what Timothy was saying about driving and shopping, and the bathroom, but a twenty-spot he understood perfectly.

'I'll be five minutes,' Timothy said, over his shoulder.

He felt better after urinating, and so walked to the front desk in good spirits. It did not last. The line was eight-people deep, and the two clerks on duty were harried, trying to keep up with the customers anxious to check out. One couple was arguing with a clerk about their bill, yelling about the local phone charges, proclaiming them 'absurd' and threatening that the hotel would regret trying to take advantage of them.

Timothy suddenly felt angry, too. He was not

going to wait in line, just to look for Katherine's silly pair of sunglasses. They were her sunglasses, after all. So why was he here, searching for them?

Besides, the sunglasses could cost no more than – what? – two hundred dollars? Four hundred dollars? It wasn't worth the aggravation. In thirty years of traveling across North America, of staying in countless hotels, of checking in and checking out, Timothy had never once left something in a hotel room. Why did she?

'All right,' Timothy said, out loud. He left the hotel and climbed back into his BMW.

When he returned to the art gallery he had a story ready, about how he asked the front desk for the sunglasses, and even bribed a housekeeper to let him into the room to search, but that they were nowhere to be found.

But he did not need the story. Katherine was standing in the parking lot, waiting for him. Under her arm she held a framed painting wrapped in newspaper. On her face she wore her sunglasses.

Timothy stopped the car beside her. She leaned over and put her elbows on the open window frame.

'You're going to kill me,' she said. She tapped the bridge of her sunglasses. 'I found them in my pocket.'

Timothy shook his head.

'Are you mad?'

'Get in,' he said. They didn't talk for the first

twenty miles, but by the time they reached Monterey, Timothy decided that he had been silent long enough, and so he asked her what she wanted to eat for dinner.

CHAPTER 7

When Timothy returned to work on Monday morning at a quarter past nine, Tricia was not at the front reception area. Instead there was a man underneath Tricia's desk, bent over, with his blue-jeaned ass in the air.

'Hello,' Timothy said, to the ass.

'Oh.' The man knocked his head against the desk as he stood. It was Tran, their computer consultant. He was thin and Vietnamese, and he looked like he was seventeen years old. 'Hello, Timothy,' Tran said.

'What's happening in the world of technology today?' Timothy said, disappointed that during his triumphant return to the office after a long weekend, he was being greeted by his computer technician, and not Tricia.

'Disaster,' Tran said, in a heavy Vietnamese accent, staccato and guttural. 'Contingency plan.'

'Okay, Tran,' Timothy said, nodding. 'Keep up the good work. Where's Tricia?'

'Coffee,' Tran said, as he went back to work beneath her desk.

Timothy walked on, toward his office. Jay appeared in the hall and swept along behind him.

'Hi, Timothy,' Jay said. 'The yen's down to seventy-two, thank God.' And then, remembering: 'Oh, how was your weekend?'

Timothy said: 'Fine, fine.' He wanted to stop talking about it before Tricia returned from her coffee run. He entered his private office and held the door open for Jay. He closed the door behind them. 'What's Tran doing out there? I never understand a word he says.'

'We talked about it last week. You gave your okay. He's installing a network backup system. In case there's a disaster, you know? A fire, or theft? We'll back up the computers each night, and then rotate the backup media off-site once each week. That way, worst case scenario, we'll only lose a few days' worth of data. It's part of our Investor Agreement with Granite Partners. They require disaster contingency planning by all the funds they invest in.'

'Okay, whatever,' Timothy said. Technology was really the Kid's specialty, after all.

Timothy removed his suit jacket and hung it behind the door. He said, 'Tell me about the yen.'

'I've heard reports that the BOJ is buying dollars. Now they're suddenly concerned that their exports are uncompetitive because of the strong yen.'

'Okay,' Timothy repeated. All he cared was that the yen was moving down, and that was Good. At the current level of seventy-two, Osiris had a paper profit of – he tried to do the math . . .

65

'We're up three million dollars now,' Jay said. It was as if the Kid had read his mind.

'That's a start,' Timothy said.

'The only thing is,' Jay said, 'that we're fully margined. I mean fully margined. If the yen moves against us, or if any clients want to withdraw cash, then we're screwed.'

'Who said anything about withdrawing cash?' Timothy asked.

'No one,' the Kid said. 'I'm just saying.'

On Timothy's desk, his phone rang. It was the internal ring tone – warm and quiet – which meant it was an intercom call from Tricia. He clicked on the speakerphone.

'Yes?'

'Hi, Timothy,' Tricia said.

'Hi,' he called out. It was hard to be flirtatious on a speakerphone. And with the Kid standing right there . . .

He reached over and picked up the handset. 'How are you?' he said, as plainly as he could.

'Timothy, I have Pinky Dewer on the line,' she said into his ear, warmly. 'He says he's in town.'

'Please tell him I'm in a meeting and take a message.'

'Okay, Timothy.' She hung up.

'Pinky Dewer's in town,' Timothy explained to the Kid.

'How long can we keep avoiding him?'

'Depends. When's his flight home?'

The Kid nodded and left. Timothy reached

below his desk and turned on his computer. He waited for it to boot, and then called up a five-minute chart on the Japanese yen. The sharp green lines spiked downward, little phosphorescent needles. Each tick down represented a million dollars. That was the kind of technology Timothy appreciated.

Before lunch, Timothy's phone rang softly again. The text display said: 'Station I. Tricia Fountain.' Timothy picked up.

'It's me again,' she said. 'I have a Mike Kelly on the line. He's from Union Bank Private Banking.'

'Okay, put him on.'

There was a soft click and Tricia's voice was replaced by a man's, phlegmy and hoarse. 'Mr Van Bender?'

'Yes, Mike. Please call me Timothy.' Mike Kelly was Timothy's point of contact at Union Bank. He took care of Timothy's banking: traveler's checks, credit cards, lines of credit, the jumbo mortgage on his home. Timothy had called him on the car phone during the ride to work. He'd told Mike to transfer two hundred thousand dollars from his general account to Katherine's checking account, so that his wife could begin her redecorating project.

Timothy asked: 'Did you take care of that matter for my wife?'

'I did,' Mike Kelly said. 'That's actually the reason I'm calling.' He sounded hesitant, uncomfortable.

Timothy had met him twice in the past – once a year ago, when Mike visited Osiris' office to have Timothy complete a new signature card, and once during Christmas, when Mike personally delivered a gift basket filled with champagne, fruit cake, and caviar. Bankers were terribly appreciative at Christmas time if they earned point two-five percent of all assets.

'I want to make sure you are aware of something,' Mike Kelly continued. 'I feel a bit uncomfortable calling like this, but it is a service that I feel obligated to provide, as your Union Bank representative.'

'Okay, okay,' Timothy said quickly. Much more banker talk and he would fall asleep right there on his desk. 'What's going on?'

'We transferred the funds from your general account to sub-account 0812 as you instructed. Ten minutes later, we received further direction from your wife, to wire those same funds to another account.'

'To whose account?'

'That I don't know,' Mike Kelly said. 'It's a Citibank account. For further credit to, let's see . . . Armistice LLC.' He rattled off an account number.

'Who's Armistice LLC?'

'I don't know.'

'How much did she wire?'

'One hundred and fifty thousand dollars.'

'Jesus Christ,' Timothy said. So much for his

instruction not to spend the money like a drunken sailor.

'Mr Van Bender, I want to make sure you understand something. Since you are both co-signers on the account, it's not a violation of our privacy policy to inform you of this transaction. At Union Bank we pride ourselves on our care and discretion. Typically we have very strict rules about what we can reveal about account activity. We take those rules very seriously. I hope I haven't overstepped any lines here.'

'What's that?' Timothy's mind was occupied by figuring out how Katherine could spend over a hundred grand in less than ten minutes.

'I said: Since you are both co-signers on the account, it's not a violation—'

'Right, right,' Timothy said quickly. 'I understand. That's fine.'

'Would you like me to call our wire transfer department and see if there's still time to stop the transfer? There's a chance we could catch it.'

Timothy sighed. 'No . . . no.' He thought about it. 'I'm sure it's nothing terrible. Probably the decorator, or contractor, or who the hell knows. Either that, or she's in hock to her London bookie again.'

Mike Kelly was silent on the line.

'I'm just kidding, of course,' Timothy said. 'Her bookie is not based in London.'

Mike Kelly chuckled.

'Mike,' Timothy said, 'I appreciate your bringing

this to my attention. I will be sure to thrash my wife later tonight.'

Now in the proper spirit of things, Mike chuckled again, 'Okay, Mr Van Bender. Okay, Timothy. You do that.'

'Cheers,' Timothy said.

'Cheers, Mr Van Ben—'

Before Mike Kelly could finish, Timothy hung up.

He dialed Katherine. The phone rang. No answer. Where could she be? Probably buying lunch at Spago for her decorator. While he sat in his office, pondering financial ruin.

There was a knock on his door.

'Come in,' he said.

Tricia entered the room, balancing a cardboard egg-box with two coffees. 'I brought you some coffee,' she said, and pushed the door closed behind her with her shoulder. With Tricia's appearance, Timothy's anxiety about Katherine vanished.

'You're the best,' he said. She wore tight red cotton jodhpurs and a black turtleneck, with a silver choker around her neck.

'How was your weekend?' she asked. She removed one cup of coffee from the cardboard box and placed it on the desk in front of him. He wondered: who was the second cup of coffee for? She answered the question by opening the lid and taking a sip. It was her own. Had she really brought two cups of coffee into her boss's office so that she could join him for a little coffee-break banter?

This was daring, he thought, suddenly feeling the rush of blood to his penis, the constriction in his throat, the prickles of excitement on the back of his arms. Tricia leaned against the corner of his desk, practically sitting on it now, the soft rounded wood pushing against the back of her thighs. Those tight red pants were just feet away from him.

She sipped her coffee, and continued her line of questioning. 'Did you rekindle the magic?'

It took him a moment to realize that she was asking about the anniversary weekend with his wife.

He said, 'I bought her an expensive diamond necklace for our anniversary. That seemed to rekindle things pretty well.'

'Jewelry will do that.'

'What makes you think we need rekindling?'

She smiled, pulled a strand of dark hair behind her ear. 'I'm sorry. I just thought, you know, being married for fifteen years . . .'

'Twenty years,' he corrected her.

'Twenty? Wow. That seems like a long time.'

'Hmm,' Timothy said, noncommittally.

She pushed herself back further onto his desk, and was sitting comfortably on it now, her back at an angle to him. She sipped her coffee.

'And how about you?' Timothy asked. He felt like a schoolboy, nervous that he needed to fill the silence, to say something clever. 'How's that boyfriend of yours?'

'What boyfriend?' Tricia said.

'You know, the one you drove to San Francisco with. From LA? You told me about him.'

'I did?' For an instant, she seemed surprised that he knew anything about her personal life. Then her face went blank and she said flatly, 'He's gone.'

'Gone?' What did that mean? he wondered. That he left her? That she dumped him?

'Gone,' she said simply. She took another sip of her coffee and stared straight ahead.

Timothy looked at the smooth skin at the back of her neck. Her skin was pale and tight, like a child's, with soft blonde peach fuzz shaped like an arrow pointing down her back. Did she dye her hair black? he wondered.

'I'm sorry to hear that,' Timothy said.

'Are you really?'

'No,' he said, 'I guess not.'

She folded one leg over the other at the knee, then bounced it gently up and down. She turned to him and smiled over her shoulder. 'Listen,' she said. 'Tonight after work, I'm going with some friends for drinks at the BBC. Why don't you come?'

'Sort of like adult supervision?'

'It'll be fun,' she said. 'They're nice.'

'What would my wife say?'

'I wouldn't tell her,' Tricia said. It wasn't clear to Timothy if this was advice or a promise.

'I don't know,' he said. 'Let's see how the day goes.'

★   ★   ★

72

How the day went: badly.

At three o'clock in the afternoon, Timothy was staring at the yen chart on his computer screen, using his limited telepathic powers to wish it downward. It had now sunk to a little above seventy one, which meant that Timothy's huge gamble was paying off. Osiris was up three and a half million dollars. If the yen kept plummeting at this pace, in a matter of a week or two he'd be able to cover his position and end his bet with a profit, and none of his investors would be the wiser.

His intercom rang. It was Tricia. 'I have Pinky Dewer here,' she said.

'Take a message,' Timothy said.

'No,' she said quietly. 'He's *here*, in reception.'

Timothy hung up the phone. He grabbed his jacket from the back of his office door and slid it on. He fixed his cufflinks, straightened his tie.

In the liquid-asset food chain, Timothy was a carnivore, wealthier than most of the people he saw or talked to during the course of a day. He was wealthier than the clerk that served him coffee in the morning at University Café. He was wealthier than Frank Arnheim, his nouveau riche lawyer at Perkins Coie, who had spent fifteen grueling years climbing to the rank of partner. He was wealthier than his pretty assistant, Tricia, and his young Jewish employee, Jay. He was wealthier than his wife – their prenuptial agreement guaranteed that. He was wealthier than virtually anyone he saw, or talked to, or even thought about. This is what it means to be wealthy: to be assured that no matter what room you enter, and no matter who rings on the phone, you can outspend any person, and solve any dispute in your favor.

But Pinky Dewer was a different matter. What Timothy had in common with Pinky Dewer was that both men had received a large amount of money from their fathers. Where they differed was that Pinky had taken that money, around forty million dollars, and multiplied it fifteen-fold, through some mysterious financial alchemy that Timothy only vaguely understood: something to do with leverage and arbitrage, with buying public companies and taking them private, or perhaps buying private companies and taking them public – Timothy could not remember which. What Timothy had managed to do with the Van Bender nest egg was different: he had managed to hold on to it and make it grow by about five percent per year. The Van Benders were, when it came to both money and sex, conservative. Financial and bedroom activities were to be carried out in a way that would not be embarrassing to explain to children.

So when Pinky Dewer showed up at Timothy's office, Timothy understood that he was temporarily demoted down the food chain from financial carnivore to financial prey. It was a role Timothy was unaccustomed to playing, but Pinky was the largest investor in Osiris, having placed twenty-four million in Timothy's fund. Through the magic of his hedge fund's one percent management fee, Timothy earned two hundred and forty thousand dollars each year simply by holding onto Pinky's money. That was twenty thousand dollars per month. Which was enough to make Timothy amenable to switching places on the food chain for a day.

Timothy strode into the reception area with his hand already outstretched. He reached for Pinky's hand and pumped it aggressively. 'Pinky!' he practically shouted.

'Timothy, old boy!' Pinky swung his left hand and grabbed Timothy's right, thus controlling the pace and duration of the shake. 'How are you?' Timothy tried to extract his hand, but Pinky kept shaking. 'It is great to see you, old friend.'

'And you,' Timothy said. Pinky kept pumping his hand, and he smiled at Timothy and stared into his eyes. Pinky had cold, blue, smiling eyes.

Timothy smiled back and kept pumping. It was pointless to try to retract his hand. Pinky would not let him go.

Pinky was a big, colorful, bear-like man. His hair was once bright red, but now auburn and gray. He wore perfectly polished penny loafers, bright green slacks, and a pink Oxford shirt. His face was bright red. For as long as Timothy had known him – since their days at Yale together – Pinky's face had been red. This, Timothy understood, was the inevitable result of spending days sailing his catamaran through the windswept Atlantic; of sunning in Naples, Florida; and of drinking bountiful gin and tonics – sometimes all three before noon.

'I'm so glad you could take the time to see me,' Pinky said. He said it without a trace of irony, which surprised Timothy. 'And I apologize for dropping by unannounced, but I'm flying out tonight, and I simply had to say hello.'

'It is a pleasure, Pinky,' Timothy said. 'You are always welcome here.' He continued pumping Pinky's hand. Over Pinky's shoulder, he saw Tricia sitting at her reception desk, watching him.

Pinky dropped Timothy's hand suddenly, leaving Timothy grasping at air. 'Can I buy you some lunch?' he asked.

'Absolutely not,' Timothy said. 'You will never be able to buy me lunch. But I would love to treat you.'

Pinky laughed, 'All right, then. Where to?' He put his hand around Timothy's shoulder.

'Come this way,' Timothy said, as he allowed Pinky to lead him to the elevators. He didn't want to turn to Tricia, to see her watching him. He was glad to be able to slink out of the office, to go far from her, to hide his obsequiousness. He was ashamed of having to act like this, ashamed at his new position on the food chain. Being prey was no fun.

CHAPTER 8

Timothy took Pinky Dewer to the Menlo Circus Club for lunch.

The Circus Club was an exclusive country club in the middle of Atherton, California, which was itself an exclusive suburb in the middle of democratic Silicon Valley. During the Internet boom, newcomers to Silicon Valley liked to think they had found a high-tech Shangri-la, a perfect meritocracy, a place where people lived wherever they liked, and worked wherever they liked, and ate wherever they liked, no matter how peculiar their last name, and no matter what color their skin. This was true as far as it went, but what these newcomers did not know was that, when they weren't looking, the Circus Club had quietly seceded from Silicon Valley without telling anyone. A four-acre throwback to twenties glamour, the club was a playground of the rich and the white, a place where people stabled their horses and played polo, and had a Tanqueray before heading off to a game of tennis on clay. Black was an acceptable color at the club, but only for a tuxedo – and tuxedos fortunately never applied for membership on their own.

Timothy drove Pinky to the club in his BMW. They sped through the club grounds, past the polo field, where eight horses in blue and green leg bandages were trotting, warming up before a match, in the afternoon sun. He pulled into the cobblestone reception circle. A valet approached the car, opened the door, and gave him a ticket stub. 'Welcome back, Mr Van Bender,' the valet said.

'Thanks, John,' Timothy said. 'What's the soup today?'

'Lobster bisque, Mr Van Bender.'

'Terrific, John.'

Timothy helped Pinky from the car. Pinky unfolded his legs, stood up, and lifted his pants belt over the bulge in his gut. He stared at the polo field. 'Beautiful,' he said, fiddling with his gold belt buckle. 'You play?'

'Betting's the only thing I do on a horse,' Timothy said.

'Right!' Pinky slapped him on the back. 'Right, old boy! Imagine the two of us on horses! Now that would be a sight!'

Timothy tried to imagine Pinky balancing precariously on a horse, his stocky frame clad in a pink shirt and green pants. Yes, that would be a sight, indeed.

He led Pinky into the clubhouse. The building was octagonal, surrounded by floor-to-ceiling windows on all sides. To the north were the tennis courts, ringed with azalea bushes. To the west, the stables and the polo field. To the east was the Olympic-sized swimming pool, studded with chaise longues and white umbrellas.

'Shall we eat outside?' Timothy asked.

'Terrific,' Pinky said.

They sat on the veranda overlooking the polo field, and ordered drinks just as the first polo chukka started. A whistle blew, and ponies thundered up the grass, following a red wooden ball.

'A beautiful club,' Pinky said. 'I'm surprised you haven't taken me before.'

'Pinky,' Timothy said, 'any time you're in town, I will take you here. I had no idea you liked horses.'

'Beautiful,' he said again.

On the polo field a blue player rode off a green player – galloped his horse alongside his opponent and pushed him off the path of the ball. 'Turn it! Turn it!' his teammates shouted. He raised his mallet high in the air and, with a thwack, sent the ball careening down the field toward the other team's goal.

As they watched the game, the glass door from the clubhouse slid open and another couple joined them on the veranda. It was Michael S. Stanton and Wife #2, whose name always eluded Timothy. Stanton was formerly the CEO of a high-flying medical device company which made stents used in heart surgery. The good news was that the company had reported five years of record-breaking profits. The bad news was that last October the company reported that those five years of profits were the result of accounting chicanery, and the profits had, chimera-like, turned into five hundred million dollars of losses. And so Michael S. Stanton went from CEO to ex-CEO. Two months later he was indicted by a federal grand jury. His trial for securities fraud was scheduled to begin in two weeks.

'Michael,' Timothy said, 'great to see you. How are you doing?'

The question was vague enough to be an invitation to talk about anything Michael cared to talk about: Michael's health, his car, his marriage – and, oh yes, maybe even the indictment that might send him to Pelican Bay for ten to fifteen.

'Timothy,' Michael said, walking to Timothy's table. 'Enjoying the weather?'

'California dreamin',' Timothy said. They shook hands. 'Michael, I want you to meet Pinky Dewer. Pinky and I are old friends from Yale.'

Michael smiled. 'From back before they had light bulbs in the dorms, right?

'Absolutely,' Timothy said.

'Nice to meet you,' Michael said to Pinky.

'Likewise,' said Pinky, distracted. His vodka gimlet had just arrived, and he was more interested in the beaded tumbler than in Michael Stanton and Wife #2.

Michael said: 'And I'm sure you remember my wife, Susan.'

Timothy was grateful for the introduction, because he remembered everything about Michael's wife *except* her name. He remembered the fact that she was blonde, pretty, and thirty years old, which made her twenty-five years younger than Michael Stanton. He remembered how she looked as she walked off the tennis courts, dressed in tight little whites, the way her skin glistened with sweat, the way her short skirt hiked up over her ass when she kept tennis balls in her panties between serves. He remembered how she had appeared at the Circus Club a week after Michael Stanton had divorced his first wife, the elegant but, alas, old Nancy Stanton, and how people had talked, but only for a few days. And then Susan Stanton came to the cocktail parties instead of old Nancy, and was wearing some of the same jewelry that Nancy had worn (had Michael simply bought duplicates of each piece? people wondered. Or did he snatch the bracelets from his first wife's arm as he ran from their house?) – and then people stopped talking about how strange it was that Michael was married to someone so young, and Susan became another fixture at the club – one the older male members enjoyed looking at – and Michael Stanton, despite his indictment and likely jail term and newspaper notoriety, became simply envied.

'Yes,' Timothy said to Susan Stanton, 'I remember you very well.'

'Pleased to meet you,' Susan said.

81

'How's the hedge fund business?' Michael asked.

'Funny you should ask,' Timothy said. 'That's exactly what Pinky and I are about to discuss. The brief answer – one word or less – *fantastic*. Isn't that right, Pinky?'

'Sure,' Pinky said, agreeably.

'That's great,' Michael Stanton said. 'As soon as I put this unpleasantness behind me –' he waved his hands around vaguely, as if discussing the summer chigger problem here on the veranda – 'I'll ring you up, and we'll talk about how I can chip into your fund.'

'Terrific,' Timothy said. What he thought was: At Pelican Bay, there will be a lot of unpleasant-ness behind you.

'Take care,' Michael said. He took Wife #2's hand and led her away. Over his shoulder, he called to Pinky, 'Nice to meet you!'

'Right!' Pinky said, mostly to his gimlet glass. Timothy noticed that he had finished the entire drink.

'Let me get you another one,' Timothy said. He pulled a drink chit from the lucite stand in the center of the table and wrote his club account number. 'Another vodka gimlet?'

'That's sounds perfect, friend,' Pinky said. He looked flushed. Whether it was from the afternoon sun or the gimlet, Timothy was unsure. Timothy wrote down the words 'VODKA GIMLET' and waved the card in the direction of a young waiter.

The waiter appeared, read the card. 'Right away,

Mr Van Bender,' the young man said. He turned to leave.

'Make that a double,' Pinky called to him. Then, pointing at Timothy: 'He's driving, you know.'

'Yes, sir,' the waiter said. He hurried off to the bar.

The two men sat quietly for a moment, watching the polo game. Two players rode into the corner of the field, chasing the ball. They hooked their wooden mallets in the air, and they tangled like umbrellas in a Manhattan wind. Then another green player rode up from behind and knocked the ball forward. The spectators clapped.

After a moment, Pinky said: 'Let me tell you the reason I'm here.' It seemed to Timothy that the gimlet had loosened him up a little. He sat hunched in his chair, squinting into the sun. From the polo field came cheers from scattered spectators, then a thwack, and then an umpire's whistle – the green team scored.

'By all means,' Timothy said.

Pinky said: 'As you know, Timothy old man, I've been one of your biggest supporters. How much did I invest in Osiris, when you started it?'

'Twenty-four million,' Timothy said. He had a bad feeling about the way the conversation was heading.

'Twenty-four million!' Pinky agreed, loudly. 'Twenty-four million dollars. That's a lot of confidence, I hope you know.'

'I do appreciate it, Pinky. Your support means a lot to me.'

'I know it does. That's why I wanted to talk to you in person. I didn't want my accountant to call you, and I didn't want to do this over the phone.'

'Do what over the phone?'

'Timothy, you know I've been very happy with your fund's returns. They've been excellent. If I was ready to sit on my laurels and collect interest, I'd keep my money riding on you.'

The waiter arrived with the second vodka gimlet. Before he could lay it on the table, Pinky intercepted the drink and took it from the waiter's hands. 'Here you are,' Pinky said to the waiter, prying the drink loose. A true business person, Timothy thought – always cutting out the middleman.

Timothy said, 'It sounds like you have other uses for your money.'

'That's exactly right!' Pinky cried out, excitedly. 'Exactly right!' Twenty yards away the Stantons, seated at another table, looked up at the strange ruddy guest in green pants and pink shirt, as he called out, sloshing his gimlet in his glass. 'That's what I want to say, old friend. That I have other uses for the money.' He enunciated the words slowly, as if he liked that particular turn of phrase. 'You see, I intend to put together one last deal – one last LBO. I need to scrape together all available cash in order to do it. This will be our biggest one yet.'

'Fair enough, Pinky,' Timothy said, amiably. 'You don't have to apologize to me. It's your money, and I'm merely providing you with a service. If there's something else you need to do with the cash, it does not affect me one way or another.'

'I'm so glad you said that.'

'So how much of the twenty-four do you want to withdraw?'

'All of it,' Pinky said. He thought about it, then shook his head. 'Well, leave one hundred thousand in, just to keep some skin in the game.'

'Terrific,' Timothy said. Pinky had just signed Osiris' death warrant. All of the fund's cash was riding on the second gigantic yen gamble. If Timothy returned cash to an investor now, he would first need to close down the bet, recognize the first failed trade, and admit that he would never be able to make back the money he had originally lost. It would mean certain destruction for Osiris, and professional ruin for Timothy. As soon as he reported the first staggering loss, investors would flee, withdrawing their money almost overnight. His reputation would be destroyed, and he'd never be able to manage money again. It was, in other words, one of the most ruinous things Pinky could possibly say.

Timothy asked, 'How soon do you need the money?'

'Tomorrow,' Pinky said.

No, Timothy thought. *That* is the most ruinous thing Pinky could possibly say.

'Tomorrow?' He couldn't prevent the sound of alarm creeping into his voice. 'But Pinky, that's impossible. The money is deployed. It's not liquid right now.'

Suddenly the vodka haze around Pinky vanished, and he looked at Timothy with clear blue eyes. 'I do vaguely remember our Investor Agreement, old man. You carved out an exception for me, since I was the first investor. Money on call within twenty-four hours. Am I mistaken?'

'No, no, of course not,' Timothy said. Pinky was correct. Legally, Pinky had the right to redeem his cash at any time.

'How are we doing this month?' Pinky asked. 'Problems? Why isn't the fund liquid?'

'No problems,' Timothy said. 'None. It's just, I would have preferred to wind down the positions the way I planned.'

'Sorry, friend,' Pinky said. He took another swig of his gimlet. 'That's the nature of the beast you ride. I need to put down cash for my deal. But I'll tell you what. What's a legal agreement between old friends? You need a little time? Take a few days.' He smiled, waved his hand magnanimously. 'How about you wire me the money on . . . I don't know. Wednesday? That should be plenty of time to extract yourself gracefully from whatever position you're in. I mean, it's not as if the whole fund is invested in one single position, right?'

'Right,' Timothy said weakly.

'Then it's settled.' Pinky was back to being amiable and inebriated. He stared at the horses galloping downfield. 'You have no idea how much

I love this club.' And then: 'How about another gimlet?'

Timothy drove Pinky to SFO to catch a six-thirty flight. After dropping Pinky at the departures level, Timothy pulled back onto 101 North and sat in bumper-to-bumper traffic. To his left, the sun was setting over the Bay, over the marsh grass and salt ponds, over the marinas and high-tech billboards. Timothy tapped his left foot against the clutch pedal. It was the only part of the car that moved during rush hour on 101.

Timothy pondered the decisions he needed to make. First, there was Pinky and his request to withdraw money from Osiris. Of course, Timothy would allow no such thing. He would delay: Wednesday would come, and he would do nothing, and Pinky would call several times, increasingly angry, but Timothy would be unreachable. He could stretch the game out for a week or two before Pinky threatened to sue. And while surely it would be a blow to turn Pinky Dewer, his biggest supporter, into a legal adversary, even worse was the alternative: to give back the money and close down the yen trade prematurely, before making back the initial loss; to admit to all the investors – not just Pinky, but all twenty-four wealthy, powerful men who invested in Osiris – that Osiris was a bust, that Timothy had lost a large portion of their money; and that he had become a public failure for the first time in his life. A lawsuit from Pinky would be ugly and would tarnish him, but he could always talk his way around it – he was good at talking his way around inconvenient facts – and he could chalk it up to a misunderstanding, or he could roll his eyes and imply that Pinky was a great guy, but simply not *all there* anymore. The important thing was to be in control, to keep the money within his grasp for as long as he needed it, and not to lose his nerve. It was the one business lesson Gabriel Van Bender had bothered to explain to his son: Never lose your nerve.

So solving the Pinky Dewer problem was not difficult at all, because Timothy had no other option. There was only one choice he could make – to keep the money riding on the yen trade, and to hold on, no matter how many phone calls Pinky made, no matter how threatening the inevitable lawsuit.

The other decision Timothy needed to make was more difficult, because it did involve a choice. He looked at the BMW's dashboard clock. It was a little past six o'clock in the evening. At that moment Tricia would be sitting down in the cool, dark bar called the BBC, drinking with friends, looking at the doorway occasionally to see if he had chosen to accept her invitation and join her.

Timothy mulled it over. He tried to imagine what would happen if he did show up. Almost certainly, he could sleep with Tricia. And then what? He thought about what would happen the following day, at work. Would Tricia be overly familiar? Would she tip her hand to Jay? Would she accidentally reveal their secret if Katherine called the office? Katherine was clever and wily, and she could read people far better than he could – in fact, he relied on her to do so, to tell him when associates were lying, to see through the inconsistencies of their stories, to hear the stress in their voices. It was one of the many things he loved about her – her street-smart cleverness. It was something he never learned, something he never needed to learn, growing up in the Van Bender cocoon of Atherton and Exeter and Yale and the East Side of Manhattan. The only street-smart he possessed was knowing where to park the Beemer in the Mission District so it wouldn't be keyed.

The three lanes of traffic on 101 were being squeezed together by pink florescent flares, and finally merged into one. Up ahead, Timothy saw the cause of the jam: an accident, a little BMW roadster, identical to his, even down to the same black color, had been wrecked. It was overturned and crumpled against the concrete pylons that separated the highway. Ambulances and police cars, siren lights flashing, stood by. Timothy craned his neck to look inside the car, to learn the fate of the driver. He couldn't see. But the front and rear of the BMW had been smashed like an accordion, and the windshield hung limply from the frame, snaked with silver and white cracks like crumpled Christmas wrapping paper. The EMS technicians stood lethargically beside the ambulance. Their demeanor said it all: there was no longer any reason to hurry.

Timothy passed the wreck, and the traffic started to move. His mind snapped back to Tricia. He thought about how she looked that morning, in her red shin-high jodhpurs, her tight black turtleneck, that little silver choker around her neck. He remembered the way she had leaned backward against his desk, how her body had been so close to his, how he could look at her breasts in profile without her being aware of his stare. What had she told him? That she wouldn't tell his wife? And how could Katherine really know?

He pressed the button on his steering wheel marked Voice Dial and then said aloud, 'Call home.'

On speakerphone, his home phone rang. He expected it to keep ringing, that Katherine wouldn't be home, that his plan – half-formed now under a cloud of testosterone and alcohol – would never be executed. But, instead, she picked up the phone. 'Hello?'

'Katherine,' he said, 'it's me. You're not going to believe this.'

'What's wrong?' she asked. He tried to imagine where she was at that moment: sitting on the patio, writing her diary? Unpacking groceries into the refrigerator, with the phone cradled under her neck? Cooking dinner? Upstairs in the bedroom, lying down in the dark, suffering from one of her frequent migraines?

'Nothing's wrong,' Timothy said. 'Well, nothing terrible. But guess who's in town?'

'Who?'

'Pinky Dewer.'

She was silent on the line. He hadn't told her about the yen, about the devastating loss, about the fact that he was teetering on the verge of ruin. But he had told her about avoiding Pinky, about trying not to take his call. She said finally: 'You're kidding.'

'No, he just showed up.' Now the plan grew solid and visible in his mind, like a distant shoreline as the morning fog burned off. He had known he would have a plan, even before it formed in his mind, even before he made the phone call. He said: 'So now I'm heading over to the Circus Club, where I'm going to meet Pinky for drinks.'

It was a good plan, because it gave him an alibi, although the time sequence was slightly off. But the alibi would work, because people had seen him at the Circus Club, and anyone who related the story to Katherine would not bother to say exactly when they had seen Timothy – only that they had indeed seen him with Pinky, having drinks on the veranda.

And so now Timothy put in place the last piece of the plan, saying: 'So why don't you come by and join us for drinks? We'll be at the pool.'

This served two purposes. First, he knew she

hated sitting at the pool, in the heat, with the old grand dames of Atherton in their sun hats and one-piece bathing suits. He knew it was unlikely she would agree to come along. And second, the story offered one last bit of insurance, in case she decided to drop by the club and pay a surprise visit to the pool: he could always say later that evening that he and Pinky had in fact been on the veranda, and that Katherine had simply missed them – and what a charming mix-up it all was!

He waited for her to answer, waited for her to tell him that she didn't want to join him and Pinky Dewer for drinks at the pool.

But instead she was silent.

'Katherine?' He didn't want to push too hard, but he needed to make a show of it. 'Do you want to join us?'

Still, she was quiet. Was she testing him? Weighing the probabilities, the possible reality behind his words?

'I don't know,' she said, alarmingly. Her voice trailed off. 'I suppose I could.'

'Pinky would love to see you,' Timothy said calmly, although now he was verging on panic. He would have to abort the plan, would have to race to the Circus Club, meet her for drinks and pretend that Pinky went AWOL, or changed his mind, or had to return to San Francisco early.

'Oh, Timothy,' she said. Her voice was soft and tired. 'Would you mind terribly if I didn't come?'

'Mind?' He swallowed hard. 'Of course not.'

'Well . . .' She sighed. 'It's nothing. I'm just exhausted and not feeling well.'

'Do you want me to come home?'

'No, no,' she said, 'it's okay. It's important that you meet with Pinky. I know he's a big client.'

'The biggest, actually,' Timothy said.

'Then you should go.'

'All right,' he said. His heart began to race as the reality of what he was about to do hit him. His pumped the clutch and shifted into fifth gear. He thought about Tricia, the way she had a habit of cocking her head and pulling a strand of dark hair behind her ear. For the first time, he tried to picture her naked: her firm, lithe thighs; her pubic hair; her buttocks.

Katherine said: 'I love you, Timothy. You know that, don't you?'

He did know that, and he appreciated her love, but – at this point – flying down Highway 101 with the sulfur smell of the Bay in his dashboard vents, and the sun on his face, her words were small and far away, and when the cell phone cut out he didn't bother to call back.

CHAPTER 9

The British Bankers Club, or BBC as it was known to people who lived on the Peninsula, was housed in an old bank building on El Camino Real. The bank had been built in an age when people still seriously considered keeping their money in a mattress, or buried in the backyard behind the juniper tree, and so bank buildings needed to make a certain statement to reassure the skeptical farm folk, which was: I am massive, and my iron and marble and stone will outlast your money by a thousand years.

Except of course that the Pacific Bank on El Camino lasted exactly twenty-three years, until the Depression, at which point its marble columns stood guard over empty vaults, and it took another thirty years for the building to find a more suitable use: that of a brew-pub catering to Silicon Valley dot-commers and the staff that supported them, as they labored to write the software that ran the banks where the farm folk finally did keep their money after all.

The BBC was an anachronism, an old-fashioned stone tomb, next door to a Kinko's Copy Shop, in the middle of the most technologically advanced suburb in the world, and it was decorated to further fool time – with burnished wood and brass, and overstuffed chairs and couches, like a London drinking club from the thirties. Union Jacks hung on the walls, and dartboards and snooker tables were found where the old bank vault used to be, and at the doorway where one entered, one read an age-worn painted sign: 'Gentlemen are kindly asked not to urinate in the umbrella stands during asparagus season.'

When Timothy entered, the BBC was dark, with heavy green felt curtains pulled tight over the windows, and candles on the tables, flickering. He looked around the room, past the young men in chinos and white shirts – either entrepreneurs or waiters, Timothy could never tell – past the secretaries, hopelessly dressed in spandex and cheap girandoles, and past the crowd at the bar, two deep, waiting for drinks. Monday night in Silicon Valley: too much money, everywhere. Money had become democratic, so much so that people with real money had to start thinking about fleeing, as if from apocalypse, into the mountains, where the Blackberries and emails and chinos could not catch them, where they could start a new society based on caste and class, and the good days of knowing one's place could return again.

Timothy saw her – *there* – in the back, with a group of men and women surrounding her like drones around the queen bee. One of the faces was familiar: Jay Strauss, the Kid, and for the first time Timothy realized something that had escaped him until that moment: that the Kid was infatuated with Tricia. Timothy could tell from the way he was smiling at her, the near rigor mortis on his face, the forced laughter when she spoke. He was hopelessly in love.

When Timothy strode halfway across the room, Tricia saw him. Her reaction was exactly what Timothy had hoped. She opened her mouth, smiled, and waved her hand. She said something excitedly to the kids around her. Jay looked up. His face dropped momentarily, and then he too smiled – a forced, pained smile.

'Timothy!' Tricia called.

Timothy approached their table. 'Hello, ladies and gents.'

'Awesome! You made it!' Tricia said. 'Everyone, this is Timothy, my boss. Excuse me, Mr Van Bender.'

'Call me Timothy,' he said.

Tricia introduced her drones. 'This is Rachel,' she said, pointing to an overweight brunette with huge breasts, wearing a sundress. 'And this is Jack,' she said, pointing to a young man with curly hair and wire-rimmed glasses. Jack waved. 'And of course you know Jay.'

'Of course I know Jay,' said Timothy.

'Hi, Timothy,' Jay said, deflated. He couldn't hide his disappointment; his boss had arrived.

'Hi, Kid,' Timothy said, and then thought better

of it. The decent thing to do, when around his peers, would be to call him by his real name. 'Hi, Jay,' he said again.

Jay nodded.

'We were just talking,' Tricia said, 'about work.' She gestured to the table behind Timothy. 'There,' she said, 'pull up a chair.'

Timothy slid an oak armchair from the table nearby. He sat down across from Tricia, who was perched in the center of the overstuffed red felt settee, with Jack and Rachel on each side. Poor Jay could barely squeeze on the small couch; his thigh rested precariously on the edge. 'Anyway,' she continued, 'everyone was saying how they hated their jobs, and how their bosses were total loads . . . except for me, of course.'

Jay said, 'And me.'

Timothy ignored him. To Tricia he said: 'You don't say.'

'I was telling everyone how great my boss was. Then, who should walk in, but my boss!' She smiled. 'What's the chance of that?'

'Slim, I'd say.'

'Slim,' she agreed.

A waitress came to take drink orders. Timothy ordered Dalmore on the rocks. Tricia ordered a second Cosmopolitan, though she had not finished her first. Rachel, Jack, and the Kid ordered beers.

'I just happened to be driving by,' Timothy said, continuing their game. 'I hope I'm not intruding.'

He looked at Tricia. He tried to figure out what was different about her since he had seen her that afternoon. She wore the same tight red pants, the same snug black turtleneck. Perhaps it was that she now wore lipstick, a dark ochre, the color of blood on sand.

Then he realized: her glasses. She was not wearing the black-framed librarian spectacles. Did she trade her glasses for contact lenses when she went out at night? Or were the glasses just a fashion accessory – a non-prescription prop? How many people, Timothy wondered, wore fake glasses if they had perfect eyesight?

Rachel, the girl in the sundress, said, 'So what do you do, Timothy? Tricia is always so vague about her job.'

Tricia laughed. 'I told these guys, I don't even *know* what you do!' She said it proudly, stupidly, and it made Timothy cringe. Why were pretty girls so dumb? What kind of society do we live in, when someone intellectually incurious can flit through life easily, simply because she has a tight body and the face of Venus?

'What I do,' Timothy said, 'is manage money. Rich people give me one hundred dollars, and a year later, I give them back a hundred and twenty.'

Tricia piped up, tried to help Timothy impress her friends: 'But they give you more than a hundred dollars, right?'

Timothy exchanged a pained look with the Kid.

'Well, that's right,' Timothy said. 'We're talking

about millions of dollars. A hundred million dollars, actually.'

'Cool,' said Jack, the curly-haired kid with the glasses. He had the shaggy amiability of someone who had done his part to support the Mexican economy by smoking a lot of pot. 'A hundred million dollars. That's a lot.'

'You see?' Tricia said to her friends. 'Isn't he the coolest boss? Out here drinking with us? On a school night? Awesome!' She reached across and put her hand on Timothy's thigh. She left it there. Timothy felt that old familiar stir: an erection. God, she was good looking, Timothy thought. Those blue eyes, the red lipstick, the tight shirt. Her hand crept up his thigh a bit. Now it was a few inches from his crotch. He dared not look down, to see her young fingers on his slacks. If he looked, he would be forced to admit what was happening. Until then, it could be a simple misunderstanding: Oh, was your hand on my penis? I hadn't noticed.

'I work with Timothy, too,' the Kid said. Timothy thought: God, you're hopeless. He made a mental note to take the Kid aside, give him some pointers about how to impress women. The Kid would need to lose this particular contest over Tricia, of course, but once this was over, Timothy could spare honest advice. The Kid would have money some day, Timothy thought, no doubt about it. He was bright, and a bit of a shark. As his mentor, Timothy owed him. He should help ease the Kid's entry into his world, the world where money always let you win. But not tonight.

Timothy glanced around the room one more time. He peered into the darkness, tried to make out the faces at the bar, at the tables around him. Was there anyone familiar? Any friend of Katherine's? Anyone from the club? Anyone from church? It was unlikely, since this was a young person's place, and his friends were no longer young. But he had to be sure.

Satisfied, Timothy said, 'I wonder where those drinks are.' He stood from his chair, made a show of looking for the waitress. Then he sat back down, and, as he did, pulled his chair closer to Tricia, so that he sat nearly between her legs. She spread them wider, reached over, guided his chair closer. Now his knees rested on the inside of her thighs. Timothy took her hand within his. Her skin was soft and dry, her fingers cold. She intertwined her fingers in his. And then he knew that he would have her, that she was his, and that money always let you win.

Her friends left, one by one. First, the Kid, who skulked off muttering cursory goodbyes. The stoner, Jack, stood up five minutes later and said, 'I gotta go.' Tricia didn't argue. Jack vacated the seat beside Tricia on the settee. Tricia pulled Timothy's hand and guided him to sit down beside her. He fell backwards into the sofa. She pushed up against him, snuggled into his side. He felt her breast against his shirt.

Rachel looked uncomfortable. 'Well,' she said, 'I should head out.'

'Okay,' Tricia said.

Rachel leaned over, pressed her cheek to Tricia's, kissed the air. 'Good luck,' she said. Then, to Timothy: 'It was nice to meet you.'

'And you.' Timothy had his arm around Tricia's shoulder. He could smell her shampoo, lemon and rosemary, and he felt her hair, like silk, under his chin.

When Rachel left, they sat together, still. The bar was full now, packed with kids blowing off steam after work, and getting louder. A bunch of beefy boys in baseball caps gathered around the snooker table, shouting.

'Well, this is interesting,' Timothy said.

But she was not the type to engage in self-reflection. 'Come home with me,' she said.

'Okay.' He stood up, opened his wallet, and threw a hundred dollar-bill on the table. They left the bar and walked out into the night.

They each drove their own car; he followed her yellow Celica.

He tailed her out of the BBC parking lot onto Ravenswood Drive, and then along Middlefield and Willow – until he was back on Highway 101. They traveled south for twenty minutes. Palo Alto was the zenith of real estate value on the Peninsula; it was – literally – downhill from there. Each mile south on 101 knocked another ten thousand dollars off the median home price and, as he drove, the houses along the highway changed, from red Spanish bungalows and sprawling ranches, to white clapboard houses, to concrete slab apartments built over open carports. Finally, she took Route 85, the corridor that carried the secretaries and personal assistants and firemen and police into and out of Palo Alto each morning and night – the renal artery of the Peninsula.

She pulled off the highway onto surface streets. He followed her down Stevens Creek Boulevard, where all evidence of a namesake creek had disappeared long ago beneath asphalt used car lots, balloons, and neon signs promising nought percent APR. Off Stevens Creek, she turned left and then right, until Timothy was sure he was lost and would never find his way home.

Finally, she pulled over to the side of a tree-lined street and stopped her car. He parked behind her and got out.

'Here we are,' she said, indicating an old yellow four-plex across the street. Two balconies had black charcoal grills; a third, a scrawny orange tree in a clay pot.

'Cute,' he said.

'A little different than what you're used to, I bet,' she said.

'Pretty much like where I started out,' he lied.

She led him up two flights of concrete stairs. He followed close behind and stared at her ass as they climbed. The stairs stopped at her apartment door, which was marked with a cheap plastic letter D. The top nail holding the D in place was missing, so the letter had flipped upside down. She took her keys from her purse and jingled them until she found the right one. She turned the lock, giving the door a shove with her shoulder. It didn't budge. 'Always sticks,' she said. After another shove, the door opened and they walked inside. She turned on the light.

It was much cleaner than the exterior had led him to expect. Plush medium-pile brown carpet, newly painted white stucco walls. An air conditioner in the window was going full blast, so the living room was icy. A sliding glass door led to a patio. Near the apartment entrance there was a small galley kitchen, with clean pots on the stove.

'Nice,' he said.

He saw her looking around the apartment. What was she looking for?

A thought occurred to him. 'Do you live alone?'

'Most of the time,' she said vaguely. She seemed nervous. Perhaps she had not left the air conditioner on when she left in the morning. In which case, he wondered, who had?

'Come into my bedroom,' she said.

'You sure?'

She took his hand and led him around the corner into the bedroom. The bed was made neatly, a blue denim duvet pulled snugly under the mattress. Why had she made the bed? Was she expecting him as early as this morning, when she left for work? Had she known even then that he would return with her?

She closed the bedroom door, turned the lock.

The bedroom was small, unremarkable. A beechwood table, probably from IKEA, was pushed against the far wall, with a computer on top. On the table, and on her bureaus, there were no photographs, no mementos.

'How long have you lived here?' he asked.

She pushed herself into his chest, pulled him down by the neck and kissed him. He felt her ochre lipstick rubbing off onto his lips.

'Do you really care?' she said, all breath and silky hair. Her mouth smelled like mint and Triple Sec. She kissed him again, pushing her tongue into his mouth. Her kiss was hard, violent. He felt her teeth under her lips. Her hand stroked his thigh and worked its way up his pants leg. She grabbed his penis. 'I've been wanting to fuck you since the first day I met you.'

Her words shocked him. He had never been with a woman that used the word fuck. Even the few whores he had been with had more class.

'I want your cock inside me,' she whispered. She stuck her tongue in his ear and pushed him backward onto the bed. He fell across the mattress with his head halfway up the bed, his Cole Haan Carnegies still firmly on the floor. She climbed on top, straddled him, pushed her pubic bone into his penis. 'You want to fuck me, Timothy?'

'I do,' he said. But felt like adding: 'If you would only stop talking.'

She unzipped his pants. She moved her hand down his abdomen, and lifted the elastic band of his cotton briefs. Without thinking, Timothy grabbed her hand, hard, stopped it from moving.

'Hey,' she said. She looked surprised. 'What's wrong?'

He sat up on his elbows, pushed her gently off him. She climbed down from the bed and stood over him.

'Nothing,' he said. 'It's just . . .' He didn't know what to say, because he truly did not know what was wrong. But it was something. He didn't want to continue. He had cheated before, and had never had difficulty doing so. But for some reason, tonight, he couldn't go through with it. He said, for lack of anything better: 'I'm married.'

'It'll be our secret,' Tricia said. She wore a sly smile, the one she always tried when she spoke about his wife.

'But . . .' he said, and he waited for an explanation to form, so he could relay it to her. None came. He needed to tell her about Katherine: about how she could be a pain in the ass, but that he loved her; about how her mood swings often made marriage into hell, but that he had learned how to cope with them; about how sometimes they hated each other, but only for the briefest of moments; and about how, after every fight, he, improbable as it sounded, loved her even more.

105

Maybe it was the anniversary weekend just passed, in which he could feel her weakness, merely by touching her – the way a boy can hold a field mouse and feel its tiny bones and frantic breathing, and know that one hard touch can destroy it. Maybe he needed to drive to Tricia's apartment that night, to come this close to betraying Katherine, to understand how fragile she was, and how much she meant to him, and how much he needed to protect her.

He wanted to tell Tricia all these things, but the thoughts remained jumbled, and by the time he could tease out the strands of an explanation, Tricia had already turned away from him.

He rose from the bed, pushed his shirt into his waist, re-zipped his pants. 'You are an incredibly beautiful, sexy girl, Tricia. I would love to stay here and . . .' He didn't want to use the word fuck. '. . . keep going,' he said. 'But it's not right.'

'Then why did you come?' She stuck out her chin, defiant. But he thought perhaps there were tears in her eyes.

'I don't know,' he admitted. 'Because I'm attracted to you. But how would this work? What's our plan?' Timothy liked having a plan, and he couldn't see one here. 'I'm practically fifty years old.'

'You're not fifty,' she said, as if the three years' rounding error was what mattered.

'I have a wife,' he said. 'I'm not a saint; I never have been. But she's waiting for me at home, for Christ's sake. I can't do this to her.' He walked to the mirror hanging over her bureau, wiped the lipstick from his face. He patted down his hair, adjusted his shirt collar. He turned to her. 'Look, I will see you tomorrow morning in the office. Let's pretend this never happened. You're a great girl, and I don't want to lose you.' Then, to avoid any misunderstanding, he added: 'As an assistant. Okay?'

She sat down on the bed and didn't answer. He wondered: could this be the first time in her life that a man fled from her, even after she touched his penis? Perhaps this was a new experience for this young girl.

'Okay?' he asked again.

She didn't answer, but he didn't care, because he needed to get home. He left her in the bedroom, and ran from the apartment before he changed his mind.

CHAPTER 10

He raced out of Cupertino as fast as traffic on 85 allowed. The clock in the BMW dash said 8.30 p.m. He reviewed the alibi he would offer Katherine. He would take the events of the afternoon, shift the timeline by two hours, make Tricia disappear. So: he had drinks with Pinky Dewer at the Circus Club at around six. When they were on their second vodka gimlet, Pinky used his cell phone to call his airline, at which point he learned his flight back to New York was canceled. Timothy would not give Katherine any details: neither the name of the airline, nor the cause of the canceled flight. Nothing for her to research, if the spirit moved her.

He continued building the story. So Pinky was trapped in the Bay Area. Timothy was upset, but he had no choice; Pinky was his largest investor, and he had to keep him entertained. So they left the Circus Club and traveled two miles down El Camino, from Atherton to Menlo Park, to the BBC. There they had a few more drinks. Finally, Pinky called his airline one more time and complained. Lo and behold, they found him a seat in first class. He raced out of the BBC and back to SFO to catch the flight.

It wasn't Timothy's best story, but it would do. There were a few weak spots, joists that didn't hang together, mortises that didn't fit. She would surely ask why Timothy didn't call her before heading over to the BBC. He thought about it, and then decided that his cell phone battery had, unluckily, died. He removed his cell phone from his jacket pocket, and – one-handed – opened the back battery compartment. The lithium block dropped into his lap. He put it in the BMW glove compartment. There, he thought. No more juice.

When he got off 101 at University Avenue it was a quarter to nine. He sped through East Palo Alto, onto Waverly, and north into the Old Palo Alto neighborhood.

Five blocks later, he pulled into his driveway. Their yard was unkempt, with spiky brown ornamental grasses and wildflowers. Apricot trees stood on the left side of the house. It was an old 1930s Tudor, with high gables and thick half-timbers crisscrossing white stucco. The windows were tall and narrow, old-fashioned lead glass, beneath a steeply pitched roof.

Timothy raced up the slate garden path, through the grasses, and to the front door. The night was warm and dry. Crickets chirped in the yard. He rang the doorbell and started for his own keys. Moths fluttered around the entryway light. Timothy half expected Katherine to pull the door open even as he turned the key in the lock. But no one answered the door. Instead he pushed it open, and was greeted by an empty foyer.

He entered, closed the door. He flipped on the light switch. 'Katherine?'

He listened for the sound of water running through the old pipes, a sign that maybe she was in the bedroom, showering. Nothing.

'I'm home,' he called out.

He walked into the foyer, his heels clicking on the ceramic tile. Before moving in, they had gutted the interior and redone it in a modern style she favored but which he found cold and unwelcoming. A black lacquered table sat at the side of the foyer, displaying the abstract white sculpture she had bought in Big Sur.

'Oh, Katherine?' he said, the first hint of worry creeping into his voice. This wasn't what he expected. He was accustomed to her pouncing on him immediately when he entered, to fending her off with hurried, breathless explanations. But now he was greeted by silence and darkness. It threw him off balance, and he felt like a Marine, on point, sensing an ambush.

But the ambush didn't come. He walked down the hall, turning on lights as he went. The only sounds were his own footsteps echoing off the plain white walls.

He climbed the carpeted stairs and walked into their bedroom. She wasn't there. The big flat-screen television stood near the bed, mute and dark. Timothy peered into their master bathroom. Empty.

He wondered where she could have gone. He glanced at his watch. It was almost nine o'clock on a Monday night. She had said nothing about having plans. When they last spoke, she was lying in bed with a migraine. But now the bed was empty, neatly made.

He walked back downstairs into the kitchen and glanced at the refrigerator. Sometimes she left him a note there. But the refrigerator door was empty, a lone magnet ('Think before you eat') askew on the metal.

He paced across the kitchen and out the rear door, which led to the garage. He turned on the garage light and descended three steps onto the concrete floor. Katherine's car, a two-year-old Lexus sedan, was gone.

He returned to the bedroom, called his cell phone voicemail, and then his office voicemail. The only message was from the Kid, who drunkenly explained that the yen had fallen to sixty-eight, but then started moving back up. He probably left the message after slinking out of the BBC, to show that he was still a team player, and that there were no hard feelings.

Timothy sat down at the foot of the bed and loosened his tie. He tried to think what this could mean. Only one thing: that Katherine suspected he was cheating and, angry, had stormed out of the house.

Her car was gone, so she had driven somewhere. Perhaps through the neighborhood, blowing off steam. Or maybe she had stopped at a girlfriend's house, where she was commiserating about how Timothy was a shit-head.

Timothy picked up the phone and called information, asked to be connected to Ann Beatty down the street. Ann was a forty-two-year-old divorcee who lived alone in the big house that used to belong to Apple Computer's CEO, Steve Jobs. Her husband, who had earned the money to buy the house, had been effectively transferred by a California divorce court to a small one-bedroom condo in San Jose, where the closest he now came to Steve Jobs was passing the Apple billboard on Highway 101 during his one-hour commute to work.

'Hello?' Ann Beatty said.

'Ann, this is Timothy Van Bender, from down the street.'

'Oh hi, Timothy.' Her voice could freeze water.

'I'm sorry to call you so late. I'm looking for Katherine. I'm wondering if she's there.'

'Your wife?' she said. He pictured her at the other end of the line, smiling bitterly. She had closely cropped graying hair and tiny eyes. She looked like a nun. He imagined the things that Katherine told her. Ann Beatty must hate me, he thought. He could hear contempt drip from her voice. 'No,' she said. 'I haven't seen her. In fact, I haven't seen her since you went to Big Sur. I hope everything's okay.'

The sing-song tone with which she hoped everything was okay indicated that she believed nothing was.

'I'm sure everything is fine,' Timothy said. 'Probably just got our wires crossed, that's all. Listen, if you see her, or if she calls, please tell her I'm at home waiting for her.'

'I will, Timothy.'

'Thank you, Ann.' He hung up.

He looked at the clock on his nightstand. It was ten past nine. He sat on the foot of the bed, waiting for his wife. He listened for the click of her heels on the slate path to the house; the tinkling of her keys in the front door; the sound of her voice echoing off the ceramic tiles in the foyer. But there were no sounds except for the crickets outside, and except for his breath, thin and ragged.

CHAPTER 11

He slept fitfully, half-dreaming, and woke at seven o'clock in the morning. The sun streamed through the tall windows onto his face. He had not drawn the curtains.

When he opened his eyes, the events of the last night rushed back to him in a jumble, and for a moment he felt as if they too had been part of a dream. But then he looked to his left, at her side of the bed, and saw that Katherine was not there, that the bed was still made, and that he was sleeping on top of the covers.

He was hungover. He hadn't realized last night how much he'd drunk. First there was the afternoon at the Circus Club with Pinky, drinking vodka in the sun, and then the hour and a half at the BBC with Tricia and her friends – three Dalmores more.

He remembered what had happened with Tricia. How he followed her back to her apartment, with the upside down letter D on the door; how she climbed on top of him, unzipped his pants. He remembered that they had kissed. That her lipstick rubbed off onto his lips.

He stood up – too suddenly – and the room whirled around him. He sat back on the bed, took a breath, tried again to rise. He stumbled to the bathroom, looked in the mirror. As if he was in an old, bad soap opera, he saw lipstick stains on his collar. He took off his shirt, put the collar under the faucet and scrubbed it with a bar of soap until the lipstick vanished, then crumpled his shirt into a ball and threw it into the hamper.

He unzipped his pants, and, with one hand on his hip, urinated.

As he stood there, pissing, the phone rang. He stopped, snapped his underwear back up. Urine dribbled down his leg. He waddled across the bedroom with his pants bunched at his ankles, to the phone. He picked up the receiver. 'Hello?'

'Timothy,' she said. 'It's me.' It was Katherine. She sounded far away, and there was noise in the background – a rhythmic static, rising and falling, alternating loud and soft.

'Where are you?'

'You have to listen to me. I need to tell you something.'

Timothy's stomach coiled into his throat. Could she know about last night? Was she leaving him? Had he destroyed his marriage of twenty years in a fit of craziness, a mistake, with a stupid secretary?

She continued. 'I'm dying, Timothy. I don't have long.'

'Dying?' He was confused. 'What are you talking about?' Her words did not fit the neat story he had already constructed: Angry Wife Walks Out on Pathetic Cheating Husband.

'I didn't want to tell you before. I didn't want to drive you away. I've known for a while.'

The only thing he could think to ask was: 'Katherine, where are you?'

'At Big Sur. Near the rocks.' And then: 'It will be easier this way, you'll see.'

On the phone he heard the static, loud and soft, rising and falling. He finally understood the source of the noise. It was ocean crashing against the shore. 'Better like what? What do you mean?' But, inside, he already knew the answer. A sick feeling grew, and he felt a wave of nausea sweep over him. He said weakly: 'Katherine, what are you doing?'

'I love you, Timothy. Everything will be okay. You'll see.'

'Katherine, wait—'

She hung up the phone. 'Katherine!' he tried to scream into the receiver, but it came out a hoarse croak. His heart pounded in his ears, and he tasted vomit at the back of his throat. He dropped the telephone and lunged across the room toward the bathroom, but couldn't make it. Vomit poured out of his mouth, a torrent of yellow mucus and phlegm and bile, splattering the hardwood floor. He stopped in the middle of the room, vomit dribbling from his chin, his hands clenched at his sides. He was powerless. In his whole life, forty years and seven, he had never felt like this, never felt so small, so little, so out of control, so helpless.

CHAPTER 12

The Palo Alto Police Department sent an officer, Detective Neiderhoffer. Neiderhoffer was short and muscular, a little plug of a man, with close-cropped salt-and-pepper hair and a black caterpillar mustache.

Palo Alto property taxes bought the best services in San Mateo County, including: a city-owned cable TV franchise which, in addition to delivering HBO and Showtime, also dug up city sidewalks and ran a fiber-optic TI cable to any home that requested it; the only city-owned electricity generating co-op in the country; and a suburban police department whose officers called citizens *customers* and which annually surveyed city residents to determine its 'customer satisfaction score.'

Detective Alexander 'Ned' Neiderhoffer had been promoted twice in four years – and had seen his pay rise from forty-five thousand to eighty thousand dollars per year – largely because he knew how to keep his customers satisfied. He followed two simple rules: he always said, 'sir' and 'ma'am,' and he treated every citizen that he spoke to as if that person were a millionaire, because, odds on, they were.

Neiderhoffer arrived at the Van Bender house and Timothy led him to the kitchen. The policeman sat down at the table, but Timothy paced back and forth in front of the patio doors. He stared through the glass into the backyard, as if Katherine might come walking through the yellow sedge at any moment, with sand on her shins, dripping seaweed.

'Mr Van Bender, sir,' Neiderhoffer said, 'I appreciate that this is a very difficult time for you. But it's important for you to bear with me. I want to get to the bottom of this.' He placed his clipboard on the kitchen table and stared at it intently, as if it was the clipboard he wanted to get to the bottom of. Then he pushed open the metal clamp and flipped over the stack of papers. He removed a pen from his suit pocket and clicked the ballpoint.

'I have a few questions for you. I know you may have answered these questions before, when you spoke to my colleagues. But please be patient.'

'That's fine,' Timothy said.

'Now – when was the last time you actually saw your wife?'

'Yesterday. In the morning. Before work.'

Neiderhoffer wrote something on his clipboard and muttered, half to himself, 'Monday morning.' He looked up at Timothy. 'How did she seem to you?'

'Seem?' Timothy shrugged. 'Fine. The same as usual.'

'Does your wife work, sir?'

'No.'

'Did she have any appointments yesterday?'

'No. I don't think so.'

'Okay,' Neiderhoffer said. He looked up from his clipboard. 'You told the reporting officer that your wife called you this morning on the telephone.'

'Around seven o'clock.'

'Did she say where she was calling from?'

'Big Sur. She . . . I think she killed herself.'

'Did she actually say she was going to commit suicide, Mr Van Bender?'

Timothy thought about it, tried to recall the exact words of their conversation. It seemed so long ago. 'No. She said she was very sick, and that she didn't want to tell me about her illness. She said, "It'll be easier this way." I know my wife. That's what she meant.'

Detective Neiderhoffer scribbled something on his clipboard. As he looked down, writing, he asked: 'Why Big Sur?'

'What do you mean?'

Neiderhoffer looked up. 'It just seems far away. To drive so far away just to commit suicide. There are a lot more convenient places. Places around here, for instance. Don't you think?'

Timothy shook his head. 'I don't know. We went there last weekend for our anniversary. She loves

it there. Loves the ocean. The rocks, the cliffs.'
Timothy looked at his watch. She had called him
only two hours ago. She could still be there, in
the sea, maybe even treading water, still alive. 'I
really should go down there . . .'

'Please, Mr Van Bender. Relax. I've already
called the Big Sur Police, and the rangers at Point
Lobos. They're looking. If she's there, they'll find
her.'

'What do you mean, "If she's there"? Where do
you think she is?'

'I'm not doubting you, Mr Van Bender. Maybe
she is there. But maybe it's not as bad as you think
– maybe she drove down there just to scare you
a little. Maybe she's in a hotel, taking a nap. Or
maybe she didn't go south at all. Maybe she's
driving north up 280 right now, to visit a friend
in Modesto. Where's her family?'

'Boston.'

'Parents alive?'

'Just her mother.'

'I'll need that phone number.' And then: 'Was
your wife mad at you, Mr Van Bender?'

'Mad?' He thought about it. 'Not more than
usual, I guess.'

Neiderhoffer jotted something on his clipboard.
'Did you fight recently . . . more than usual?'

'No.'

'Did you do anything that would upset her?'

'No.'

'The reason I ask – nine times out of ten, in

cases like this, the person turns up, perfectly fine. Usually it's just a fight. Or one spouse decides . . .' He stopped in mid-sentence.

But Timothy knew what he meant. 'One spouse decides to leave the other,' he said.

'Divorce is very common, Mr Van Bender.'

'My wife is not divorcing me.'

'If we had to choose between divorce or suicide, I think we'd both choose the same. Right?' He looked at Timothy, but didn't wait for an answer. 'Has your wife ever attempted suicide before?'

'No.'

'Is she mentally ill?'

'No.'

Detective Neiderhoffer put down his clipboard and clicked his pen closed. 'Okay, Mr Van Bender, let me tell you what's going to happen. With your permission, I'd like to look around your house. Sometimes I see things that catch my eye, but which seem unremarkable to the person that lives here. Also, I have two officers going door-to-door to your neighbors, with your wife's photograph. I have Officer Karpsky calling the taxis, the bus stations, Caltrain, the airlines. We're speaking to the hotels and motels in the Big Sur area. We've put out a notice to the regional sheriff departments and CHP to look for your wife's green Lexus. I am willing to bet dollars to donuts that we find your wife, Mr Van Bender, and that she is fine. So I want you to stay calm. Okay?'

'Okay,' Timothy said.

'One more thing, Mr Van Bender. When your wife called, she told you she was very sick. Do you know the name of her doctor?'

Timothy thought about it. Who was it? The name was on the tip of his tongue. Then: 'Yes . . . Dr Charles. Something Charles. At the Palo Alto Medical Foundation.'

'Great,' Neiderhoffer said. 'Right down the street. That'll save me some gas.'

The morning, which began with high hopes as Neiderhoffer departed, promising a rapid and probably happy end to the search – ground into tedium and despair. Timothy sat alone in the house, mostly in the kitchen, waiting for the phone to ring. He tried to take his mind off Katherine by making himself a pot of coffee, but that task was usually Katherine's responsibility – there was always a pot waiting for him when he rose in the morning – and he wasn't entirely sure how to operate the drip machine. He guessed the ratio of water to beans, and the result was a deadly brew: acrid, bitter, like an industrial solvent. He drank the whole pot anyway. Afterwards, he felt sick and had the runs, and he crapped in the bathroom four times before his bowels finally emptied.

The phone rang at one o'clock in the afternoon. Timothy raced from the bathroom to the kitchen and lunged for the receiver. He half-expected to hear Katherine, but it was only Neiderhoffer.

123

'Mr Van Bender, it's Ned Neiderhoffer. I don't want to alarm you. I have no news for you.'

Timothy's heart dropped. 'Have they looked near Point Lobos like I said? Have they at least found her car?'

'I just checked again with Big Sur. Nothing has turned up. But they're still looking. I wanted to call and give you an update so you weren't sitting by the phone. Is there anything I can get you?'

'Just my wife.'

'I understand. Mr Van Bender, we're working hard on this. This is what we're trained to do.'

Timothy wondered how many missing persons, how many suspected suicides, the Palo Alto Police Department had ever handled. Their expertise seemed to involve recycling bins left out on the front lawn too long, loud high-school parties, feral cats. Wives jumping off cliffs was probably not on Neiderhoffer's CV.

'I need you to be calm,' Neiderhoffer said. 'I want you to stay in the house, in case she calls.'

'I understand.'

Neiderhoffer hung up. Timothy went into the living room and turned on the television. He flipped through the stations – past home remodeling shows, past cooking shows, past a gardening tutorial – now suddenly the entire broadcast spectrum was filled with scenes of tranquil domesticity. He landed finally on a Nascar race. He liked the mindlessness of it, the blur of the colors, the thunder of the engines, the cheering crowds. As he watched, his mind kept returning to Katherine. Could she really be dead? When he spoke to her at seven in the morning, he was sure of it; he knew from her voice exactly what she intended to do. It seemed so real, so imminent. He could taste the salt spray, feel the ocean mist on his forearms. But now, after talking to Neiderhoffer, who seemed so blasé about his wife's whereabouts – now, sitting in his living room, with stock cars whizzing around the Deep South on his television, it seemed crazy, improbable.

What had Neiderhoffer said? It just seems far away to commit suicide. He was right. Would his wife really drive ninety miles in the dark to kill herself? Katherine would barely drive five miles to a super-market to pick up a ham. Or was she punishing him, tormenting him, trying to teach him a lesson about how much he needed her? Was she going to waltz in through the front door an hour from now, hoping for a warm and tearful embrace? Now, as he thought about it – about the smug expression she no doubt had when she made the phone call, the feeling of power she must have enjoyed – Timothy began to have that old familiar feeling: the heat on the back of his neck, the tightness in his throat. What he felt, more than anything, was anger.

The doorbell rang. Timothy shuffled to the front door. He opened it to see the Kid standing there with a box of Krispy Kreme donuts and two cups of coffee.

'Cholesterol delivery,' the Kid said. He smiled. 'I thought you might need some sustenance.'

'Thanks, Kid,' Timothy said. 'Come on in.' He stood aside to let him enter and led him into the living room. The Kid looked at the Nascar race on the television.

'You watch Nascar? Jews don't get Nascar. It seems kind of pointless, driving around in a circle.'

'For once,' Timothy said, 'I agree with the Hebes.' He took the remote control and muted the television. Now the doughy Southern fans – little boys in flat-front trucker caps and men with cans of Miller – cheered silently.

Jay laid the donuts on the stone coffee table. Timothy gestured for him to sit on the sofa, but Jay shook his head. 'I won't stay. I just wanted to see if you needed anything.'

'Please, sit.' It occurred to Timothy that he had never had the Kid over to his house before. It had seemed inappropriate to show him his personal world, to let him see the rooms where Timothy walked in his pajamas, the toilet where he pissed before going to work. It was a form of weakness. And also: letting his business world into his home had other dangers. What might the Kid say to Katherine, even accidentally, about Tricia?

'We miss you at work,' the Kid said. 'I mean, I can't believe this is happening. And Tricia, she's . . .' He shook his head. 'She's devastated, obviously.' He looked sidelong at Timothy, testing.

Timothy thought: Obviously? What did that mean? The Kid wanted to see how Timothy would respond: would he provide details about what

126

happened last night at the BBC, after he'd left? What had Tricia told him? Timothy wondered. Had she revealed that he went home with her?

The Kid said: 'I heard about last night.'

Timothy wasn't sure about that. The Kid was too interested, too eager to learn more. Tricia had probably spoken in generalities. Jay, after all, was a suitor, too. One thing slutty women know how to do, Timothy thought, is to keep everyone in the game, keep the losers thinking they still have a chance to win.

'Well,' Timothy said, vaguely. He reached over and opened the box of donuts. He took a maple glazed. 'Good choice on the donuts. Maple glazed are my favorite.' He bit into the donut and wiped his mouth with the back of his hand. 'How are our Japanese friends doing this morning?'

The Kid shook his head. 'The yen's up again, unfortunately. Back to seventy-five, where we started. That wipes out any profit. And you know Pinky Dewer called. He said he spoke to you. He wants to withdraw everything but a hundred thousand. What do you want to do?'

'Nothing. Absolutely nothing.' Timothy smiled at him. Even now, with his wife either dead or missing, with his career tottering on a precipice, with his world possibly about to change forever, and for the worse, he knew to stay confident. Never show uncertainty. Never show weakness. 'We need to stay the course,' Timothy said, with sudden vigor. 'We keep Pinky's money, and we

127

keep it all short on the yen. Fuck Pinky Dewer, fuck the Japanese, and fuck the yen.'

Jay nodded. But for the first time, Timothy noticed it: a narrowing of the eyes, a hint of uncertainty in his face. For the first time, the Kid doubted Timothy's answer. And who, Timothy thought, looking at the Nascar race on the muted television, and then down at his own unbuttoned shirt collar and rumpled pants – who could blame him?

The day passed.

Neiderhoffer called again at five thirty, to tell Timothy that he still had no news, and that Katherine's car had not been found. He told Timothy that the Big Sur Police would continue the search in the morning, and that Timothy should stay confident, and not give up hope, and that, if he could, he should get some sleep.

Timothy tried. He ate a bowl of leftover pasta from the previous Thursday. He poured himself a glass of Dalmore twenty-one-year-old Scotch, neat. He watched TV. After a few hours of staring at the television, not paying attention to the programs, he poured himself another glass of Dalmore and headed upstairs.

It was ten o'clock. He undressed down to his underwear and then lay on the bed, over the blankets, and turned off the nightstand light. The August moonlight glowed through the window. Timothy felt dizzy, and the bed rocked as if on a dark ocean. Timothy turned his head, burying one eye in his pillow, to look at Katherine's spot on the bed. In the gloaming, with the half-moonlight, the vision beside him shifted. First the space was empty, just a dark indentation in the bed. Then, as he stared, the space grew darker, and he could imagine someone there, in the shadows. He could imagine *her* there, suddenly in the darkness, sleeping beside him, with her arm thrown across her forehead, her mouth open, asleep. He wished it, wished he could make it happen, make her appear through sheer force of will. He reached his arm toward the shape in the darkness – and touched nothing but cold bedspread.

What have I done? he wondered. What have I done? But the Dalmore was merciful, and sleep came.

CHAPTER 13

Timothy woke and shaved. He put on chinos and a blue pinpoint shirt, then padded down to the kitchen. The sun was bright in the backyard; he could see the day gathering in the sky, hot and sticky, real summer, unforgiving.

Timothy tried again to make coffee. This time he adjusted the ratio of beans to water, tried one tablespoon per cup of water. He flipped on the coffee maker.

The doorbell rang. It was Detective Neiderhoffer. 'No news,' Neiderhoffer said, right away.

Timothy led him into the kitchen. 'I have some coffee brewing.'

'That sounds great.' Neiderhoffer sat at the kitchen table and removed a notepad from his jacket pocket, flipped through the pages.

Timothy sat down in the chair across from him.

Neiderhoffer said, 'I got in touch with Dr Charles at the Palo Alto Medical Foundation this morning. You were right. He was your wife's doctor.'

Timothy nodded.

'When your wife called you yesterday, she told you she was very sick, right?'

'Yes.'

'According to Dr Charles, your wife hasn't seen him in the last year. Her last appointment was, let's see.' He flipped through his notepad. 'June 1998. And she was in perfect health.' He looked up at Timothy. 'Which is odd, if she was really sick.'

'Yes,' Timothy said. He tried to remember the last time Katherine had mentioned anything to him about a doctor appointment, about her health. He remembered almost nothing – he vaguely recalled a few gynecologist appointments, a check-up at the optometrist. She never said anything about being seriously ill.

'Of course that doesn't mean anything,' Neiderhoffer said. 'She may have switched doctors and not told you about it. I mean, I guess you two had secrets from each other, right?'

Timothy stared at Neiderhoffer. Neiderhoffer looked at him benignly. He stroked his caterpillar mustache. Was Neiderhoffer testing him? What was he getting at?

Then, from the detective's pocket came an electronic jingle: Tchaikovsky's 1812 Overture in tinny computer tones. Neiderhoffer pulled out his cell phone. He looked at the caller ID, held up one finger at Timothy, as if to say, 'This is the call we've been waiting for.'

He flipped the phone open and said: 'Neiderhoffer.'

Neiderhoffer nodded. He listened to the voice

131

at the other end of the line. Timothy saw the corners of his mouth tighten, and Neiderhoffer closed his eyes. Timothy felt his stomach drop.

'Okay,' Neiderhoffer said. 'I'm there now.' He nodded. 'Right. Okay.'

He snapped the phone closed, placed it gently on the table.

'That was Sergeant Billings from the Big Sur Police. I have some bad news, Mr Van Bender. They found the Lexus. It was on Mule Canyon Road, near Wells. The car was parked on the ridge, overlooking some rocks. Just like what you told us to look for, near the ocean.' He stroked his mustache. 'They found a woman's clothes, folded neatly, on the cliff. It matches the outfit you said your wife was wearing. She must have undressed before she, um . . .' His voice trailed off.

'Before she what?'

Neiderhoffer answered a different question. 'They found some blood on the rocks below. Of course we'll test it. Make sure it's hers.'

Timothy stared into the backyard, past the tall bunches of grass and gnarled apricot trees. The sun was bright, the sky perfectly blue and cloudless.

'Mr Van Bender, they didn't find the body. They may never find it. If your wife jumped, and it was low tide, she could have been carried out to sea. We're going to keep looking – we've already called the Coast Guard . . .' He waited for Timothy to react. In vain. Then: 'Mr Van Bender?'

Timothy closed his eyes. 'Yes,' he said.

'Until we find the body, we can't label it a suicide. Legally speaking, this is still a missing persons case. But, I need to be frank with you, now. It's not likely that your wife is alive.'

Timothy folded his arms and put his head down on the table. He tried to stay perfectly still, to lose himself in the darkness of his shirt sleeves and the quiet of the moment. What had he done? he thought again. He had ruined everything. And then a thought came to him with strange, sudden lucidity: How odd that I feel self-pity, and not sadness. What is wrong with me? I am the most awful person that I know.

CHAPTER 14

Palo Alto Daily News, August 19, 1999

Palo Alto Resident Missing, Apparent Suicide

Palo Alto police reported that Palo Alto resident Katherine Van Bender, of Waverly Drive, is still missing. Mrs Van Bender's car was found in Wells, near Big Sur, ninety miles south of Palo Alto. Although her body has not been located, the case is being treated as a suicide, said Detective Alexander Neiderhoffer, because Mrs Van Bender reported she was depressed, and there is physical evidence that Mrs Van Bender jumped to her death into the ocean near her car. The Coast Guard has been assisting in the search for the body, so far unsuccessfully.

Katherine Van Bender was 43. She is survived by her husband, Timothy Van Bender, who owns Osiris Capital Management in Palo Alto, and by her mother, Faith

Sutter, 66, of Cambridge, Massachusetts. The family has scheduled a memorial service for Saturday at 11.00 a.m. at Alta Mesa Memorial Park on Arestradero Drive in Palo Alto. They request that donations to Lucille Packard Children's Hospital, in the name of Katherine Van Bender, be sent in lieu of flowers.

CHAPTER 15

Katherine's mother, Faith Sutter, flew to SFO on Thursday morning. Timothy waited for her downstairs at the baggage carousel.

She appeared in a line of arriving passengers, between an Armani-clad businessman straightening his tie and spraying aerosol breath mint, and a Sikh in a sky-blue turban. Timothy walked to her. He opened his arms and pulled her toward him.

'I'm so sorry, Faith.'

She started to cry into his shoulder.

She pulled back from him and looked into his face. She was a handsome woman, with dyed blonde hair, clear blue eyes and Katherine's thin aquiline nose. Her skin hung loosely from her neck, wrinkled and soft. She looked at Timothy for a long moment and was about to say something, but stopped. Instead, she shook her head. Then she hugged him again. They held each other in the middle of the baggage claim area, as the rest of the passengers filed past them and continued their lives.

★   ★   ★

The journey to the house in Palo Alto took about one hour and fifteen minutes, during which time Timothy realized that she hated him.

He had not been aware of it before. They had seen each other infrequently, twice a year, at Christmas and during an occasional summer visit. Katherine and Timothy often asked her to come, and offered to pay for her travel, but Faith still worked as a second-grade teacher in Cambridge, making travel during the school year difficult. In the summer she preferred to stay in her own house, she said, tending to her tomatoes.

When she did visit, relations with Timothy were cordial, if perhaps cool. He tried to keep his distance from her, and he used his wife as a buffer, ostensibly to let Katherine spend time with her mother without Timothy's meddling. But over the years Faith seemed more and more distant to Timothy. He suspected, but never was sure, that Katherine confided in her mother, revealing her own unhappiness and pointing to Timothy as its cause.

Now, back at the house, Timothy helped Faith from the car and led her up the slate path into the house. At the foot of the stairs he gently tried to take her suitcase from her hand. She pulled it away from him. 'I'll take it,' she snapped.

'Let me help,' he offered.

'You've done quite enough already.'

Timothy took a step back. He had expected to play the role of comforting son-in-law to the old

137

woman. He was not expecting fury. 'Faith,' he began. 'What's—'

'She talked to me, you know,' Faith said. 'She told me all about you.'

Timothy was dumbfounded. What had Katherine told her?

'Faith, I loved your daughter. She was my wife, and I loved her more than anyone else in the world, whatever else you might think.'

She shook her head. 'You've always said the right words, Timothy, for as long as I've known you. But it's what's in your heart that matters.' She lifted her suitcase, turned, and headed up the stairs. After three steps she stopped and looked down at him. 'Everyone gets what they deserve. Remember that.'

Until they found her body they could not issue a death certificate, even if suicide was the presumptive cause. But, as Neiderhoffer gently suggested, they might never find the body – given the tides and the surf and the rocks near Big Sur – and so, even without a final cause of death, the family had every right to hold a memorial service to honor Katherine, and to bring closure to the tragedy.

Ann Beatty, Katherine's friend from down the street, offered to arrange the memorial service on Timothy's behalf. He gave her a few phone numbers, the friends he could think of off-hand, and she said she would take it from there. She called these friends, and together they assembled a further list of people to contact. By the time the

Friday service was held, more than a hundred people had been called, and Timothy was surprised by the number of friends and acquaintances that turned out.

They held the ceremony at Alta Mesa Memorial, a pretty cemetery near Foothill Park. They gathered in the indoor chapel, a studiedly non-denominational room, with pews facing the front, where Ann had placed a large photograph of Katherine on an easel, and two massive flower arrangements – sprays of white gladiolas, daisies, and carnations – on either side. The photograph, grainy from being over-enlarged, showed Katherine smiling, squinting into the sun. Timothy remembered taking the picture ten years earlier, during happier days, as they vacationed in the San Juan Islands. They were riding the ferry from Bellingham to Orcas Island. Katherine was leaning over the iron railing, her elbows supporting her body, looking into the sea. She was younger then: there was none of the sadness in her eyes that Timothy remembered. Now, enlarged and sepia-toned, ten years too young, the photograph made her look otherworldly, a ghost, frozen in time.

During the ceremony Timothy sat alone in the front pew. Sunlight streamed through the stained-glass windows, filtered by abstract shapes that could have been birds, or flowers, or perhaps nothing at all. Reverend Clark, the Rector at All Saints, spoke first. He described Katherine as a vibrant woman, a loving wife, and a woman of great faith. He said that she would be missed by all the people who came in contact with her love. He said that surely the members of All Saints, and other friends of the Van Benders, would stand beside Timothy and support him during his hour of need.

Then Reverend Clark said, 'I've been told that Timothy Van Bender would like to say a few words about his wife.'

Timothy stood up. He had not prepared a eulogy, but he knew the words would come to him, as they always did. He nodded, walked to the front of the room, and stood beside Katherine's photograph.

He began quietly. 'First, thank you all for coming. It still hasn't sunk in, that she's gone. I feel like I'm in a dream, and that I'm going to wake up soon. But I guess I won't.'

Timothy looked around the room. Faith Sutter sat immediately in front of him, in a wide-brimmed black lace hat pulled down over her eyes, her lips clenched. Next to her sat Ann Beatty, dressed in a black suit. In the next row he saw members of the Circus Club: the indicted Mike Stanton and young Wife #2, the Greenhills, even the club General Manager, Gary Currie. He saw Frank Arnheim, his attorney, a pudgy bald man with a bullet head, a double-chin, and a shiny pate. In the back row, among other faces he didn't recognize, Timothy saw one he did: Detective Neiderhoffer. Neiderhoffer wore a surprisingly good suit, dark and well-tailored, with a handkerchief in his pocket. Near him, Timothy saw the Kid and Tricia Fountain. She wore a tight black dress. Tricia nodded at Timothy. Was it a gesture of agreement? Of complicity?

Timothy continued. 'I love my wife. We were married for twenty years. That's a long time. I miss her already. I'm so terribly, terribly sad that she's gone.' He turned to the photograph. 'I love you, Katherine. I wish I could have you back.'

From the audience, Timothy heard a woman cry, but he didn't want to look into the crowd to see who it was. He was on the verge of breaking down himself, and decided to end his eulogy there. He held up his hand, nodded, swallowed, and returned to his seat. Before sitting, he glanced at the back row. Neiderhoffer stared at him. It was a friendly enough stare – with an open, sympathetic face – but it made Timothy feel uneasy, so that he looked down quickly, took his seat, and, for the rest of the morning, refused to look at Neiderhoffer again.

After the ceremony, when he returned to the house, a crowd followed him so he would not be alone: Faith Sutter, smoldering with sadness and anger; Anne Beatty from down the street; the Greenhills from the club; Reverend Clark, glancing at his watch to see how much longer he had to stay to make a decent showing; even the Kid, who looked like a wide-eyed doe, as if death was a new and shocking experience.

141

Cars filled the driveway and the street, and the house buzzed with voices and activity and women expertly preparing food, keeping the quiet of death at bay. So when he walked through the house, interrupted by people offering condolences and shaking his hand and hugging him, Timothy hardly noticed that the window in the den was open, and that the slatted Levolor blinds were swaying in the wind.

He passed the window and noticed too that the screen was askew, as if it had been replaced sloppily, and somewhere in the back of his mind he thought it was strange, because he never left the windows open.

But other than that, the house was fine. Nothing was missing. There were no muddy footprints or ransacked bureaus. And so he thought nothing more of it, and decided that he had been forgetful, and in his rush to the memorial service, he had not properly locked the house.

CHAPTER 16

Life returned to normal. Or at least, as normal as life can be after your wife throws herself from a rocky precipice.

Timothy returned to work after spending five days at home popping valiums and watching daytime TV. The Kid had done well, running the office, telling investors what had happened to Timothy, handholding them and answering their questions. Their condolences, no doubt sincere enough, were tinged with ice and steel: would this tragedy adversely affect Timothy Van Bender and Osiris LP? Would it change the strategy? Would it alter Osiris' returns? These people had not become rich by allowing themselves to brood. The Kid reassured them that Timothy's absence would be brief and that when he returned to the helm of Osiris, he would continue doing what he did best, making money on their behalf. That was all they wanted to hear.

What the Kid did not tell them was that, with or without Timothy Van Bender, Osiris was facing imminent ruin. The yen, which had so agreeably started moving down the moment that Osiris went short, had, almost on the day of Katherine's death, reversed and began moving upward with alarming speed.

The three-million-dollar paper profit that Timothy had already counted on to make back his first loss had slowly dwindled, first to two million, and then one. On the day of Timothy's return to the office, the huge yen trade was back in the red, and the twenty-four-million-dollar loss had, somehow, preposterously, grown to twenty-five million dollars.

This was what the Kid explained to Timothy as he greeted him at the elevator on Wednesday morning, his first day back to work. First, that the yen had risen past seventy-five; second, that all the other funds that had shorted the yen were now buying to cover their positions, further increasing the speed of the yen's ascent; that Osiris' loss had grown to twenty-five million; and, finally, that Pinky Dewer had called several times, asking for his money. After all this, the Kid said: 'Welcome back. You look good. How are you feeling?'

'Like shit,' Timothy said. He pushed open the glass doors leading to the Osiris offices. Tricia was there, at the front desk. Timothy had not spoken to her since the night he fled her apartment – the night Katherine disappeared.

'Hi, Timothy,' she said. 'Welcome back.'

'Thank you, Tricia.' He nodded. 'I'm glad to see you.'

But the Kid was right behind him, staring at

144

them, trying to figure out what it all meant. Timothy wasn't sure what he would say to Tricia, anyway, even if the Kid were not gawking. It seemed beside the point to tell her that their affair, however abortive, was over. Somehow, being a sudden widower made cheating less fun.

So he said, 'Thanks for standing by me during this time.'

That seemed sufficiently vague, even conspiratorial – maybe just what she needed.

'You know I'm here for you,' she said.

'I'll be in my office,' Timothy said. 'Kid, why don't you join me?'

It didn't take long – only an hour – for Pinky Dewer to call. Tricia announced him on the intercom, and Timothy decided to take the call, hopeful that the sudden death of his wife might make Pinky more empathetic. It did not.

'Timothy, old boy,' Pinky said, 'I know you've recently had a terrible tragedy. I'm sorry about Katherine. Did you get my flowers?'

'Hmm,' Timothy said. 'I'm not sure. What did they look like?' There had been a lot of flowers, and he couldn't remember who sent what, but he wouldn't put it past Pinky to expect as much and then send only an imaginary bouquet.

'They were very floral,' Pinky said, his voice echoing on the speakerphone. 'Very flowery.' He cleared his throat. 'Timothy, the reason I'm calling is that I still have not received any funds wired into my account, as I requested. This is now becoming a rather serious matter.'

Timothy winked at the Kid, who sat silently in the chair across the desk.

'Jay,' Timothy said, 'I thought I told you to take care of Mr Dewer's request to redeem all but a hundred thousand dollars of his investment in Osiris.'

The Kid said theatrically: 'I'm sorry, Mr Van Bender. It's completely my fault. With all the events happening here – the tragedy – I just completely forgot. I'm so sorry.'

'Jay,' Timothy continued, masturbating a giant imaginary penis in the air above his desk, 'I'm very disappointed with you. My personal life should not affect your ability to do your job.'

'Yes, Mr Van Bender, I'm sorry.' The Kid joined in, masturbating his own giant imaginary penis.

'All right,' Timothy said. He rose from his chair and walked to the door of his office. 'Now get out of here.' He opened the door and slammed it shut. The Kid remained seated, silent. 'Pinky?' Timothy called. 'You there?'

'Yes.'

'I'm sorry about that, Pinky. The Kid's an asshole. I will wire the money this morning. If I hurry, I can make the twelve noon cut-off.' But I won't hurry, Timothy thought.

'I would appreciate that,' Pinky said.

'Thanks for your patience, Pinky.'

'I understand.'

Timothy returned to his desk, and his finger hovered over the End Call button, ready to hang up. Before he could, Pinky's voice called out. 'Timothy?'

'Yes.'

'I'm sorry about Katherine. She was a lovely woman. I can imagine how you must miss her. It's not easy, losing your other half, is it?'

Timothy felt ashamed. A moment ago he was pantomiming masturbation, and now Pinky was consoling him about losing his wife of twenty years.

'It's not easy,' Timothy agreed, quietly.

'It gets better,' Pinky said. 'Not right away. It takes years. You were married for what, twenty years? Keep in mind: twenty years is longer than people used to live, not so long ago. So it may take time. But it will get better. And then one day you'll wake up, and it will seem like a lifetime ago. All the hurt, all the memories – they'll fade. She'll fade. You'll see.'

'Thanks, Pinky,' Timothy said. And then he hung up.

CHAPTER 17

The nights were the hardest.

During the day, at work, he could lose himself, staring at the green phosphorescent chart of the yen, or backslapping brokers at Il Fornaio over lunch, or taking an investor phone call, or shooting the breeze with the Kid – or even flirting harmlessly with Tricia. Even the failure of his yen bet was not unpleasant – the worry, the fear at least kept his nerves jangling, and kept him from thinking about Katherine.

But at night, alone in the big Tudor, he had nothing but the quiet. When the sun set, he made a point of walking through the house and turning on all the lights: every low-voltage point spot, every overhead chandelier, every floor torchiere, every under-cabinet fluorescent, every nightstand lamp. But even with the lights, it was futile; even with the white high-gloss paint and the gleaming ceramic tiles, the house seemed too dark, and it felt like the night was pressing in on him and his house, that he was being swallowed by it, a tiny pinpoint of light on a vast black ocean.

Drinking helped. Timothy had always had a

drink at night, after work – a glass of wine with dinner, a Scotch while watching television with Katherine. But now, alone, without anything else to do or think about except his dead wife, he drank heavily, so much that he would finish an entire 1997 Flora Springs before bed, or polish off a quarter bottle of Dalmore while sitting at the kitchen table, eating spaghetti. The drinks dulled him so that the sharp, sickening feeling in his gut, that inexpressible sense of something lost – of anger and sadness – became nothing but a dull pain, a regular everyday feeling of warm melancholy.

For nine days after her death, Timothy was able to control himself, but on the tenth, after drinking far too much – a bottle of cabernet from his wine cellar and three neat glasses of Scotch – he made a decision, as much as you can make a decision when you can barely walk, that he would read her diaries.

He stumbled up the stairs and into the bedroom. Her closet, a large walk-in, was separate from his, a small arm's-length box. He had not touched any of her belongings since her death. When he pulled open the doors he caught her smell, that sweet familiar odor of apples and honey, which clung to her clothes and, for a moment, made him think that she was still there, behind the blouses and dresses, ready to come forward and display a new outfit. He closed the door behind him to preserve the smell a few days longer, to prevent it from dissipating into the house, to keep from losing her completely into the air.

The diaries – that neat stack of identical leather-bound journals with gold leaf pages – remained meticulously stacked on the top shelf, among her sweaters and handbags, completely visible and in the open, protected by no more than the threat of her ire. He took the top-most volume and sat down with it on the carpeted floor. He landed on one of her shoe heels, which dug into his thigh. He pushed it aside, into another pile of her shoes, and all the heels clicked together softly, and now, down on the ground, he could smell the shoes too, the odor of leather and polish, the smell of undressing at night after an evening out, of unfastening a shoe strap before having sex, of kissing her ankle and calf and thigh.

What was he looking for in the diary? He did not know. The last time he had summoned the courage to read her journal, years ago, he was surprised and hurt by her words, by her withering criticism of him, by her icy secret hatred. Now, he didn't care what he found; he just wanted to have her back in some way, to stare at her tiny meticulous handwriting, to read her thoughts, to relive a day with her, even if through her eyes, and even if it meant seeing himself as a cad, a fool, a bastard.

He started from the back, flipping through empty pages – white space that represented days, and then months, of sadness; of his shuffling through the house, alone; of drinking himself into a stupor at night; of sleeping beside an empty dark space in bed. Finally, midway through the book, he saw her writing, in that sky-blue ink she always used, the tight letters coiled on themselves, and he stopped flipping and licked his thumb, and began flipping forward instead of back, until he found one of the last entries in the book.

Thursday, August 12, 1999
Breakfast: wheat toast and jam, grapefruit. Timothy went to work, oblivious. Tomorrow, we drive to Big Sur. Twentieth A. at Ventana Inn! Twenty! Does he remember? I love him anyway. Sometimes he can be a dummy. Underneath, he is a kind man, and love means accepting. So I accept. Maybe we will find something white for front table in foyer. Marble? We'll see. Spoke to Mom. She went on and on and on about her tomatoes. She's like George Washington Carver with her tomatoes. I can't wait until winter comes to the Northeast and those plants wither so we'll have something else to talk about. Am I terrible? Yes.

Well here he comes. Home early. One day you look up and it's twenty years. Imagine that.

Timothy smiled. He could picture her writing those words, that last afternoon before their trip to Big Sur. It was only two weeks ago, but it seemed like forever, as if years had passed. What had Pinky told him? One day you'll wake up, and it will seem like a lifetime ago. Could it seem so long ago, already?

Timothy flipped backwards through the pages, through August and July, and then through June, and he imagined the Northern California seasons running in reverse, the dry heat and undulating hills of brown grass changing back to the bright wet green of spring – and then, in March and April, the rainy season coming, day after day of gray skies and drizzle and bone-chilling winds.

He skimmed her words as he turned. He flipped a few pages, and then slowed down, read an entry, and then continued flipping the pages. He was looking for some hint of sadness, some explanation about why she killed herself, but there was nothing. Just wheat toast and jam, every day – so often that he wondered why she bothered recording it – and lunches with Ann Beatty, and tennis and riding at the Circus Club. Gifts purchased for friends; gifts returned. A shopping trip to the Stanford Mall. Dinner at Spago.

Every now and then, a jibe at Timothy – his callousness, his selfishness – always thinking about himself and not her. The way he flirted with the Asian hostess at Tamarine (how had she noticed that, Timothy wondered?) – and the suspicion, occasionally lurking under her words, that Timothy was not very smart, that he had managed to get where he was by sheer accident of birth ('Thank you, Gabriel,' she wrote meanly one day, in an imaginary paean to Timothy's father, after Timothy bought her a new dining room set). But interspersed with those flashes of anger was the Katherine he remembered, the kind woman, the accepting wife, who was ready to forgive him for being who he was – who was more likely to see her husband as kind rather than slow ('I think Timothy would have been a wonderful dad,' she wrote, after they spent an afternoon with the Weavers and their children), who was more likely to view his success as the result of a good heart and warm smile than genetic luck ('he is full of grace, and the people around him respond to that,' she wrote about Timothy's toast to their guests at the Thanksgiving meal).

But what he did not find, as he pored over the pages, as he read entry after entry, was any mention of sadness, of suicidal despair. And there was no mention of illness. No mention of doctors or even a flu or a sore throat. This woman who was dying did not seem terribly concerned about that fact, which struck Timothy as odd, even though he was drunk on a whole bottle of cabernet and fifty dollars' worth of scotch.

He clapped the leather book shut with a thump and tried to stand. Off-balance, inebriated, he fell backwards into her shoe pile. He tried again. Now he felt very tired, but – strangely – giddy. Despite the oddness of some of her entries, he was pleased with what he had read. It wasn't as bad as he feared. She loved him. Reading her tiny handwriting was like a magical incantation, a spell that had momentarily brought her back to life. He felt close to her now – closer even than on some days when she had been alive – and it was as if he had spent a few hours with her in the dark, lying next to her in bed, in a post-coital rambling stream-of-consciousness chat.

He considered for a moment replacing the volume he had just read, and continuing with the next journal on the pile, but then he stopped and thought better of it. Did he want to spoil such a wonderful night, a pleasant evening with his wife? Perhaps the next journal, written longer ago, was less charitable to him, less kind. Maybe it would be better to stop there, basking in his love for her, and in her love for him. Why ruin it? Maybe this was a perfect goodbye, a beautiful way to remember her.

And then he made a promise to himself, the rash kind of promise people make drunkenly, full of alcoholic purpose and resolve, that he would not read her journals again until their next anniversary, and that he would put them away, safely in the attic, so he would not be tempted to read them; he would practically bury them in the upstairs darkness, to give her the kind of proper burial that her suicide at sea had unfairly denied him.

And so he gathered together the bundle of journals – years of thoughts and criticism and insecurity and happiness and hope, all contained in light-blue ink in tightly wound script – and carried the heavy pile in his two arms in front of him, like a sleeping child. He left the bedroom, his footsteps creaking across the second-floor hallway, and he came to the doorway that led to the attic.

He opened the attic door and flipped on the light switch. He walked up a cheaply carpeted flight of stairs, brown and orange like nutmeg, and the air was humid and stale, and the light dim – just a solitary bulb in an enamel socket, without a fixture. He had to bend down to avoid the steep slope of the ceiling. Bent, he walked further into the attic, past cardboard boxes full of hard-cover books that they had never unpacked after their move from New York; past two old coffee makers, for some reason being saved, perhaps in the hope that they would spurt back to life; past an old computer monitor, its power cord limply hanging over the cathode tube. He stepped past lacquered decorative baskets and holiday wreaths, through a tangle of Christmas lights, and finally to the rear of the room, where a tall, narrow window, lined with old lead caulk and brittle putty, was filled with the moon. He looked through the panes. Down below, he saw the dark outline of the old apricot tree, and further on, streetlights humming a sodium buzz.

He bent over and laid the stack of journals on the floor, and when he stood up again he knocked his head into the ceiling. He backed up a step, regained his balance. He looked again at the pile of journals.

He thought that he would return to them in exactly one year, on his twenty-first wedding anniversary. Perhaps, he thought, this will become an annual event, to be repeated each August: a glass of wine, and then a few hours alone with my wife, reading her innermost thoughts. He tried to imagine this – this secret ritual to be repeated one dark night each summer. But even then, standing in the attic, bent over, with his head brushing the ceiling, he wasn't sure he could bring himself to do it again.

CHAPTER 18

While Timothy drank in his dark house, across the world the sun was shining in Tokyo, and the yen continued its strange rise.

That it should keep rising was more than unexpected, it was unfathomable, because everyone in the world agreed that it could not possibly rise, that there was only one direction it could go: down. And this Timothy found odd, because if everyone agreed it was going down, who was buying yen futures, anticipating that it would go up, driving up the price?

By August 27, Osiris total loss had reached twenty-seven million dollars. A few million more, the Kid explained to Timothy, and the margin calls would start: the brokers – fearful about being on the hook for unrealized losses – would start liquidating Osiris' positions whether Timothy agreed or not, and of course would do so at the worst possible prices, creating even larger losses and driving the prices even further against them.

So it seemed queer to Timothy that, given the fact that his fund had lost almost a third of its value, and that nearly thirty million dollars of investor wealth had been destroyed, he was more concerned about the relatively small one hundred and fifty thousand dollars that had vanished from his bank account days before Katherine died. There was something strange about it. He started thinking about it the morning after reading her journal, after remembering what the journal did not contain: any mention of sickness, or of doctors, or – for that matter – of interior decorators. Katherine had asked him for two hundred thousand dollars in order to begin remodeling the house. But the money had vanished. No decorator called Timothy sheepishly to return it; no contractor wrote him a letter asking when to start work. One hundred and fifty thousand dollars had disappeared. And Katherine, who scrupulously recorded each grapefruit she ate for breakfast, had not written a single sentence about it.

That morning at work, Timothy called his attorney at Perkins Coie, Frank Arnheim.

'Timothy,' Frank said. 'How are you holding up?'

'I've been better, Frank,' Timothy said. Over the past week he had refined his answer to that question, since he had been asked it, in one form or another, hundreds of times. He appreciated that people bothered to ask, but he knew that, secretly, they did not want to be burdened by the truth, which was that he blamed himself for his wife's death, that he was sad and lonely, and that he drunk himself into a stupor each night and often cried. On the other hand, Timothy knew he could not simply ignore his grief or make light of it. So he had settled on the 'I've been better' line – a laconic, honest admission that he hurt like hell, but business was business – and so let's not waste too much time on facts that we can't change. Like the fact that my wife killed herself.

'I understand,' Frank said. 'I can't even imagine what you are going through.'

'Thanks, Frank.' With that out of the way, he got down to business. 'Frank, the reason I'm calling is that I need a little help tracking down some money.'

'Tell me.'

'About two weeks ago, I wired a hundred fifty K into a Citibank account, for the benefit of a company called Armistice LLC. I want you to find out who owns the account – who exactly is Armistice LLC? – and how to contact them.' Timothy rattled off the account number at Citibank that Mike Kelly at Union Bank had given him. 'Can you do that?'

'Give me a couple hours.' And then: 'Got any lunch plans?'

He had somehow managed to avoid Tricia his first days back at work – just a terse hello as he walked to and from the elevator, a brief exchange of pleasantries when she brought him coffee in the morning – and she too at first tried to keep her

159

distance, as if standing too close or talking too much might somehow shatter his fragile recovery, might remind him of the Monday night before Katherine died, and start the pain rushing back.

But that afternoon Tricia came to his office and brought him coffee, and turned to leave. She stopped at the doorway and turned to him. 'I'm worried about you.'

He sipped his coffee and looked up at her. She wore a snug black-and-white striped pullover and a cotton skirt, and her hair was pulled back in a prim tight bun. Her librarian glasses were perched on her nose, and she looked very different from the woman who had climbed on top of him a week earlier and said, 'I want your cock inside me,' and stuck her tongue in his ear.

'Worried?'

She shut his office door. 'You seem so sad and lonely.'

'I am sad, Tricia. I am lonely.'

'I feel partly responsible.'

Timothy wanted to tell her that she was incorrect, that she was not partly responsible – she was, rather, completely responsible. Her flirtation, her infatuation, her come-ons, had caused his wife's suicide. She had tempted him even though she knew he was married. 'You're not responsible,' he said.

'If you're lonely, maybe you'd like some company. I can come over, cook you dinner.'

He tried to picture her in his kitchen, rattling

pans over his stove, sautéing vegetables and braising meat. 'I don't think that's such a great idea.'

'I know,' she said, 'it's too soon, right?'

She was looking, Timothy realized, for some kind of confirmation that he was still interested in her. Maybe his wife's death was too recent, she seemed to think, to begin an affair, but perhaps soon?

How could he tell her that this was not the case, that it would never be the case, that he considered her dull-witted and vulgar and foul-mouthed – and perhaps sexy, yes – but nothing more than a little girl, a trashy, slutty, little girl who said 'awesome' too frequently and who probably was great in bed, but who – when that was done – had nothing much to offer a man like himself.

'It's too soon,' he agreed.

She nodded. 'Awesome,' she said. The word probably meant she was glad he would be open to the idea in the future, but it sounded ridiculous to Timothy, and confirmed his worst suspicions about her: that she was just a dumb girl from LA.

There was a knock on the door, and Frank Arnheim, Timothy's lawyer, stuck his bald bullet head into the office. 'Hello?'

'Hi, Frank,' Timothy said.

Frank said apologetically, 'There was no one at reception so I just thought . . .' His voice trailed off as he looked at Tricia.

She smiled pleasantly at him. 'I should probably get back to the front desk.'

'Okay,' Timothy said.

She nodded and squeezed past Frank Arnheim in the doorway. 'Excuse me,' she said.

Frank glanced down at her breasts as she walked past, and then his eyes followed her ass as she departed down the hall. He closed the door behind her.

'God,' he said, 'killer ass. That is the hottest receptionist I've ever seen. And I'm a bit of a connoisseur.' He put a hand to his mouth. 'Sorry. I guess that's kind of inappropriate, especially right now, isn't it?'

'It's okay,' Timothy said. 'I agree with you. She's not my type, though.'

'Oh, yeah?' Frank said, suddenly interested, as if this freed him to try to get Tricia for himself. He thought about it a moment, then snapped back. 'I have that information you wanted. Pretty interesting stuff. I'll tell you over lunch.'

They ate at Il Fornaio, just across University Avenue. The restaurant was filled with tables of two, and all were nearly identical – a bug-eyed young man dining with an older, better-dressed, more distinguished-looking gentleman. The young men laughed eagerly at every remark of their dining companions, and tried to stare into their eyes, and to please them. In any other city in the world it would have seemed like a room full of gigolos entertaining their sugar daddies, but here in Palo Alto, at the height of the Internet boom, everyone understood that it was something very different: the tables were filled with young entrepreneurs trying to charm a venture capitalist, or a board member, out of money, or into a job.

Timothy and Frank sat in the corner, overlooking the courtyard. Frank opened his briefcase and took out a yellow legal pad scrawled with notes. 'I had two associates look into Armistice LLC, as you requested. I thought it would be a simple thing, you know, one hour of billable time, tops.'

'And?'

'Not so simple,' Frank said. He bit into a piece of bread and tore it with his teeth. 'So don't be surprised when you get the bill.'

'Your bills never surprise me, Frank.'

Frank wasn't sure what to make of that. He looked up at Timothy, then shrugged. 'So here's where it comes out. Armistice LLC owns the Citibank account that you gave me. Armistice LLC is a Delaware corporation – but really, it's a nothing: no assets, no income, no taxes, no place of business. Not really uncommon. But –' He started reading from his notes now. 'Armistice LLC is in turn owned by a company called Chelsea Partners. Chelsea Partners is not a partnership, incidentally, just another corporation, this one registered in Nevada. Okay, so Chelsea Partners is in turn owned by a company registered in the Bahamas, called Keystone Group. You following this?' Without waiting for an answer, he

163

continued. 'Keystone Group is just a shell – all the contact information points to an offshore corporate services company in Nassau, and they have no idea who Keystone Group is, and – even if they did – they probably wouldn't tell me. By the way, that's where most lawyers would stop. They'd tell you, that's all I can find out; the search ended at Keystone Group in Nassau. And then they'd hand you a bill right then and there.'

'But you didn't stop there, Frank, did you?'

'Of course not.' He turned the page on his legal pad. 'So we did a legal search on Keystone. It turns out that you can find references to Keystone Group in the registration of a Panamanian shell company called Stillwater Group. Stillwater and Keystone are joint partners in a third company, Amber Corp. Still with me? Amber Corp is registered in the State of Florida. They're totally legit, by the way, in good standing with Florida Secretary of State, all taxes and fees up-to-date and current.'

'That's it?'

'Well, yes, "That's it"' – he made quotation marks in the air – 'as you put it so dismissively, but I think you might be interested in one more thing.'

'What's that?'

'Amber Corp. is a Florida corporation, right? Why Florida, you ask? I have no idea. But they have another business office listed in their annual filing. Want to know where it is?'

'Sure.'

'Their office is on Sand Hill Road, right down the street from here, in Menlo Park. 3625 Sand Hill Road. What are the chances of that?'

CHAPTER 19

At three o'clock in the afternoon, Timothy pulled his BMW out of the underground parking garage and drove toward the Stanford University campus.

Stanford began at Palm Drive, which was both an avenue and a triumph of stage management. Broad, lined by majestic Canary Island Palms, it ushered people onto the campus, rising at a gentle grade – perfect for rollerblades and ten-speeds – and ending, to the west, at the Oval, a green space filled with taut Stanford men and women playing frisbee. Behind them was Memorial Church, a terracotta cathedral, with a giant exterior mural of Jesus ministering to his disciples among what clearly looked like Northern California foothills. Every time he drove toward the mural, Timothy half-expected to see Jesus, robe flying, catching a frisbee between his legs.

In August there were few students on campus, just a handful of rollerbladers, gliding lackadaisically down Palm Drive. Timothy drove past them, then cut across the campus to Sand Hill Road.

Sand Hill was as famous, in its way, as Park

Avenue or Champs-Elysées, except instead of storefronts and cafes, it offered nondescript low-rises and fields of California oatgrass. It was the most expensive real-estate in the state, costing more per square foot than downtown San Francisco or Los Angeles, but was spectacularly nondescript: a two-lane street in a prairie formerly known for its excellent cattle grazing.

But the cattle were gone now. They had been replaced with two other commodities: cash and brains. For within those plain office boxes congregated the world's smartest people – computer scientists, biologists, genetic engineers – and, in the same buildings, the highest concentration of venture capital anywhere on the earth. It was this combination that gave Sand Hill its frisson; Sand Hill was a street where a scientist could run into a financier at the hot-dog stand at noon, off-handedly mention the project he was working on, and be offered twenty-five million dollars to start a company before dinner.

Sand Hill Road cut through Timothy's world like the lifeline on a crone's hand. He had driven it hundreds of times, in his continual search for new money and new investors. When you are a successful venture capitalist, and each year your share of your partnership's profits, twenty or thirty million dollars, drops into your lap like a sack of potatoes, then you have a problem: what to do with the cash? Venture capitalists are the only people in the world who do not want to invest their wealth in venture capital: it means too many eggs in one basket – and a single industry down-turn will ruin them.

So Timothy was a problem-solver. Osiris took the cash, fed it back into the financial markets, and made it grow by between fifteen and twenty percent a year – not exactly venture capital returns, but respectable enough, and certainly better than any bank or real estate investment could offer.

Today Timothy drove down Sand Hill Road searching not for other people's money, but for his own. There was that small, curious matter of the hundred and fifty thousand dollars that he had given to Katherine on the day before her death, money which was somehow, apparently with Katherine's permission, transformed into bits and bytes and then beamed through fiber optic cables and microwave towers, first into the Bahamas, and then into Panama, and then, according to Frank Arnheim, back to Menlo Park. Not exactly, Timothy thought, the typical way home re-modeling gets done.

Timothy found the address he was looking for, turned left across two lanes of traffic and pulled into the parking lot at the 3600 complex. He got out of the car and locked the BMW with his keychain remote. Even at three o'clock the August sun was high overhead, baking the asphalt, making the air beside his hub-caps shimmer.

There were two buildings on opposite ends of the

parking lot. Timothy followed a flagstone path past the first building, which said: '3700–3799.' He continued on through a courtyard into the shade of newly planted sycamore trees, and then past a bronze sculpture shaped like an automobile-sized egg. Ahead he saw the second office building, and a sign above the entry that said: '3600–3699.'

Timothy bounded up three shallow steps leading to the building. He pushed open the glass doors and found himself in an empty lobby, all cool air and marble. Across the lobby he saw a directory.

He scanned the directory, running his finger over the small plastic letters inserted into black corduroy. It took him a moment to find what he was looking for. There, between Aegis Capital and Angus Biotech, he saw: 'Amber Corp. – Suite 301.'

Timothy studied the directory: all venture capital partnerships, law firms, and vaguely futur-istic-sounding research companies. Another line of the directory caught his eye: 'Ho, Dr Clarence – Suite 301.'

Suite 301, Timothy thought, must be a very crowded place.

Timothy decided to pay Dr Clarence Ho a visit. He walked across the lobby, his shoes echoing on the marble floor. At the far end he found a concrete staircase and started to climb. At the second floor, his bad knee began to ache. The change in temperature – the heat of the parking lot, then the sudden chill of the lobby – must have aggravated it, he decided.

On the third floor the stairs stopped at a carpeted hallway. Timothy wandered past Suite 304, and then 302. The hallway was lit with buzzing fluorescent bulbs, and had the familiar smell of a dental office – disinfectant and perfume.

He came to Suite 301. A small plaque on the door – easily removed and replaced, Timothy noted – said: 'Amber Corp.' Timothy turned the knob and pushed open the door.

He entered what looked like a doctor's office: a small waiting room with padded chairs lined against the wall. A glass window separated the waiting room from a receptionist station. Behind the window, the reception area was dark and deserted. A sign in front of the window said, 'We prefer payment at the time services are rendered.'

In the corner of the waiting area, near the chairs, there was a low, white Formica table, the kind of table that doctors use to display magazines, to keep waiting patients occupied. But this table was empty, and so too was the waiting room. No magazines, Timothy thought, and no patients.

Timothy called out, 'Hello?'

No answer. Timothy heard only a soft buzzing sound coming from somewhere behind the reception area. 'Hello?' Timothy called again.

A door leading to the back room swung open. A Chinese man with a slight, pipe-cleaner body leaned his torso into the waiting room. He wore a white lab coat, pens in his chest pocket, and small wire-frame glasses. 'Yes?' he said. 'May I help you?'

170

Timothy took a step toward him. 'Dr Ho? Dr Clarence Ho?'

The Chinese man was noncommittal. He kept the door pulled tightly beside his body, as if ready to pull back inside and lock Timothy out. 'Yes?'

'I'm here to talk to you about Katherine Van Bender. Do you know her?'

But even before he could finish asking the question, Dr Ho pushed open the door, waved his hand, and beckoned Timothy inside. It was clear that he did.

Dr Ho led Timothy down a florescent-bathed corridor, past rooms marked simply Lab #1 and Lab #2. He stopped at an open doorway, reached around the wall, and flipped on the lights.

He showed Timothy into a small office. Not much larger than a closet, it was crowded with bookshelves on three walls, and piles of paper on the floor. There was barely enough room for a desk, which itself was crammed high with stacks of manila folders. Ho stepped over a pile of folders on the floor and squeezed behind his desk. He gestured for Timothy to take one of the two seats across from him.

'Excuse the mess,' Ho said.

Timothy sat down. The doctor, like many Chinese men, was of indeterminate age. His skin was smooth, without wrinkles, but his hair was streaked with gray. His tiny spectacles were too tight, buried deep into the bridge of his nose, so the wire frame became almost a part of his brow.

'Well, well,' Ho said. He looked at Timothy wearily. 'You must be Mr Van Bender.'

'I am.'

'I've been expecting you.' With a sudden burst of energy he leaned across his desk and began flipping through a pile of manila folders, searching for one in particular, like a card sharp working his way down a deck to find his assistant's chosen card. As he flipped, he said: 'I figured you'd be paying me a visit. I'm sorry about your wife.'

'How exactly did you know my wife?'

Ho didn't answer. He kept working his way through the pile, picking up each folder, looking at its label, then tossing it aside. 'Let's see. It should be here . . .' He flipped another folder from the pile. 'Ah, here. Katherine Van Bender.' Then, holding the folder up for Timothy to see: 'Your wife.'

He opened the folder, riffled the papers inside. From Timothy's view it seemed that Ho was skimming medical charts and hand-scribbled notes. 'I am your wife's doctor,' Ho said, finally answering Timothy's earlier question. 'Did your wife tell you about her illness?'

Timothy shook his head.

'No,' Ho said, 'I thought not. She had mentioned to me that she wanted to keep it from you. Often my patients make that decision. I neither encourage nor discourage it.'

172

'Exactly what kind of doctor are you, Dr Ho?'

Ho looked up from the folder, a faint smile playing on the corners of his mouth. He looked down again at the medical chart in front of him and answered a different question. 'Your wife suffered from a very rare and very deadly form of ovarian cancer. She came to me seeking an experimental treatment that I – and my company – have pioneered.'

Timothy looked around the room, the whirlwind of papers and sagging bookshelves. It seemed hard to believe that a man in this three-by-five cubicle, with papers stacked haphazardly and shin-high, was pioneering anything, let alone a treatment for ovarian cancer. But then Timothy's eye landed on a row of diplomas hanging on the wall behind Ho, and the large calligraphy told him something different: that Dr Clarence Ho had, first, graduated in 1982 from the Massachusetts Institute of Technology with a B.S. degree in biochemistry, and then received an M.D. from Stanford University in 1985, and then further completed a Fellowship in neurology from Stanford in 1992. Dr Ho was, apparently, a well-educated man.

Ho saw Timothy staring at the diplomas. 'You see?' Ho said. 'Not acupuncture or herbal medicine. Was that your fear?'

'Did my wife pay you one hundred and fifty thousand dollars?'

'She did.'

'For what, exactly?'

Ho closed Katherine's folder. He clasped his

173

hands together on top of his desk, and leaned back in his chair. 'I'm afraid that at the present time I'm not at liberty to discuss your wife's course of treatment. This is a very gray legal area, Mr Van Bender, since you are her husband. I can appreciate that it must be painful for you. But I hope you understand my position.'

Timothy looked at Ho. 'I'm not sure I understand what your position is,' he said. 'Did you know my wife was going to kill herself?'

'Again, Mr Van Bender, at the present time I cannot discuss my treatment of your wife.'

'I asked about her suicide, not her treatment.'

Ho was silent.

'Exactly what kind of treatment did you perform on my wife, Dr Ho?'

Dr Ho stood up and gestured at the door to his office. It was clear the interview was over. 'I'm afraid I'm out of time. I'm certain that I must have other patients to see.'

Timothy thought about the pristine, empty waiting room – no magazines, no receptionist, no patients – and wondered exactly where those mysterious patients were that Dr Ho was in a rush to see, and exactly what Dr Ho would do to them, if they ever turned up.

When Timothy returned to his office, Tricia was packing her purse, getting ready to leave for the day. Timothy looked at his watch and was surprised to see that it was already five o'clock.

'Jay's gone,' Tricia said, peering into her purse. 'He went to meet some friends at Zibbibos.'

'When the cat's away . . .' Timothy started, but immediately thought better of it. She might take that the wrong way.

'I'm leaving too. Is that okay?' She finished re-arranging her purse, then tossed it over her shoulder.

'Of course.'

She stood up, circled her desk, and walked toward the office door. She stopped near Timothy and stared at him. Timothy wondered if she was looking at the circles under his eyes, something he had been noticing with increasing interest himself. She asked, 'How do you feel?'

'Okay.'

She considered what she was going to say next. She started speaking, just a syllable, and stopped.

'What?' Timothy asked.

'I was going to invite you out. As a friend. You know, for drinks, maybe to the BBC, just the two of us. Casual. No pressure.'

'Last time we did that, it didn't really work out.'

She shrugged. 'That was last time. How about later this week?'

'Maybe,' Timothy said.

She slid past him. Timothy held the glass doors open for her, and she exited to the elevator bank. He looked at her body as she went. Dumb as a wall, he thought, but what a body.

In the hall, she pressed the elevator call button and turned to him. 'You know, if you won't have a drink with me, I might have to ask you for a raise.'

'You can ask, but you're not going to like the answer.'

Behind her, the elevator chimed. The doors opened. She looked over her shoulder, then backed into the car. She flipped her purse over her shoulder. She said, 'But I always get what I want,' and then the elevator doors closed.

It wasn't clear if she was talking about a raise, or about Timothy, but either way, he thought: Yes, I believe you do.

CHAPTER 20

The next morning, things began to fall apart. First came the phone call from Pinky's lawyer in New York. He reached Tricia first. When she refused to put the lawyer through to Timothy, he played an old trick: Try to Make the Secretary Cry. He launched a diatribe – an electric, shocking, verbal torrent – alternately berating Tricia, muttering ominous legal threats, and scoffing at Timothy's hiding behind a receptionist. The speech was, Timothy knew, when Tricia came to him cowering, a rehearsed piece – the attorney's equivalent of a Hamlet soliloquy. But it accomplished exactly what it was designed to: it made Timothy pick up the phone.

The Kid was in Timothy's office when Tricia came to him, helpless. Timothy nodded and waved her out. She shut the door, then he picked up the speakerphone. 'This is Timothy Van Bender.'

'Timothy Van Bender,' the voice shot back, 'I represent Pinky Dewer. You must send my client his money as he requested. There will be consequences if you refuse.'

'What kind of consequences?'

'Dire, Mr Van Bender. Are you aware that the only thing standing between me and a phone call to the CFTC is your friendship with Mr Dewer? And I might add that your friendship is in a very precarious state, at this moment.'

'So Pinky found out the fruitcake I gave him for Christmas was a hand-me-down?'

'Mr Van Bender, no doubt you think you are clever, and funny, but I am making this phone call because Pinky is gracious, and he asked me to give you one last chance. This is your final warning. Simply return Mr Dewer's money, as he requested, and there will be no further consequences.'

'I'd like to. The problem is, Mr . . .'

'Allen. John Allen from Shearman and Sterling.'

'The problem, Mr Allen, is that I can't do that. The money is not exactly in a liquid form.'

'Then I suggest, Mr Van Bender, that you make it liquid – soon. I won't be phoning again.'

With that, the line went dead.

The Kid whistled through his teeth. 'Wow,' he said. 'Sounds pretty serious.'

'Just a little saber-rattling,' Timothy said, but secretly he thought the Kid was right. He had never meant for things to get this far. He had always expected the yen to fall fast, and for Osiris to make back the original trading loss before investors realized anything had happened. But now it was heading in the opposite direction, and the loss was growing. And Pinky Dewer, who had

178

a mean streak as wide as the Mississippi, had just sworn vengeance.

'Where is the yen?' Timothy said.

'Eighty,' said the Kid. 'We're going to get a margin call tonight, if things don't change.'

'What's the total net loss?'

'We're down by thirty million dollars since the start of the month. What do you want to do?'

Timothy was relieved that he didn't need to answer the Kid, because his intercom rang. It was Tricia. He picked up the receiver. 'Yes?' He expected Tricia to say that Mr John Allen from Shearman and Sterling was calling to issue further threats. But instead she said, 'Timothy, I have a Dr Ho on line two. Do you want to take it?'

'I'll take it,' Timothy said. He put his hand over the mouth-piece and said to the Kid, 'Give me a minute, okay?'

The Kid nodded, and quickly left the office – too eagerly, Timothy thought. It occurred to him then that the Kid had already begun sending out resumes, and perhaps was even interviewing at other hedge funds. Maybe that's where he was yesterday afternoon. Maybe the Kid was starting the process of distancing himself from Timothy, getting off the sinking ship, explaining to prospective employers in conspiratorial tones that Timothy was responsible for 'certain problems' at Osiris, which the Kid was not at liberty to describe, but which the employer would no doubt hear about soon enough.

'This is Timothy Van Bender,' Timothy said, into the phone.

'Mr Van Bender, it's Clarence Ho. Thank you for taking my call.'

'What can I do for you, Dr Ho?'

'I recently had the opportunity to speak with my client. She has agreed that . . .' His voice trailed off. Then he started again: 'It's important that you come to my office tonight. Please come alone.'

CHAPTER 21

H e agreed to meet Dr Ho at eight o'clock in the evening on Sand Hill Road. Timothy drove from his house with the windows of his BMW open. The smell of Northern California summer – of rosemary and jasmine – swept down the foothills into the valley.

Timothy parked in the Sand Hill parking lot, which was now empty, save for a few cars, perhaps those of janitors and cleaning staff. He walked beneath the sodium arc lamps, following the flagstone path along the edge of the office park, past the giant egg sculpture, and into the 3600 office building. He trotted up the three flights of stairs as fast as his legs would take him, but they were old legs, and in the last long month they had grown older. On the third floor he came to Suite 301, and the door marked 'Amber Corp.'

He knocked, turned the knob, and entered Dr Ho's office. Again, he was greeted by an empty waiting room and dark reception area. No magazines. No sign of any patient having visited, perhaps ever. This, Timothy thought, is one strange doctor.

Timothy called out. 'Dr Ho?'

The door to the reception area opened, and Dr Ho was there. 'Thank you for coming, Mr Van Bender.' He gestured for Timothy to follow. 'Please.'

He led Timothy down the hall. They stopped at the door marked 'Lab #1.' Ho removed a set of keys from his pocket and turned the lock.

They entered the lab. It was a large windowless space, sixty feet long on each side, with exposed ceilings snaked with cables and piping and ventilation ducts. In the middle of the room were two laboratory islands, black enamel, with sinks and sawtoothed gas nozzles, out of a high-school chemistry class. On the nearest island, beside the sink, sat a computer keyboard and two giant screens – big twenty-one-inch plasma monitors with bright yellow and green pixels, displaying neatly indented lines of computer code.

In the back of the room, on metal racks, Timothy saw them: rows and rows of computers – black Dell machines; sleek new Suns, the size of pizza boxes; even old clunky beige cases, fossils from an earlier computer epoch. The computers were stacked on top of each other, sometimes three high, bulging from the racks, filling every inch of space. It was high-technology squalor: haphazard piles of CPUs, some vertical, some horizontal, in no particular order. The racks themselves stretched from wall to wall, the width of a football field, as broad as the bow of a ship. The computers were linked by orange Ethernet cables, a thicket of wires, poking messily from the racks and into patch-boards, where hundreds of LEDs blinked green and dark, epileptically, displaying the ones and zeros of network traffic in a ceaseless, ever-changing pattern: true becoming false, false becoming true, thousands of times per second.

The whirr of the computer fans, hundreds of them together, sounded like water racing through a concrete sluice. The room was cold. There must have been dedicated air conditioning, Timothy thought, keeping the machines cool, adding to the rushing sound.

In the back of the laboratory was another door, forbidding cold steel, with a sign that said, simply: 'Keep Out.'

Timothy said, 'Maybe you're the guy to ask. I'm having trouble setting up my wireless home network.'

Ho smiled.

'Okay,' Timothy said, suddenly tired of trying to be charming. He let his voice deflate. 'Tell me what this is about.'

'This is about your wife.'

Timothy stared at him. It was like a key turning a lock. Now it all made sense. He was being black-mailed. It fit: the hundred and fifty thousand dollars Katherine had paid to Dr Ho. Her sudden suicide. And now Ho was calling him to a dark office in the middle of the night, making cryptic comments about Katherine, and about to ask for more money.

Timothy wondered: What had Katherine gotten herself into? Did Ho have photographs of her, some sort of pornography? Were there drugs involved? Perhaps something more awful? An accidental death? Manslaughter?

Timothy thought about how to respond. He needed a Plan. He decided quickly: he would never parlay with a blackmailer, never negotiate, but instead simply walk away. Because once you start, it will never end.

'You look alarmed,' Dr Ho said. 'Don't be.' Ho walked to the computer screen near Timothy, tapped the keyboard. The yellow cursor jumped down a line. 'Do you use computers, Mr Van Bender? In your line of work, I'm sure you must.'

'Sometimes,' Timothy said. His mind was elsewhere. He was still trying to figure out Ho's blackmail plan. He ran through the various angles: Katherine in trouble. Katherine killing herself. Was she in debt? Is that why she needed the two hundred thousand dollars? What kind of mess did she get herself involved in? What kind of secrets did she keep from him?

But no: it was impossible. Katherine was too clever. Even if she did get involved in something unsavory, she would never allow herself to be put in a position of weakness. She was too strong, too smart . . .

Ho said: 'What I'm about to tell you must remain in the strictest of confidence. If anyone should find out about my work – about my company's work . . .'

184

His voice trailed off. 'It would be premature,' Ho said, simply.

'Are you blackmailing me, Dr Ho?'

Ho laughed. 'Oh God, no.' He removed the tiny spectacles from his eyes, virtually unpeeled them from his skin. They left a bright red line in his brow. Ho rubbed his eye sockets. His eyelids made a clicking sound as he rubbed. Now, with his eyes red and puffy, he replaced the glasses. 'I can see, in retrospect, why you might think that. But, no, Mr Van Bender. That's not what I'm doing. Not at all.'

'Then why am I here?'

Ho turned his back to Timothy. He walked to the racks of computers. Only twenty feet from Timothy now, he had to raise his voice to be heard over the rushing fans. 'Three hundred and fifty machines. Nothing fancy. Just off-the-shelf components. Some fast, some slow. Whenever we get our hands on one, we just plug it in. If a machine fails, we leave it in the racks. They're too cheap to bother with.'

Ho ran his fingers over an Ethernet cable absent-mindedly, like a man stroking his lover's hair. 'That's all Amber Corporation is: a few hundred computers. I founded it four years ago. It grew out of research I've been involved in, on and off since . . .' He thought about it, laughed. 'Since forever, really. I've been doing this as long as I can remember.'

He removed his hand from the computer cable

almost longingly, and turned again to Timothy. 'I gathered a group of investors, men not unlike yourself, Mr Van Bender. Wealthy men. Men who could appreciate the promise of what I'm developing. For reasons that I'm about to explain, they would prefer not to be identified. Not exactly typical Sand Hill Road VCs.'

Timothy wondered: if this isn't blackmail, what is it? And then he understood. Was this crazy Chinaman selling him a business plan? Could he possibly want Timothy to invest in his company? Was he using Timothy's dead wife as a convenient entrée? Was this entire episode – the meeting this afternoon, the sinister night-time appointment – was this all a hopeless pitch meeting, a desperate Hail Mary by a cash-strapped entrepreneur?

Ho continued. 'My company has pioneered a rather interesting technology. A kind of backup technology. As you no doubt know, computers are prone to failure. And when computers fail, catastrophically, it is possible to lose critical data. That's why companies like yours, for example, implement a backup policy. You make a copy of all your data so that, if something terrible happens, you'll be able to start your work again. In the worst case, maybe you'll lose a day's worth of work. It's upsetting, obviously, but it's better than losing a year's worth of work. It's better than losing all your customer records, your correspondence, your financial transactions, your software. I'm sure you understand.'

Timothy nodded. He did understand. Since installing the automated backup system, each night the hard disk drive of every computer at Osiris was copied and stored on an optical drive. Once a week, the Kid removed the optical disk and brought it home for safe keeping. If there were ever a fire, or an earthquake – which was not far-fetched in Northern California – and the Bank of America building was destroyed, then Osiris would be able to rise again. Unless, of course, everyone who worked at the company happened to die in the accident. Which was the small but glaring problem with the backup plan that Tran had designed.

'If you understand that,' Ho said, 'then you will appreciate what I am about to tell you. It is very simple. You –' he pointed at Timothy's forehead – 'your mind, your brain, your memories, your personality . . . you –' he waved his hands around Timothy's chest – 'are a glorified computer program.'

Ho stopped. He looked at Timothy to see if he understood the implications of this statement. Timothy's face remained blank.

'Well, not exactly a computer program. Not identical. Computers are binary, of course – ones and zeros – on and off. That was an arbitrary decision by the earliest computer designers, just an artifact of 1940s transistor technology. But there's no reason computers need to be binary. In fact, we can design a perfectly good computer – a much faster one, incidentally – that uses sliding scales, not just on and off, but very on and slightly on and somewhat off. That's how your brain works, too, Mr Van Bender. The rate of neurons firing is a like a sliding scale. Very fast means one thing. Very slow means something else.'

Timothy was about to interrupt, to snap the conversation closed like a bank teller's shade, to say something snide about how fascinating this all was, but that he really needed to go home and perfect his latest hobby: solitary night-time drinking. Ho must have sensed this too, that he had lost his audience, so he tossed the meatball into the lion cage, right then and there. He was, Timothy later realized, pretty good at the pitch meeting after all.

'What I'm saying,' Ho explained, finally, 'is that I have made a backup copy of your wife.'

CHAPTER 22

Ho's words knocked Timothy backward. He took a step, then held on to the cool black enamel lab island to keep his balance. He wasn't entirely sure what Ho was saying, but the doctor was doing it again, mentioning his wife off-handedly, in a way that made her sound like the subject of a medical experiment, like someone not-quite-dead.

Now that he had Timothy's attention, Ho told his story. The problem with science, he explained, was over-specialization. Brain experts knew a lot about how the brain functioned, but knew nothing of the work of chemists, who in turn knew nothing of the work of computer scientists. Each field read its own journals, went to its own conferences, awarded prizes and grants to its own experts. It was as if science took place in separate, hermetically sealed boxes. There was no Science, with a capital S; there were, instead, lots of little sciences, dozens of intricate and precious mechanisms, pointless contraptions, beautifully built and maintained, but absolutely useless. There was no interchange, no attempt to put the

189

machines together to form a larger, more useful whole.

It was a just a fluke that Ho happened to be interested in three extremely different fields – electrochemistry of the brain, computer science, and physiology – and that he had stubbornly pursued these fields concurrently, despite the protest of his professors and supervisors and fellowship advisors, who warned Ho that dabbling in many fields was the same as mastering none, and that his career would suffer as a result.

They were right. From MIT and Stanford, Ho traveled Silicon Valley in the downhill direction, working on small, one-off NIH grants thrown to him when the competition didn't bother to apply. Unable to find a tenure-track position, barely scraping by, Ho worked as a contract employee at a few biotechnology startups, in Berkley, in Oakland, in San Jose. It was at one of these now-defunct firms that he met a mysterious benefactor, who encouraged him to pursue his Big Idea, and who offered to throw cash his way, for a small equity stake in his company.

Amber Corporation was the result. It was a money-losing, research and development company that employed a dozen people – graduate students, technicians, software programmers – but in small, separate roles, so that no one knew exactly what the company was building, nor what the ultimate result of their work would be. No one, that is, but Dr Ho, who understood exactly what he was doing, which was nothing less than changing the nature of what it meant to be alive, and what it meant to be dead.

'Look,' Ho said. 'Did you know that the neurons in your brain live on average twelve to eighteen months? Then they are replaced by new neurons. Do you understand the implications of that?'

Timothy said that he did not.

'It means that, statistically speaking, your brain upgrades itself every three years. The neurons in your skull today are almost certainly completely different from the neurons that were in your skull three years ago. Yet you still have the same memories from childhood, the same personality, the same likes and dislikes. You're still yourself. Human beings don't become different people every three years. Which is rather amazing, when you think about it.'

Ho smiled. Timothy realized that this was a rare opportunity for him, a chance to explain the work that he had labored on for perhaps twenty years, alone, unable or unwilling to share it with anyone. How many times, Timothy wondered, had Ho rehearsed this speech in front of a mirror, while driving down a highway, or while drifting off to sleep? Now, finally, he was having his Blofeld moment, explaining his diabolical plot to James Bond as the secret agent dangled by his ankles above a death ray.

Except that Ho was a bit different from the typical super-villain familiar to Timothy. Thin and waif-like, of indeterminate sexuality, with a precious manner and neatly clipped syllables, he seemed more like an interior decorator than a world destroyer. 'You see?' Ho said. 'Your personality is just software. Completely separate from the hardware it runs on. And just as we copy software from one computer to another, we can do the same with our minds, our personalities. And that is what Amber does. We preserve the contents of a human mind. We store it, back it up, put it away for safe keeping. Everything is digitized.'

Timothy was a bit lost. He followed the doctor only partly. Of more concern to Timothy was what Ho wanted from him. More money? An introduction to other venture capitalists? Advice about how to build his business? Timothy squinted in consternation. Ho read his expression as frightened.

'No,' Ho said, 'it's nothing disgusting – no surgery, no wires, no holes in the head. No wetwear. It's basically an MRI – we simply read the electrochemical pattern that is stored in the brain. Of course it's much more computationally intensive than a plain MRI. That's what these are for.' He indicated the rows of humming computers behind him. 'It's the opposite of three-D rendering. It's kind of like three-D de-rendering, if you follow me.'

Rendering, de-rendering, Timothy thought. I could use that Scotch that's waiting for me back at home. He said, 'I'm sorry, Dr Ho. I'm no technology expert. I can read my email. That's about it. Sometimes, if no one's looking, I play online checkers. That's my level of interest in computers.' In truth, Timothy realized, this technology talk was a little over his head, and was boring him. Normally, if confronted with a technical matter he didn't understand, Timothy just called the Kid into his office and said, 'Take care of it.'

Ho tried a different tack. 'I met your wife six months ago. We were introduced by a mutual acquaintance.'

'Who?'

Ho ignored him. 'She had just learned she was very ill. She was dying. She heard I might be able to help. Not the way most doctors would try to help. I wasn't going to cure her disease. But I explained to her that I could make a backup.'

'A backup? Of what?'

'Of her.'

'Of . . .' Timothy's voice trailed off. Suddenly, the technology gibberish made sense. MRIs, wetwear, rendering . . . those terms were just so much mumbo jumbo. But now, with the context of Katherine's illness to latch onto, Timothy understood what the doctor was saying. He claimed to have a copy of Katherine's brain.

Timothy said, 'You're lying.'

'I made her promise not to tell you, until the process was done. You must understand, my work is not exactly complete. There are . . .' He waved his hands. *'Issues.'*

'What did you do to my wife?'

'Nothing,' Ho said. 'Your wife was dying, Mr Van Bender. She had perhaps one or two months left. Then things were going to become painful. Her cancer had spread. It was in her ovaries, her colon, even her brain. She would need drugs, morphine constantly, just to make the pain tolerable. She would lose control of her bodily functions. Dementia would set in. She would begin to lose her mind. And so she made a decision while she still could make a decision. I offered her an alternative to all that.'

'You offered a desperate and sick woman a fairy-tale . . . a science fiction story.'

'This is no science fiction story, Mr Van Bender.'

'Are you a con artist?'

'No. I'm an entrepreneur.'

Ho sat down in front of a computer screen, tapped the keyboard twice. The cursor appeared again, a yellow blinking square.

'I want to show you something,' Ho said. He typed:

cd ~/amber/v1

amber

'Pull up a seat,' Ho said. 'And say hello to your wife.'

Ho typed: I have Timothy here.

It took a moment, and then the blinking yellow cursor zipped across the screen, leaving behind a trail of phosphor:

Hi, Timothy.

The cursor waited, blinking, patiently.

'Go ahead,' Ho said, 'you can type.'

'You motherfucker,' Timothy said, but he couldn't help himself. He typed:

Who is this?

After a moment, new words appeared:

Who do you think, Gimpy? It's me.

That was enough for Timothy. Dr Ho was a huckster, a carnival barker, a charlatan. Timothy had no doubt that, at that very moment, one of Ho's associates was sitting in the next room, the one conveniently blocked by the Keep Out sign, pecking at a computer keyboard, pretending to be Timothy's wife.

It was one of the lowest, most despicable things Timothy had ever heard of. He wasn't sure of the angle. What did Ho hope to extract? Money, no doubt, but how? Or maybe he had already made his money from the Van Benders – that cool hundred and fifty thousand dollars that disappeared into a series of shell corporations – and this exercise was part of an escape plan, a kind of giant distraction to keep Timothy hopeful and placated while Ho and his associates had a chance to flee.

In any case, Timothy knew that this son of a bitch had quite possibly encouraged Katherine to commit suicide. Perhaps he had convinced her to jump to her death. Perhaps he had indeed promised she would be backed up, that she would have eternal life in silicon. How desperate and frightened she must have been, Timothy thought, to be taken in by this monster.

The cursor flew across the screen:

I love you, Timothy.

That was it. Timothy windmilled around and punched Ho in the face. It was the only punch Timothy had ever thrown in his life, and he felt a sickening thud, the feeling of his fist hitting a half-filled sandbag, and Ho fell backwards with a surprised look on his face, as if this was the only punch he had ever received, too. His glasses were askew – one earpiece hung preposterously from his skull like an antenna. Timothy grabbed the computer monitor and wrenched it off the table, pulling wires loose. The screen crashed to the ground, the glass panel popping out of its bevel like a high-tech jack-in-the-box.

Timothy kicked the monitor. His shoe crashed through the screen, breaking it in two. He headed for Ho, who was scrabbling on the concrete floor, trying to stand. Timothy bent down, grabbed Ho by the white lab coat lapel, and pulled him up. Ho tried turning away, but he was off balance, and didn't have any purchase on the floor. He raised his hands over his face feebly.

'You despicable man,' Timothy said. 'You lied to my wife. You encouraged her to jump.'

'No,' Ho said. 'You misunderstand.'

Timothy raised his fist. He thought about punching Ho one more time, but decided against it. He tossed Ho to the ground, instead. The doctor fell to the floor like a limp roll of carpet, his palms slapping concrete.

Timothy turned to leave. He gave the computer screen, now a pile of plastic, one more kick, sending it skittering across the floor. Then he walked out.

CHAPTER 23

He could not sleep.

He tried, first by keeping his appointment with Mr Dalmore, twenty-one years old, and then by popping a valium, and finally by falling backwards into his mattress with his shoes on, tight and sticky around his ankles.

In the dark, the empty space on the bed beside him seemed to grow, like ink racing across a shirt pocket, sending tentacles of black outward, threatening to swallow him and the bed.

His mind raced. His heart still fluttered, even hours later, giddy and surprised about the cold ruthless violence that had surged through him – the way he punched Ho, the snap of the doctor's jaw, the sting on Timothy's hand, his kick of the computer screen that sent it skidding across the concrete laboratory floor.

And there was something else. The hoax itself. So elaborate and so perfect. When had Ho decided to carry it out? How long had he been planning it? Months? How long had he known Katherine? How long had he been toying with her, tantalizing her with the promise of eternal life? How had he convinced her to keep the entire matter from her husband of twenty years?

It was brilliant. There was a moment – just a moment – when Ho almost had him. Almost. The off-hand display of the computers. Not *too* science fiction. And then the words appearing on the screen. It was as if Katherine was there, on the other side of the screen. What had she said?

Who do you think, Gimpy? It's me.

And that was the troubling bit. How did Ho know her nickname for him? Perhaps Katherine mentioned it accidentally, or maybe Ho extracted it from her under more direct questioning. 'We need to know everything about your relationship with your husband, Mrs Van Bender, before we can offer you eternal life.' That might have done it.

And yet. And yet. Even as phosphorescent pixels, the words seemed so true to life, so natural, so much like her own. That was exactly what she would have said. And exactly how she would have said it. Looking down her long thin nose at him, regarding him with cool amusement: 'Who you think, Gimpy? It's me,' as if he were the most stupid person in the world, but she still loved him anyway.

Yes, it was almost as if Katherine was there tonight, talking to him.

But of course it couldn't have been her. Because his wife was dead, and Timothy knew that there was no bringing her back, no matter how much he wanted to, no matter what he was willing to give up.

When sleep finally came, he dreamed: of Katherine, of Dr Ho and his tiny spectacles, of the racks of computers, and the yellow flashing cursor. They were drunken, wild dreams, and when he woke he realized he was bathed in sweat, his shirt soaked, and that his fist was clenched, as if he had punched Dr Ho all over again.

CHAPTER 24

He rose from bed and showered.

When he wandered downstairs to the kitchen, the answering machine light was flashing. He must have missed the call when in the shower.

He pressed play. Dr Ho's voice – punctilious and effete – filled the kitchen, playing over the ceramic splashboards and making the glass patio doors vibrate. Too loud. Timothy turned down the volume.

'Mr Van Bender, this is Dr Ho. I'm calling to apologize about last night. I can understand why you must have been quite upset. This is the first time I've had to deal with – with the feelings of family members, in the work I do, and I didn't think it through. Frankly, I didn't realize how things would appear to you.'

Timothy noticed with satisfaction that Ho's speech was slurred. He could picture the doctor wearing spectacles held together with Scotch tape, holding his swollen jaw as he spoke.

Ho continued. 'I'm calling to apologize, but I'm also calling for another reason. It is vital that you do not contact the authorities. It could mean ruin for my work, and – frankly – danger for your wife. I promise you, sir, I am not interested in any money from you. I am not trying to steal from you. I am not trying to trick you. I am simply performing the service that was requested of me. I do not want any further trouble, Mr Van Bender.'

I bet you don't, Timothy thought, since you left a paper trail a mile wide showing a hundred and fifty thousand dollars disappearing from my bank account and landing in yours.

'I will not call you again,' Ho's voice said. 'You have my word. I will not bother you. If you want to contact me, you can do so at your own choosing. Here is my phone number.' He gave a Peninsula phone number, and then said, 'Again, I'm terribly sorry, Mr Van Bender. I was only trying to help.'

The message ended, and the machine beeped.

Timothy walked across the kitchen to the coffee maker. He spooned the beans into the drip basket, filled the carafe with water, and poured it into the machine. He had given up trying to measure. It was hit or miss now. Usually miss.

The doorbell rang. Timothy walked to the foyer and peered out the keyhole. A pleasant-looking black woman, all smiles, wearing corn rows and a happy pink blazer, grinned back at him. He opened the door.

'Mr Van Bender?' she asked.

'Yes,' he said, 'what can I do for you?'

From behind her back she pulled a quarter-inch

stack of papers and pushed it into his chest. He took it. 'You just did it,' she said pleasantly. 'Have a good day.' She turned and trotted down the stairs to the driveway.

Timothy looked at the papers. It said: 'SUMMONS (Citacion Judicial) – Notice to defendant: Timothy Van Bender; and Osiris LP – You are being sued by Plaintiff: Peter Dewer; Dewer Family Trust I' and proceeded to list, in twelve pages, the exact nature of the lawsuit, in which Pinky Dewer was requesting both the return of his money, and damages in the amount of twenty million dollars.

CHAPTER 25

At the office the Kid delivered another piece of bad news: that Refco had overnight raised its margin requirements – that is, the amount of collateral it insisted on holding while Timothy and Osiris gambled on a risky trade – and had issued a margin call. At noon it would begin to liquidate its portion of the yen trade unless Osiris could deposit another ten million dollars cash in its brokerage account. The yen, apparently, had had a busy night, rising briefly to eighty before settling down at seventy-nine.

Refco's demand for another ten million dollars was of course impossible to meet. Osiris' loss had now grown to thirty million dollars since the beginning of the month. Refco rightly suspected that Osiris was in trouble, and that the trouble would only grow larger with each passing day. They realized that soon Osiris' other brokers would issue margin calls, too, and that the last broker to do so might be left holding the bag, on the hook for millions of Osiris' losses, without enough collateral to make good. In this game of million-yen musical chairs, no one wanted to be left standing when the Hagaku stopped.

It was only a matter of time, Timothy understood, before the other brokers would follow suit with their own margin calls – perhaps they would do so as early as that afternoon. They would insist that Osiris buy back the yen contracts that it had sold short – but at the price of seventy-nine, or even eighty – which would turn that hazy, ephemeral, *potential* loss of thirty million dollars into a concrete, actual fact. Once that loss was reported to investors, that would be the end of Osiris. When investors learn that they have lost forty percent of everything they have invested, practically overnight, it is hard to convince them to stick around a while longer to 'make it back.'

It did not take long for the phone calls to start. As Timothy sat down at his desk, Tricia patched through Hans Drexler, another Yale classmate, who had invested five million in Osiris a year earlier.

'Hans, my friend,' Timothy said, as he picked up the receiver. 'How are you doing?'

Hans had a vaguely European accent. He was actually American, but the product of Swiss boarding schools, and so sounded like he had been raised somewhere between the two continents. Perhaps, Timothy thought, on a yacht in the middle of the Atlantic.

'Timothy, I am hearing some disturbing things about Osiris.'

Which meant, Timothy understood, that he had

heard them from Pinky Dewer. Pinky was now out to destroy him.

'What kind of disturbing things?' Timothy asked.

'Would it be possible to get some transparency into the fund? I know August statements will arrive shortly. But perhaps you can fax me some kind of interim results? Surely you must know where you stand at this moment, give or take.'

Oh, I surely do, Timothy thought. I stand in a pile of shit about knee high, and the elevator is going *down*. But he said: 'Hans, you've got to be kidding me. You want me to spend a couple hours putting together make-work financials for you, instead of earning you money? August P&Ls are coming out in just a few days.'

'But what I've heard—'

'You've been talking to Pinky? That son of a bitch is playing hardball with me. He wanted me to cut my management fee to a half a percent. When I refused he threatened to call the rest of you and make life difficult. You know why he's doing this, don't you?'

'Why?'

'You must have heard about his . . . troubles? With the takeover?' Timothy had no idea what he was talking about. But it sounded sufficiently ominous, and vague enough, that Hans would be able to read into it whatever he liked. For good measure he added: 'With the SEC?'

'I hadn't heard.'

'Well, there you go. I'll tell you what, Hans. I

will make sure you get the August statements first, before anyone else, hot off the presses. When are you coming out west? I owe you some drinks.'

'I don't have plans.'

'That's a shame. The weather out here . . . well, you know.'

'Yes.'

'All right, Hans. You want me to call you when the August statements are ready?'

'I would appreciate that, Timothy.'

'All right, my friend. I'll speak to you soon.'

'Cheers.'

Timothy hung up. He leaned back in his chair, stared at the ceiling, and exhaled.

'Timothy?' It was Tricia, leaning her head into his office. She smiled at him.

'Yes, Tricia?'

'I have Frank Arnheim from Perkins Coie on line one.'

'Put him through.'

Frank got right down to business. He was like a warrior in battle, his voice hoarse, adrenaline coursing through his blood. This was his element. He loved lawsuits. That they were directed at his client did not seem to decrease his enjoyment.

'Yeah, I got a copy of the summons here,' Frank said. 'Son of a bitch. Twenty million dollars. Holding you personally liable.' Then: 'Hey, you even *got* twenty million dollars?'

'Yes,' Timothy said. 'In gold bullion. I carry it around in the trunk of my car.'

Frank laughed. 'That's a good one. Gold bullion.' His voice dropped. 'Say, why don't you just give him his money back?'

'I was hoping to hold onto it maybe a week longer.'

'What's going to happen in a week?'

'I'm hoping Japan will throw in the towel. You know, just give up the whole industrialization thing, go back to Samurai swords and rice farming. Then the yen might fall.'

'I see.' Frank asked again: 'Can you give the money back?'

'Soon.'

Frank sighed. 'Okay, Timothy, have it your way. You're paying by the hour. I don't think a twenty-million-dollar judgment is gonna stick. But I'll give you my professional opinion.'

'Do I really want it?'

'No, but here it is. You should give him back the money. The cost of not doing it is too high. I'm not talking about this lawsuit. We'll make that go away. I'm talking about your reputation. In your business, you don't need attention. Quiet is best. Do you really want a nosy CFTC investigator poking around your files, looking at your emails?'

Timothy was silent.

'That's what I thought.'

'All right, Frank. I'll think about it.'

Timothy was about to hang up, but Frank quickly spoke. 'Hey, Timothy.'

'Yeah?'

'Forgive me. But we're going to need the monthly retainer paid in advance from now on. Let's just start with twenty thousand. Not my decision. Just policy, in situations like this.'

'I understand, Frank. I'll take care of it.'

'Thanks, Timothy.'

Timothy hung up and then said to the phone on his desk, 'You son of a bitch.'

At noon, Refco bought back a thousand yen future contracts for Osiris' account. The huge order, quickly and sloppily placed, sent the price of the yen up another half-point on the Chicago Merc – Osiris effectively paid eighty and a half for contracts it had sold at seventy-five. The loss – real and irreversible, not just a paper marked-to-market loss – was six point eight million dollars. And that was only the portion of the yen gamble that had been placed using Refco as a broker. When it made the bet, Osiris had divided the trade among five brokers. Timothy knew that soon the other four would be calling, insisting that he close out their portions of the trade, too, effectively quintupling the loss. Timothy was sure that, despite their promise of confidentiality, the brokers spoke to each other often about client disasters, and perhaps even now the phone wires between Chicago and New York were burning with talk of Osiris and its impending flame-out.

The Kid came to Timothy's office and handed

him a printout detailing the loss. Timothy pretended to study it. What did the Kid expect him to say?

The Kid said, 'It doesn't look good.'

'It ain't over 'til the fat lady sings,' Timothy said. He glanced upward and half-expected a giant opera soprano, dressed as a Norse Valkyrie, with bear-skin pelts and a winged helmet, to drop out of the ceiling onto his desk.

'I think I need to tell you,' the Kid said, 'that I'm interviewing at other firms.'

'You don't say,' Timothy said flatly, staring at the Kid's printout. He looked up. 'I understand.'

'But I'll stick around for as long as you need me.'

'I appreciate that, Kid,' Timothy said. He stood up suddenly, removed the suit jacket that hung on the back of his chair, and slid it on.

'Where you going?' the Kid asked.

'I'm calling it a day,' Timothy said, fixing his shirt sleeves. 'You're in charge while I'm gone.' The Kid's face said he had just been awarded a dubious honor indeed. 'Don't worry, Kid. It's only money. OPM. Other people's money. Important lesson. Remember that.'

CHAPTER 26

Timothy drove. He had no particular destination in mind. He simply wanted to go somewhere.

He headed north into Portola Valley. It was a town of green and gold grassland and cedar homes nestled cozily along the San Andreas fault. Strict zoning laws – large indivisible lots, low rooflines – kept it rural and thinly populated. So too did the fear that the town might simply disappear one day, swallowed by the earth.

Timothy sped down Alpine Road, through the town center – a cluster of shops offering video rentals and frozen yogurt – past horse stables, and into the foothills.

He turned left at Arestradero Road, drove another quarter-mile, then stopped his car at the Arestradero Preserve. It was a county-run open space preserve, six hundred acres of rolling hills and grassland, crisscrossed with horse and bike trails. Katherine had liked taking him here. She liked to lead him up Meadowlark Trail, to the tallest hill in the park. She would race ahead, calling over her shoulder, 'Come on, Gimpy, you can do it.'

At the top of the hill, she would wait for him. There they had unobstructed views 360 degrees around, of brown grassland and crisp blue Bay – of fog and sun – of undulating hills strewn with California poppies and buttercups.

Timothy left the BMW and walked into the park. He began climbing Meadowlark. He was wearing his suit and Cole Haan shoes. The sun was bright and hot; he started to sweat. He loosened his tie and took off his jacket, bunching it into a ball under his arm. The grade was steep, and his knee ached, but he wanted to keep going.

He had traveled there to be alone, and to think in solitude, to come up with solutions to his problems, and he was surprised that none came to him. He just walked. He knew that his company was ruined, and that soon the damage to his reputation would be irreparable. He thought about what he had done wrong. Doubling up the yen bet, hiding his original losses from his investors. It all seemed obvious now – like a pat after-school television drama, those programs designed to teach lessons to young people – but he was unsurprised when he looked inside himself and realized that he regretted nothing. If given a chance, he would do the same thing again. This is who I am, he thought.

From behind him came the sound of a rubber tire running over a pebble, sending the rock skipping over dirt. He turned to see a young woman on a mountain bike, riding up the hill toward him.

Beneath her helmet she had a pretty face, coated in sweat and dust. She was just a girl, maybe twenty years old, probably a Stanford student. She smiled pleasantly at Timothy as she passed, and said, 'Hi there.'

Timothy nodded hello. She biked past him, standing now as she pedaled, the bike rocking left and right as she struggled to push up the hill.

Like Katherine twenty years ago, Timothy thought.

Then the memories began. They came tumbling back, just one or two at first, happy ones – the memory of Katherine when he proposed to her in the Greenwich Village restaurant, by candle-light, when she was young and healthy, like that girl on the bike. And of Katherine on the day of their wedding – the way she looked radiant in her gown. But then quickly other memories began to rush in on him, one after another, a wild jumble: Katherine and Timothy in Big Sur, hiking up the switchback to the cliffs above the sea; Katherine making love to him, the feeling of the cold sheets and her warm thighs; Katherine sitting on the bed, writing her journal, and Timothy approaching from behind; Katherine cooking for him as he stood in the kitchen and watched – the memories came in no particular order, in and out of the slip-stream of time, first from twenty years ago, and then from just two weeks past.

At that moment, he understood why he had come here. It was true: he had come to be alone,

213

and to find solutions to his problem. But the problem he cared about had nothing to do with Osiris and its impending liquidation, nothing to do with his tarnished reputation as a money manager; and nothing to do with Pinky Dewer or with investors or with the yen.

As much as he had tried – to ignore the nagging doubts and unresolved questions; to focus on work, on his disloyal lawyer and employees, on the twenty-million-dollar lawsuit slapped on him by Pinky – he could not quite make one thing leave his mind: his conversation with Dr Ho, the demonstration at the computer terminal, Katherine appearing to him from within phosphorescent pixels, a silicon wraith.

The thought that kept returning to him, no matter how hard he tried to ignore it, was this. What if it is not a hoax? What if it is all true?

CHAPTER 27

He knew that he would call Dr Ho, but delayed as long as he could, because somehow he understood that once he called, nothing would be the same.

So he ate dinner, alone again at the kitchen table, another bowl of pasta and oil, and a bottle of cabernet from the cellar. When he had finished, he wandered into the living room and watched TV. He poured himself a Dalmore on the rocks, sat on the couch, and didn't bother closing the curtains. The back yard was dark, the windows open, the night air warm; and he sat staring at the television screen, comprehending nothing, running his finger along the condensation on the outside of his Scotch glass. A drop of water gathered at the bottom of the glass and fell into his lap.

When he finished the Scotch he padded back to the kitchen, where he replayed Dr Ho's telephone message, and scribbled his phone number on a yellow Post It. He dialed.

A voice answered. 'This is Clarence Ho.' There was noise in the background – voices, glasses clinking – it was probably a cell phone.

Timothy said, 'It's me.'

'Mr Van Bender?'

'Yes.'

Ho said, 'Hold on.' In the background, Ho's voice said something to his companions, and then came the sound of amplified rustling, and breathing, and a door closing. Now the line was quiet and crisp.

After a long pause, Ho said: 'I tried to explain to your wife what happened last night.'

Timothy was silent. He was leaning with his forearm against the kitchen wall, over his head. The plaster was cool. He closed his eyes.

'Are you at home?' Ho asked. 'Do you have a computer in your house?'

'Yes.'

'Write this down.' He proceeded to dictate a single, arcane computer command. Timothy scribbled it on the Post It pad. Ho said, 'Feel free to talk to her as long as you like. You can reach me in the morning.' Ho hung up.

Timothy wandered upstairs with the Post It clenched in his hand. He walked into the library. This had been her room: her oak bookshelves, her books – literary fiction he could never make it through – even her desk and red velvet divan, from her old New York apartment. On the desk sat her computer. He seldom used it. He sat down in front of it, reached under the desk and turned it on. After a moment the machine booted, and the whirr of the hard disk stopped.

Timothy followed Ho's instructions. He navigated to a command line and typed:

telnet 33.141.61.254

The cursor sat perfectly still for a moment. Then, words appeared on the screen:

Please don't throw the computer off the desk tonight.

Timothy leaned back in his chair, thought about it. He was unsure what to type. Should he give in? Could this . . . this *program* possibly be her? Was it even a program? Was it perhaps Ho, sitting in his lab, chuckling as he typed?

A new line appeared on the screen:

Now is a really bad time to be technology-phobic, Gimpy.

Then:

(You're not going to go crazy if I call you that, are you?)

Timothy closed his eyes. The wine and Scotch were doing their job. He felt nothing, except dizziness. This thing in front of him, this text purporting to be Katherine, meant nothing to him. Of course he wanted it to be her. But he refused to believe it, with any certainty. His wife was dead. And he was drunk.

He typed: I'm having a hard time believing this.

She responded: I know. It must seem crazy. But it is amazing, Timothy. It is me. I am pure thought. That's what I feel. I think about typing, and I make the words appear.

Timothy rubbed his chin. Could it be his wife, in a computer? It seemed impossible.

And yet.

And yet. How many technologies had he seen arise, in his short life, that – when they first appeared – seemed like magic? Could Dr Ho have done something as amazing as this? Storing a human mind in a computer? It sounded crazy when he thought about it like that, but then again, what technology *didn't* sound crazy when it was developed? Didn't the MRI sound crazy – the idea that you can see inside the human body without cutting it open? And didn't it sound crazy to think that you could create a computer that could beat a human at chess? And didn't it sound crazy when people started freezing their sperm and eggs in test tubes so that they could make babies whenever they chose, in a laboratory, like a Betty Crocker mix?

Now we accept those developments as commonplace, Timothy thought. But when they first appeared, they sounded outlandish.

And how outlandish is it, really, to record a human brain? The way Dr Ho described it made sense. The brain is just a bunch of software. And we can copy software.

And if there was any place in the world where such a technology could arise, this would be the place. And this is exactly how it would happen: a lone scientist and entrepreneur, laughed at by the medical establishment, but supported by a deep-pocketed Silicon Valley venture capitalist. How different was this from, say, Genentech, which pioneered gene splicing – putting a goat gene in an E. Coli bacteria – right down the street?

And even if this thing in front of him was only a pale simulation of his wife, a kind of artificial intelligence parlor trick, did it matter? It certainly seemed like her. The thing on the screen responded the same way his wife would have. Wasn't that good enough? After all, Timothy was glad to be talking to her again. He was not prepared to turn off the computer and walk away.

He wrote:

Why did you kill yourself?

He immediately regretted it. It felt like an accusation. There was a long pause, as if his words had somehow hurt her. Then her response appeared.

I don't remember. I mean, I did think about it. When I learned about my illness, I made plans to do it. But that woman who killed herself – it wasn't me. I'm the backup. I made a copy of myself the day before we went to Big Sur. Remember when I said I was going to have lunch with Ann? I went to Dr Ho's. And that's the last thing I remember.

Timothy tried to grasp this.

Then she wrote:

How was Big Sur? Did you score? (With me!) Did we have great sex?

Timothy laughed. Now he felt it for the first time: an unimaginable happiness. A furtive joy, deep in his gut. Like a child with a secret – a young boy with a crush who has just been kissed for the first time – or a job-seeker being offered more money than he even imagined asking for – he felt surprised and ecstatic. Could it possibly be her?

He knew what he had to type next. He almost didn't want to do it, because he was afraid that she would fail his test, that his happiness would be snuffed out like a candle taper, and he would never feel like this again, for the remainder of his years. But of course he had to know, to be sure. And so, very slowly – almost longingly – to avoid reaching the conclusion too quickly, he typed:

Answer one question for me.

She said: Anything you want.

What were we going to name it? The baby. The last time we tried?

The cursor sat there, hanging in the empty black space of the screen. It did not move.

Timothy's heart dropped, because he understood what the pause meant. It had all been a trick. Ho did not know the name of their baby, the child that he and Katherine had almost had, so many years ago. Ho was good: before her death he had asked her many questions, gotten a lot of the details right, even picked up her mannerisms and speech patterns. The glib 'Did you score? (With me!)' was a perfect Katherine imitation: insouciant, self-deprecating, hurt. It was a good trick. But it was only a trick.

Then the cursor sped across the screen and a new line appeared:

Connor. (I forgive you for bringing it up, Timothy.)

Timothy looked at the screen. His hands shook. Then, something he didn't expect: he started to cry. First it was just a tear, falling from his eye onto the desk, like the condensate from his glass of Scotch. But within seconds, it came, all at once, and his body shuddered and he rubbed his eyes and he wailed. His wife was there, talking to him. He had not lost her, after all. He had another chance.

'Katherine . . .' he said aloud, reaching his fingers to the screen.

His tears blurred his vision, and so at first he did not see what she wrote next. It was just a smudge of shimmering text. He wiped his eyes and then read the screen. She wrote:

I miss you, Gimpy. You need to talk to Dr Ho. He'll explain everything. I want to see you again. I want to come out.

CHAPTER 28

Dr Ho agreed to see Timothy the next day, at noon. He insisted on meeting in a public place. Apparently his last encounter with Timothy had made him think twice about meeting the volatile Mr Van Bender alone in a deserted office park.

They met at the Stanford Shopping Center, an outdoor mall adjoining the university. Ho was waiting for him at the food court, an atrium near the coffee and sandwich shops. He sat at a mesh wire table, with two paper cups of coffee in front of him.

Timothy approached. Under Ho's left eye was a purple bruise the size of an eight ball.

'That's quite a shiner,' Timothy said. He took a seat across from Ho.

'You're not going to punch me today, are you, Mr Van Bender?'

'I suppose that depends.'

'On what?'

'On whether you're going to share that coffee.'

Ho slid a cup across the table to Timothy. 'So,' Ho said. 'I take it you spoke to your wife.'

Timothy regarded him skeptically. 'If you're lying to me, what you are doing is the lowest thing any man has ever done.'

'I'm not lying to you.' Ho took a sip of coffee, snapped the plastic lid back on the cup. 'I'm not asking you for any money, Mr Van Bender. I've already received my payment for the backup procedure. I want absolutely nothing more from you: no money, no time, no attention.' He paused. 'I am only trying to do what is right. I'm trying to keep the promise I made to your wife.'

'Which was what?'

Ho shrugged. 'This isn't science fiction, Mr Van Bender. There's no magic wand I can wave. I can't bring back the dead. Your wife's body is . . . dead. Even if she hadn't . . .' He thought about how to say it, delicately. 'Even if she hadn't ended her own life, she would have died shortly because of her illness. That's the problem with the backup technique. All I am doing is keeping your wife in a kind of non-corporeal stasis. But she is not truly human, not alive in any meaningful sense, as she is currently constituted.'

Ho continued. 'Someday, when we have perfected human cloning – and I believe it is only a matter of time – well then, you can imagine the possibilities. Backing up one's mind, and storing it along with a tissue sample for safe keeping. And then, should an accident occur, or an illness, one would simply restore the mind, re-copy it into a perfectly blank clone, back into one's own body, as it were. There would be no such thing as accidental death, or sudden illness. Imagine it.'

'That would be pretty nifty.'

'That's my vision for my company. To be the company that solves a huge market need: death. Obviously it opens up a whole can of worms. Moral and ethical dilemmas. But we could work through those. There would be no stopping the technology. Who doesn't want to live forever?'

Ho looked at Timothy, as if waiting for an answer. None came.

'Which brings us to your wife,' Ho said. 'You have a difficult choice to make now, Mr Van Bender. I do not envy you.'

'What kind of choice?'

'Backing up your wife was only half of the plan. Your wife wanted to come back to you, to be with you . . . *physically*.'

'Fine. How do we do it?'

Ho shook his head, as if to say: Mr Van Bender is not a very smart man.

'Tell me,' Timothy said.

'As I said, this is not science fiction. There is no way to cure her cancer, or to bring back her dead body.'

'So?'

Dr Ho leaned over the table as if to impart a very dark secret. 'I can restore your wife. But I need a . . .' His voice trailed off.

'A what?'

'A vessel,' Ho said. 'Another person. I can simply

overwrite your wife on top of someone else's hard-ware, as it were.'

'Overwrite—' Timothy stopped and thought about it. 'What happens to the other person?'

Ho shrugged.

'You kill them?'

'No, no,' Ho said quickly, looking around the food court, to see if anyone was listening. An obese woman walked by with two fat grade-school children. Ho waited for them to pass. 'It's not like that. Their body stays alive. And their mind – well, I can simply perform a backup on that person too, so that when it is scientifically possible, we could theoretically bring that person back, without harm.'

'You've got to be kidding.'

Ho shook his head. He was not kidding.

'So you want to bring Katherine back in someone else's body?'

Ho stared at Timothy without speaking.

Timothy asked: 'Whose?'

Ho raised his index finger. 'That,' he said, 'is up to you. But please allow me to make some suggestions. The person should be young, in outwardly good health. It would be an irony of O'Henryesque proportion to go through this entire procedure and then learn that the person you chose had some sort of terminal cancer. Of course the person should be a woman; I don't think you want to live in your house with a bearded two-hundred-pound truck driver. It should be someone you find physically appealing – in the same way that you found your wife physically appealing. And finally, if I may make one more recommendation—'

'By all means.'

'It should be someone you know. Someone who you could legitimately . . . wind up with, after your wife's death. What I want to avoid – and forgive my selfishness – is the appearance of anything too unusual, anything that raises too much attention. I'm not ready to market this technology yet. So we don't want to raise any eyebrows.'

'I see,' Timothy said.

'Do you?' Ho asked. 'Are you sure you understand what a serious choice this is? Choose your vessel with care, because you're going to put your wife inside. And you're going to spend the rest of your life with her.'

'Sort of like marriage.'

Ho said, 'I have spoken to your wife about this. She is very flexible. She understands that there is no perfect choice. She will leave the decision up to you. She thinks you will choose wisely.'

CHAPTER 29

As if they were talking about how Timothy might swing by Ho's lab after a fishing trip to drop off an extra trout he had caught, they agreed that Timothy would find a suitable 'vessel' and would phone the doctor on his cell to alert him. Then they would meet at the lab.

Timothy returned to his car. He drove the black BMW through the mall parking lot, past the housewives walking to their cars and hugging ungainly shopping bags, past the high-school kids at the ice-cream shop, past the burrito joint with the outdoor tables, where the businessmen tucked their ties into their shirts. Looking at them all, Timothy felt uneasy. He could have Katherine back, but he would need to choose someone – a vessel – to put her in. He scanned the shoppers. Whom would he choose? One of the housewives at the mall? One of the young women serving coffee at the Starbucks? The pretty clerk in the bookstore?

He drove slowly, like an automaton, turning the wheel, signaling with his blinker, stopping at the red light, slowing for pedestrians. When he looked up, he had driven a mile towards home, but the time had disappeared. He felt hollow, parched – a clay cistern filled only with dust.

Timothy knew why he felt empty. He was about to do something horrible. Even without understanding the details, he knew. He was choosing someone. He was choosing a victim.

Yet wouldn't any man, Timothy wondered, do the same? Could any man – anyone who loved his wife, or his family – do different? This is what drives good men to fight wars – to napalm thatch huts, to bomb cathedrals, to talk about acceptable levels of 'collateral damage.' There are times when you love someone so much that you must drive the rest of the world from your thoughts. All that matters now: her.

His wife was coming back. He loved her more than anything, more than anyone. It took her death for him to understand, finally, what she meant to him. She was everything. She was the only woman he had ever loved. She was the only person he had ever trusted.

Without her, his life would be empty: lonely nights in a dark house, restless sleep, fading recollections of happier times.

Somehow, faintly, Timothy understood that he was choosing a path that would lead to disaster. But – just as he recognized earlier that afternoon that he would repeat the same failed yen gamble if given another chance – he knew too that, if he relived this moment a hundred times, he would choose the same way each one. He would bring Katherine back, regardless of cost, regardless of result.

Yes, I love her that much, he thought to himself. I miss her that much. I would do anything. He nodded grimly. Anything.

By the time he reached Webster Street, just a mile from home, Timothy had decided to put his plan into motion.

The first question that he needed to answer: Whom would he choose?

With one hand on the steering wheel, Timothy dialed his cell phone and stuck it to his ear.

He was surprised when the Kid answered the phone. 'Osiris.'

'Kid? It's me. Where's Tricia?'

'She stepped out. I'm glad you called. We've gotten three calls from investors who want to redeem: Sharpe, Johnson, and Hendrick.'

'What did you tell them?'

'That you'd call them when you got back. Where are you?'

'Oh,' Timothy said dreamily, 'I just left the mall.'

'The mall? Timothy . . .'

'We can hold their money for ninety days. Tell them we'll start the clock now, and then they can redeem.'

'Okay.'

'So . . .' Timothy paused, tried not to seem excited. 'Is Tricia back yet?'

The Kid sighed. First his boss was shopping at the mall while the business was crumbling around him, and now he wanted to flirt with the secretary. 'Hold on.' The Kid said something in the background.

Tricia's voice came on the line. 'Hello?'

'Hey, Tricia.'

She sounded happy. 'Hi, Timothy.'

'Remember how we talked about getting together for drinks later in the week?'

'Yeah?'

'Well it's later in the week. What are you doing tonight after work?'

'Nothing. I mean, unless—'

'So let's have drinks. You know the Dutch Goose?'

'Awesome!'

'Awesome,' Timothy agreed. 'See you there at seven thirty.'

'Great.'

Timothy said: 'Don't bring the Kid.'

'I won't.'

'Okay. Bye.' He snapped the phone shut.

Yes, he knew right away whom he would choose. Was there ever any doubt?

CHAPTER 30

The Dutch Goose was a Stanford institution: a bar on Alameda with tight booths, peanut shells on the floor, fresh beer, greasy burgers, and initials carved into tables – decades' worth of initials – gouged into the dark lacquered wood. They were runes, these initials, mysterious stories of love long lost. Over time the carvings had been lacquered over, once a year when the students left town, brushed with a thick poly gloss so many times that the gouges in the wood had healed, and all that was left was a faint scar, a barely visible story about a young boy so much in love that he needed to record it with pen knife in cedar. The young people that carved these initials had been lacquered over too, by time and distance; they were fat and old now, or far across the country, married to someone else, someone unexpected, and had children, and were living a life different from the one imagined when the love runes were carved.

What the Dutch Goose meant to Timothy was youth. He loved walking in and feeling the floor under his shoes vibrate from the jukebox. He loved the smell of day-old cigarette smoke and spilled beer. At first he wasn't certain why he had told Tricia to meet him there, but then, when he entered the place, he suddenly did understand. This was where he would be meeting his wife all over again. This was the restaurant in Greenwich Village where he had proposed, but now he was doing it as a forty-seven-year-old, and now he was the oldest man in the room by at least a decade.

He saw her sitting in the back – she always sat in the back, he realized, so she could stare at everyone else.

He threaded through the crowd, mostly students in summer session, a few professors, and went to her. He slid into her booth, and it was so tight that their knees touched. She was wearing a tight black sweater, short-sleeved cotton, and her silver choker. He could smell her perfume, a sweet floral smell, like Katherine's funeral arrangement. Her glasses were gone – she was now in evening mode, Timothy understood – and she wore lipstick, this time bright red. She was stunning, and he felt happy when he saw her. He knew that he could have her, but on his terms. She would become his wife. Or his wife would become her.

'Let me get you a drink,' Timothy said.

'A Cosmo.'

'No Cosmos tonight,' he said. 'Tonight we'll put some hair on your chest.'

He left her before she could protest, and walked to the bar. The bartender, a young blond man, pointed to him. Timothy said, 'I need two Scotches. Doubles. On the rocks. You have single malt?'

'Macallan's.'

'Perfect.'

The bartender poured, and Timothy dropped a fifty-dollar bill on the bar.

'I guess I need change,' Timothy said. 'Keep sixteen dollars for yourself.'

'Thanks,' the bartender said. He raised an eyebrow. He turned and started for the cash register.

Timothy glanced to his left and right. Two groups of people were talking, one on each side of him, wrapped in their own conversations: a middle-aged couple to his left, talking quietly, possibly arguing; and a group of thin men with glasses and dirty hair, wearing chinos and blue denim shirts – engineer's uniforms. The engineers talked intently, but did not look at each other. Instead they stared at the surface of the bar as they spoke, as if the wood grain itself were the subject of the discussion.

Satisfied that no one was watching him, Timothy reached into his pocket and pulled out three blue pills he had retrieved earlier from Katherine's medicine chest.

He held them in front of his waist, using the bar to shield them from the bartender's view. The bartender was oblivious, counting singles into a neat pile on top of the register drawer, trying to work out the complex math implicit in Timothy's generous tip. The bartender grabbed the pile, licked his finger, and began to count them again.

Timothy casually dropped the three pills into the drink to his right. He took a red swizzle stick from the bar to mark the glass, stirred it in the drink.

He turned and glanced over his shoulder at Tricia. She was looking in the opposite direction.

The bartender returned finally and handed Timothy a stack of bills. 'Thanks again.'

'I'll be back,' Timothy promised. He was about to turn. A hand landed on his shoulder. Someone had been standing behind him. How had he not noticed the person? Timothy looked up and saw a big man in a motorcycle jacket, with a square-cut beard and mustache. The man gestured with his chin at the drink in Timothy's right hand.

'Hey, pal,' the biker said. 'What's that?'

Timothy regarded him. The biker weighed two hundred and fifty pounds. There were still a bunch of them around, ex Hell's Angels, who had come to live among the Northern California redwoods of La Honda or Woodside, near Neil Young and Jerry Garcia, back before the Valley was called Silicon Valley, back when high technology still meant *high* technology, and revolved around grow lamps and hydroponics.

'What's *what*?' Timothy said.

'That drink,' the biker said. 'Looks interesting.'

Timothy turned to Tricia. Now she was looking at him, intrigued by Timothy's new, beefy friend.

'Listen,' Timothy said softly. 'I don't want any trouble.'

'You don't, huh?' The biker turned to look at Tricia. He regarded her for a moment, then turned back to Timothy and smiled. The biker grabbed a swizzle stick from the bar, stuck it in his mouth like a toothpick. He chewed. 'Okay.' Then: 'It's just that the drink looks good. What's in it?'

'Macallan's. Can I buy you one?'

The biker smiled. 'Make it two.'

'You got it.'

Timothy ordered. He opened his wallet and put another fifty down on the bar in front of the biker. 'You mind taking care of the tab?' Timothy asked.

'Not at all.'

Timothy returned to the table with the two drinks.

'Who was that?' Tricia asked.

'Local color.'

'Were you fighting over me?'

'I told him I had a black belt. Scared him off.'

'Do you?'

'Gucci,' he said. 'Alligator.' He slid the swizzle-sticked drink across the table.

'What is it?'

'Scotch. Drink up.'

'Are you trying to make me drunk, Mr Van Bender?'

'Absolutely.' He raised his glass of Scotch. 'A toast.'

She wrapped her hand around her glass, but

didn't raise it. She looked uneasy. 'You know, about the other night . . .'

He shook his head. 'No. Let's not talk about it. It was my fault. I sent out mixed signals.'

'But I . . .' She paused, thought about it. 'I came on a little strong, didn't I?'

He recalled the encounter in her apartment, how Tricia stuck her tongue in his ear and insisted that she wanted his cock inside of her. 'No, not at all,' he said. 'You were a lady. Anyway, that's all in the past. I'm sorry about how I acted.'

'Me too.' She lifted her tumbler. 'To second chances,' she said.

They tapped glasses.

She took a sip and licked her lips. She said: 'I missed you at work today. I guess things aren't going well, are they?'

'No, they're not.'

She leaned over the table to confide a secret. 'I think Jay is looking for another job.'

'You think?'

She nodded.

He asked: 'And what about you?'

'Me?' She looked surprised. 'I'm staying. I mean, if you want me to.'

'I do. I need you.' Your body, anyway.

'I know. You need a friend. I mean, first you lose your wife. And now your company is in trouble. Your investors want to leave. Your employee wants to leave. I know, I'm just a secretary—'

'Assistant.'

'Whatever. I know you think I'm just a girl. But believe me, I know what it's like to go through tough times. When everything goes wrong, all you want is a little loyalty. So I promise. You have mine.'

Her words were like a slap. For a moment, he thought about calling the whole evening off. He could still back out. He could still drive Tricia home, tuck her safely into her apartment, before the blue pills kicked in. He could call Dr Ho, tell him that he wouldn't go through with it, that he loved Katherine – yes – but he wasn't going to harm an innocent girl, for the sake of some grotesque science experiment.

'You know something,' she said, staring at him, 'you are so awesome.'

He kept smiling, even though inwardly the word made him cringe. It was a word that Katherine would never use. In two quick syllables, it reminded him how different Tricia was from the woman he loved.

'Awesome,' he agreed.

They sat in silence. He tried to keep a pleasant smile on his face. But she must have noticed a change in his posture, because she said, finally, 'What's wrong?'

'Nothing.'

'You miss your wife, don't you?'

'Oh,' he said, and he lingered on the syllable. He was surprised to hear his voice crack involuntarily. 'More than you can imagine.'

She reached across the table and held his hand. 'I'm here for you,' she said.

This talk of Katherine gave him new resolve. He was sorry for what he was about to do, but he would do it. Of course he would. He had to. Dr Ho was giving him an opportunity. He could have Katherine back. He could go back in time, correct his mistakes, do everything again. Anyone would do the same. Any man who loved his wife.

'So,' Tricia said gently, mistaking his silence for gratitude. 'I'm not leaving Osiris. I'm not going anywhere. At least, not until the yen goes back down and you land on your feet, which I know you will.'

Timothy nodded. It was a kind thing to say, but it was also curious. He had always regarded her as a glorified switchboard, a good-looking telephone operator. Yet she mentioned the yen trade. Not that he had actively tried to keep it secret from her – he had never felt the need to. Her mind kept its own secrets. She was, after all, the girl that proudly boasted to her friends that she didn't even know what Timothy did for a living. But yet here she was, offhandedly mentioning the yen, even knowing what direction he wanted the currency to move – down. Curious.

But then she took another sip of Scotch and said, 'Wow. Now this packs a punch,' and she slapped the glass down on the table so hard that it sounded like a shot ringing out, and people beside them turned to look. 'Whoops,' she giggled.

'Careful, there,' he said, laughing pleasantly.

238

He wondered how long three valiums would take to work on a girl her size. The answer, he found out quickly, was: not very long at all.

When it seemed like she was in danger of passing out, he knew it was time to leave. He said, 'Let's go home.'

Her eyes were at half mast. She giggled and leaned over the table. Now she was using the table as a crutch under her chest, to keep from sliding onto the peanut-shell floor. 'Your place or mine?' she said, sloppily.

'Mine,' he said. 'Let me help you.'

He stood and assisted Tricia from her side of the booth. Timothy glanced at the bar. He saw the biker standing there, staring at him. Tricia gripped Timothy's shoulder. Timothy put his arm around her hip, and bore her entire weight. The biker smiled at Timothy, raised two fingers to his forehead, gave a little salute. Timothy nodded.

'Come on, Tricia,' Timothy said.

They walked toward the exit. He practically carried her, keeping his face down, and tried not to make eye contact with anyone. She felt heavy and limp. He tried to smile, to seem natural and casual, as if he and this beautiful woman half his age were strolling down a boardwalk. Yes, her knees where bent and, yes, her toes were dragging across the floor, sliding on peanut shells, but this was still the most natural thing in the world. Nothing to see here, folks.

'Wow,' Tricia said. 'I don't feel so good.'

'Come on. A little more.'

He took her outside into the warm night air, and laid her in the front seat of the BMW.

'Whoa boy!' she cried out. 'Awesome!'

They drove the dark streets, from Alameda de Las Pulgas to Menlo Park. Her eyes were half closed, but she still had a general sense that they were heading in the wrong direction.

'Hey, where are we going?' she asked pleasantly.

'I want you to meet a friend.'

'Cool.'

Timothy dialed his cell phone. When Dr Ho's voice answered, Timothy said: 'I'm bringing her over.' He hung up and dropped the phone in his jacket pocket.

'Was that your friend?' Tricia asked.

'Yes.'

'You know, Timothy, I really like you,' she said dreamily. 'I'm so happy you wanted to go out with me. I know you're sad about your wife.' She glanced at him sideways. She had slid almost halfway down the passenger seat. Only her knees, pushed up against the BMW dash, kept her from falling to the floorboard. 'I know you are a very sensitive man.'

'You think?'

'Yes. I could easily fall in love with you.' She slapped her mouth with her hand. 'Whoops. Did I say that out loud?' She closed her eyes, and seemed to drift off to sleep. Timothy turned left onto Sand Hill Road. Then she woke suddenly and continued her earlier conversation. 'I mean, you remind me of my dad.'

'Great,' Timothy said. 'Thanks.'

'I mean that in a good way. The best way.'

'Okay.'

They arrived at 3600 Sand Hill. The parking lot was empty. Timothy got out of the BMW and circled around to her side. He opened her door. 'We're here.'

She looked up at him. 'Where?'

'My friend's.'

'Okay,' she said, agreeably. She held out her hand for Timothy to help her from the car. He hoisted her from the low bucket seat and she stood up and grabbed his shoulder. She was standing chest to chest with him, her arms slung around his neck, as if they were dancing across a ballroom floor. He could feel her breasts pressing against his shirt. Her red lipstick was smudged. Her breath smelled of alcohol.

'Let's go,' he said. He guided her to Ho's office.

He knocked on the door to Suite 301 and Dr Ho answered.

'Good, good,' the doctor said, glancing down the hall. 'Come in.'

She was unconscious now, limp over Timothy's shoulder. Ho led them into the office waiting room and closed the door behind them.

'Is she okay?' Ho asked. He looked concerned.

'A couple valiums,' Timothy explained. 'Is that all right?'

'That's fine,' Ho said. 'I would have sedated her myself if you didn't. Let's bring her back.'

Ho put one of her arms over his shoulder, and the two men walked with Tricia slung between them, down the corridor toward Lab #1.

With his free hand, Ho pulled a key chain from his pocket. He unlocked the laboratory door and pushed it open with his shoe.

They carried Tricia into the room. The lab was cold from air conditioning. The hum, from hundreds of computers in racks, filled the space like the buzzing of a hive. Timothy had not seen the lab since the night he punched Ho. The mess on the floor – the shattered computer screen, the dropped keyboard, the loose wires – was gone. Now, on the black enamel lab island there was only one plasma monitor instead of two.

'Let's put her down,' Ho said, 'gently.'

They lowered Tricia slowly to the concrete floor. Dr Ho put his hand beneath her skull and guided it softly to the floor. She was lying on her back now, asleep, snoring.

'Okay,' Ho said. 'That's all.' He looked at Timothy.

Timothy wasn't sure what he meant.

Ho said: 'You can go.'

Timothy was surprised. He had expected to watch Ho perform the backup procedure. 'That's it?'

Ho gestured to the door leading to Lab #2, which was marked with the Keep Out sign. 'No visitors are allowed in that area. We have a very strict confidentiality policy. Part of the agreement with my investors.'

'I see,' Timothy said. But he didn't see. He wanted to stay and watch Ho work.

'You can leave her with me. The procedure will take some time. But before you know it, you'll have your wife back.' He walked to the computer monitor and tapped the keyboard. A cursor appeared. He typed something. A string of file-names filled the screen.

Timothy said: 'And what about . . . her?' He gestured at the sleeping secretary. 'You'll back her up, right? So that some day . . .'

'Yes, yes, of course,' Ho said. Timothy noticed the flicker of a smile at the corner of Ho's mouth.

'First I'll back up your young lady friend,' Ho said, 'and then I will restore your wife's backup on top. As you can imagine, the amount of data that needs to be transferred is quite large. Unfortunately the throughput is very limited. This is not exactly high-speed data transfer. That's actually one of the things we need to solve in the future, before we can make this a mass-market procedure.'

'So, how long?'

'Go home, Mr Van Bender. It may take all night.'

'And then what?'

'And then I'll contact you. After that – after your

wife has been restored – you and I will have no further contact. Once I have carried out my agreement with your wife, then our relationship will be terminated. You must not contact me again. You must not speak to me again. Do you understand?'

Timothy glanced at the door in the back of the room, which said Keep Out. He wanted to venture back and see what was inside, to watch the procedure, to witness Ho copying Katherine's mind into Tricia. 'But Doctor, maybe I should—'

On the floor, Tricia stirred. She moaned. 'Timothy?'

'You should go now,' Ho said. 'I need to begin.'

Timothy nodded. He turned to go, then stopped.

Dr Ho looked up at him.

Timothy wanted to tell him to be careful, to be gentle with his wife, and with Tricia, and not to make any mistakes; but then he thought about it and realized that, on this night – when he had drugged a young girl to the point of unconsciousness and dragged her body into a laboratory, and asked a doctor to copy over her brain and in its place restore his dead wife's – that maybe the time for being careful and gentle had long ago passed.

CHAPTER 31

For the first time in three weeks, he slept peacefully.

He did not dream about Dr Ho and his tiny spectacles, or about Tricia's bright red lipstick, or about the cliffs above Big Sur. Those dreams that had visited him so many nights before vanished, and in their place he felt nothing, just darkness and rest.

When he woke the sunlight was streaming onto his face, and it took a moment to remember the day of the week (Thursday) and what had happened the previous night. And then he remembered the Dutch Goose, and the suspicious biker, and the valiums in Tricia's drink.

He got up and showered. He dressed and made his way downstairs.

He was about to start the coffee brewing – one more time without Katherine, he thought hopefully – when the doorbell rang.

He turned the doorknob without looking through the peephole. He did not care whom he would find. He tried to empty his mind of all hope or expectation or fear. For once in his life, he would live his life without a plan, and see what happened.

He pulled open the door.

Tricia stood in the doorway. She wore the same outfit as the previous night, the snug black sweater, but the choker was gone, and her face was freshly scrubbed, without make-up. Her dark hair was combed down in a simple bob, and, without eye shadow, her blue eyes seemed unusually pale, the color of morning sky.

Timothy looked at the driveway behind her. Dr Ho was sitting in his Acura, the driver's window rolled down, his elbow on the doorframe. He nodded to Timothy, as if to say: It is done. He turned around in his seat, looked over his shoulder, and backed the car down the driveway, then turned into the street and drove away.

'Hi, Gimpy,' Tricia said.

Timothy stared at her. It was clearly Tricia standing in front of him. But something about her was different. It took him a moment to under-stand. It was her posture. The Tricia he knew stood ramrod straight, with her breasts out – always showing off her best features – with a crook in her hip, and an 'I dare you' saunter. But the woman in front of him was different. She leaned over the doorframe shyly, her chest in, her head down. That was Katherine's posture. On Katherine's body – the small chest, the long slender limbs – it seemed unremarkable. On Tricia it seemed absurd, like a whore trying to blend in at the debutante ball.

'Who are you?' Timothy asked. It was not an accusation; it was a happy question. He knew the answer already, and wanted to wring more pleasure out of the moment by hearing the response out loud.

'It's me,' she said.

And he was more sure of it than anything in his life – that the son of a bitch Dr Ho had really done it, that his crazy technology worked, that the woman standing in front of him, with her shy smile and posture that was all wrong, was not Tricia Fountain, stupid but sexy secretary, but rather his wife, Katherine, and that somehow – as unlikely as it seemed – he had gotten her back.

She walked around the house like she owned it. Which, technically speaking, she did. She first went to the kitchen and fixed coffee expertly, like a nurse moving a patient around a bed – gently but with certain, confident motions – grabbing the filter bucket, sliding open the water canister, sticking the carafe under the drip spout. It was as if she had handled that particular machine a hundred times before. Tricia had never been in his house, had never seen his kitchen, and certainly had never made him a cup of coffee. But Katherine had, each morning, for twenty years.

When the coffee was brewing they went upstairs to the bedroom. She stared at herself in the full-length mirror. Timothy stood beside her, afraid to touch her, unsure of what to say. She held up her arms, looked at the skin under her bones, taut and muscular, turned her face from side to side, trying to catch her profile. 'So this is what she looked like,' she said finally. 'Not bad.'

'I never slept with her,' Timothy said, because he thought she would want to know.

Tricia regarded him coolly. 'Never?'

'Never,' he said. Then he realized that he had to be forthcoming with Katherine, that she knew him too well. 'I thought about it.' Another pause. 'I came close once, but at the last minute I realized I hated her.'

Tricia said, in a saccharine sing-song voice, the voice of a stupid little vixen, 'Oh, Mr Van Bender, sir, you are so unkind.' Then she laughed, meanly.

Timothy stared at her. It was Katherine, most certainly was Katherine, the way her mimicry cut through his pretension like a scythe through wheat, but the voice, the throaty laugh, was Tricia's.

'I'm having a hard time with this,' he said. But he was secretly thrilled. This was magic, the stuff of dreams.

'Don't be crazy,' Tricia said. 'Look at me. Look what I get to look like.' Then she added: 'You found her attractive, didn't you?'

'Yes,' he admitted.

'Are you glad to have me back?'

'Yes.'

She turned to him. 'Then kiss me, Gimpy.'

He leaned over and kissed her. Her tongue found

his, and moved into his mouth the way Katherine's always had, just the tip, softly. But it felt different, not at all like Katherine's mouth – the thin, freckled lips were now full and soft, and her breath was loud and hot, as it was that night at Tricia's apartment.

Tricia broke off the kiss and looked up at him. 'Now that is strange,' she said. 'To feel you through somebody else. What's it like for you?'

How typical of Katherine, he realized, to pull away from a passionate moment and ask a question about how he felt. She was always analyzing, always stepping back, always making mental notes of things she might want to record later in her journal. She always kept her distance, from him and from the moment in which they lived. She wanted to package her life up and behold it, to understand it, like a piece of crystal in the light.

'It feels,' he said, 'different.'

She smiled. 'Welcome to the new era,' she said. She might have been talking about this new chapter in their marriage, these days of strange kisses and glancing at the mirror in disbelief. Or maybe she was proclaiming a new epoch in the history of mankind, an age when technology had finally overcome mortality, and the nature of what it meant to live had radically changed. He wasn't sure what she meant. But then she pulled his face down to hers, and kissed him again.

She led him to the bed, to the expanse of sheets and duvets and pillows that had seemed empty for so long. And they made love, this couple that had been married for twenty years, as if it was the first time they had ever felt each other; and, in a way, it was.

After he made love to Tricia, she did what Katherine always did. She slid across the bed and put her head on his chest. She lay there quietly, stroking his brown and gray chest hair between her fingers, listening to his heartbeat.

'Tell me everything,' he said. He knew she would understand what he meant.

'It was like a dream,' she said. 'Have you ever had a waking dream? One where you know you're dreaming, and can steer yourself in different directions, make yourself say things to the people you dream about? That's what it was like, talking to you in the machine. I could make myself say things, by thinking. Does that make sense?'

'Yes.'

'When I woke up this morning, it was different. I wasn't dreaming anymore. I felt fine. Like waking up after a long nap. I was . . . refreshed. And I feel like me. I am Katherine Van Bender. But when I pass a mirror, or look at my reflection in a window, then it's frightening. Like a nightmare.'

She lifted her head from her chest, looked at him. 'But I would do it again. What was my choice? I was sick, Timothy, so sick. And dying. And so scared. So maybe this isn't so bad. Maybe it was all worth it.' She put her head down again on his

250

chest and hugged him tightly. 'It only seems strange because we're not used to it. Maybe in the future this will be common. Like waking up after anesthesia. That must have seemed frightening, when people first did it. You wake up with a scar and stitches and a leg missing, or an organ cut out from your belly.' She stroked his abdomen, the spot above his appendix, as if tenderly drawing an invisible scar line. 'Isn't this the same thing? I guess we'll all get used to it, eventually.'

'I'm just glad you're back. I don't care what you look like.'

She sat up and smiled. 'Then why didn't you choose an old lady? Or a homeless man?'

'I don't want to make love to an old lady.'

'I'm not upset. I understand why you chose her. She's very pretty. I could get used to this quickly.'

When they rose, Tricia said she didn't want to dress like a slut, so she searched through Katherine's closet for something to wear. The outfits she chose – elegant silk twill blouses, pleated skirts – did not fit. Katherine was four inches taller than Tricia, and slimmer.

So Tricia put on again the clothes she had worn last night, the black sweater and tight jeans.

They agreed she would have to come to work with him. Now a Plan formed: that Timothy, devastated from the loss of his wife, would fall in love with his much-younger secretary, in a desperate and sad attempt to replace Katherine.

251

Their burgeoning relationship would need to be visible for everyone to see. So they drove together to the University Avenue office of Osiris, and he parked in the underground lot. The parking lot attendant smiled at him, and nodded at Tricia; he had seen them both before, but never had they arrived together in the morning, in the same car.

They took the elevator to the twenty-third floor. When they reached the office it was ten-thirty, and the Kid was sitting at Tricia's desk, looking harried, trying to work the phones. 'Osiris,' he said frantically, as he answered an incoming call. And then he saw Timothy and Tricia walk in together, and Tricia wearing the same clothes as the previous day, and he couldn't help himself: he raised an eyebrow and smirked. 'Yes,' the Kid said, into the phone. 'I will have him return your call.' He scribbled something on a notepad, then tossed it aside.

'You made it,' he said to Tricia.

'I made it,' Tricia said.

The Kid rose from her chair and made a show of gesturing grandly at it with a sweep of his hand, welcoming Tricia back to her station. Tricia sat down at the front desk. She stared at the phones. She seemed uncertain.

The Kid said, 'Timothy, I need to talk to you.'

Timothy understood Tricia's look; she had no idea how to use the PBX. Timothy said, 'In a second, Kid. Do me a favor. Would you please run across the street and grab me a cup of coffee?'

For a moment the Kid looked shocked, and he glanced at Tricia, as if to say, Isn't that *her* job?

Timothy said quietly, his voice laden with innuendo, 'Please. Just give us a minute.'

When put that way, as a secret man-to-man communication, the Kid understood, and he relented. He nodded, and then to Tricia said, 'You want coffee too? Black, right?'

She smiled. 'Little change of pace today. Cream and sugar.' The Kid seemed surprised, but Timothy understood right away. That was exactly how Katherine ordered it. With cream and sugar.

'Okay,' the Kid said. 'I'll be back.' As he headed to the elevator bank, he turned to Timothy over his shoulder. 'But we need to talk when I get back. It's important.' He pushed open the glass door. In a moment the elevator appeared, and he was gone.

Timothy showed her how to use the phones. She sat at the front desk, and he leaned over her from behind, demonstrating which buttons to press, and describing the general fuck-you posture she would need to adopt when dealing with angry investors calling for Timothy. Standing behind her, reaching over her, he was surprised by her smell. It was Katherine's smell, the smell of apples and honey. Tricia was wearing Katherine's perfume.

'I think I understand,' she said, about the phones.

'I love you,' he said. He bent down and kissed the flesh on the back of her neck.

'Oh, Mr Van Bender,' she said. She shivered. 'How inappropriate.'

'Sorry.'

He turned and walked away. 'Hold all calls, Tricia.'

'Yes, sir, Mr Van Bender.'

When the Kid returned, they met in Timothy's office. The news during Timothy's day-and-a-half-long hooky game had not been good.

The yen had continued its relentless climb, reaching a high of eighty-two during the previous day. Bear Stearns had issued a margin call and unceremoniously closed out its portion of the yen trade, resulting in another loss of seven million dollars. Further, that morning, while Timothy was making love to Tricia, the Kid had fielded a phone call from Barclays, who had issued their own margin call and explained that they would begin liquidating their yen position within hours.

The total losses for the month were now nearing forty million dollars, and there was no end in sight. Each margin call resulted in another broker placing a frantic order to buy yen for Osiris' account, at whatever price the market was charging. This raised the price of the contracts further, as sellers smelled blood, which in turn caused further losses.

The rising yen and the margin calls were only one side of the problem, the Kid explained to Timothy. Squeezing Osiris at the other end were the investors, who were clamoring to withdraw their money. It was now more than the small matter of Pinky contacting his limited set of friends and casting doubt on Osiris. Now each investor in the fund was calling the others, and the doubt and anxiety were feeding off each other, as August statements had not yet been mailed, and Timothy Van Bender was not taking phone calls, and no one had any sense of exactly where the fund stood, or how much money had been made or lost. The thing about rich people, Timothy understood – because he was one himself – is that they do not necessarily care about searching for the absolute highest returns available, and in fact, they do not even mind a slow dribbling loss, like a leak in an inner tube. What they dread more than anything else is losing a lot of money all at once – a 'blow-up,' in industry parlance. Most rich people are not self-made men; they inherited their money from fathers and grandfathers past, and most are insecure and fearful that they will never be able to earn money on their own, as their ancestors have; and so the only thing they care about is to preserve the good fortune they have been handed, and not ruin it for the next generation. Now Timothy Van Bender, former star money manager, the man who had never returned to his investors less than ten percent per year and averaged more than seventeen percent, was clearly blowing up, and taking a lot of family nest eggs with him.

Even though Osiris had the legal right to hold onto investors' money for ninety days after redemption was requested – a right enshrined in the Partnership Agreement, to prevent the very run on assets and messy liquidations that were now taking place anyway – the Kid reminded Timothy that it was only a formality now, that the redemptions would happen in ninety days, no matter what, and then whatever was left in Osiris' coffers – and it might not be much – would be handed back to the investors, and Osiris would be left a desiccated corpse, like the shell of an insect in an old spider's web.

And then there was one other matter, which the Kid saved for last, as if he was carefully building a legal case, block by block, trying to establish beyond all reasonable doubt the utter hopelessness of their situation. He handed Timothy a single sheet of paper, a letter typed on thick vellum, from the CFTC – the government agency responsible for regulating companies like Osiris, and responsible, Timothy knew, for prosecuting fraudulent money managers and sending them to jail.

It said:

COMMODITY FUTURES TRADING COMMISSION

DIVISION OF ENFORCEMENT
VIA FEDERAL EXPRESS

Enclosed is a subpoena ad testificandum and duces tecum of the Commodity Futures Trading Commission issued in connection with the above-titled private investigation being conducted pursuant to Section 6(c) and 8(a)(I) of the Commodity Exchange Act, as amended, 7 U.S.C 15 and a12(a)(I)(1994).

This subpoena calls for your testimony on October 12, 1999.

Attached to the letter was a subpoena. It instructed Osiris to gather all relevant documents for the CFTC to study. These documents included internal profit and loss estimates, emails, memos, spreadsheets, brokerage statements, and phone message logs. The CFTC believed Timothy and Osiris had committed fraud, that it was hiding losses from investors, that it was telling them comforting stories while proceeding to lose money hand over fist. Which was, more or less, true.

'I'm named in the subpoena, too,' the Kid said. He couldn't keep the anger out of his voice. It was bad enough that his resume would forever bear the mark of Cain, a stint at the soon-to-be infamous Osiris LP, which people would from now on mention with a shake of the head and a whistle of disbelief. In addition Timothy had somehow gotten the Kid involved in financial fraud. It was the kind of crime that landed people in prison at worst, and barred from the financial industry at best.

'Don't worry, Kid,' Timothy said. 'When things are going bad, everything looks worse than it is. When things are going well, everything looks

257

better than it is.' It was a useful old saw, one that had gotten Timothy through many a depressing day. But of course none of those depressing days had ever started with a subpoena from the federal government.

'I'm giving notice,' the Kid said. 'I resign effective two weeks from today.'

It occurred to Timothy at that instant that, when the Kid testified to the CFTC, he would hang Timothy out to dry. He would describe how his boss had instructed him to commit fraud, how he had been told to mislead investors. The Kid was going to hand them Timothy on a platter to save his own skin. But at least he was giving two weeks' notice. Nice kid.

'You need anything else?' the Kid asked. And then he added meanly: 'More coffee, maybe?'

'No, Kid,' Timothy said, holding up his cup. 'My coffee's fine.' Yes, the Kid was going to hang him out to dry.

Despite the fact that he was facing a twenty-million-dollar lawsuit against his personal assets, and despite the fact that the federal government was investigating him for suspected fraud, and despite the fact that he had lost over forty million dollars in less than a month and his career as a hedge fund operator was ending in ruin – despite all this, Timothy was happy.

Katherine was back. She was inside Tricia, that was true, but even that fact – at first so queer and frightening – had advantages. The things he disliked about Tricia – her stupidity and shallowness – had been washed away in her technological baptism. Instead, Katherine – his wife of twenty years, the woman he loved – had replaced her. Somehow, thanks to the advances of Dr Ho and Amber Corp., the woman that slept beside Timothy was now twenty-three years old, in perfect health, beautiful – and, most important – was really his wife.

There was of course the matter of sex. Those next few days they made love every night, and most mornings too. It was still the same Katherine – still unadventurous, never initiating, always face-forward-and-underneath. But even the quiet sex was better with her now, and – whereas two months earlier it had been ambitious to make love once a week – now he would push her to the bed and climb on top of her at any excuse. Her new body – the full breasts that rolled down over her rib cage when she lay on her back, the taut buttocks, the smooth thighs, which he explored when he raised her ankles into the air, her neck as soft as satin – was an adventure for him, and he could not get enough of it, of the novelty, the excitement, this new woman in his house.

On Sunday morning, after they'd had sex, the doorbell rang.

'Don't answer it,' Tricia said.

'Maybe it's important,' he said, thinking that the black woman with the cornrows had returned to deliver another summons. He rose and put on his bathrobe.

But it was not important. It was Ann Beatty, Katherine's friend from down the street, bearing a paper bag that smelled like hot garlic and dough.

'Good morning,' she chirped. 'I brought you some bagels. I hope I'm not too early.'

'No, of course not,' Timothy said, even though she was in fact too early. 'Come in. I was just going to eat.'

He took the bagels from her and led her to the kitchen. She sat at the table in front of the patio doors. Behind her, sunshine filled the backyard, and the ornamental grasses along the patio swayed in the morning breeze.

'I thought maybe you could use some company,' Ann said. 'I know when Mark and I divorced, weekends were the hardest. So lonely, without anything to fill your day.'

'Would you like some coffee?' Timothy asked.

'If you're having.'

Timothy banged around the cupboards, looking for the coffee beans. Where had she put them? Ann continued: 'I can only imagine what you're going through. I know it's only been a few weeks. Things are still raw.' She touched her fingers to her short black hair, obviously dyed, and stroked the back of her head thoughtfully. 'Katherine was a wonderful woman.'

'Yes,' Timothy said, into the cupboard. Then he heard slippered footsteps approach the kitchen.

He turned to see Tricia standing in the doorway in a skimpy T-shirt, her nipples bulging beneath the cotton, and a pair of boxer shorts.

'Hello,' Tricia said.

'Oh—' Ann looked mortified. 'I'm so sorry. I didn't know you had . . . company.'

Tricia walked to Ann, held out her hand. 'Tricia Fountain,' she said.

Ann seemed uncertain. She didn't know where to look: at the young girl's face? At her breasts? Her exposed thighs? She looked past Tricia to Timothy. She took Tricia's offered hand, shook it perfunctorily, and said, 'Ann Beatty.'

'Timothy has told me a lot about you.'

Now Anne regarded her carefully. Of course it was preposterous that Timothy would tell this young girl, twenty years younger than Katherine, all about his dead wife's friend, the old neighbor down the street.

'Maybe I should be going,' Ann said. 'I'm so sorry to intrude.' She started to rise.

'Please,' Tricia said. 'Stay.'

Timothy did not want Ann to stay. In fact, after seeing Tricia appear, with her nipples showing under her T-shirt, in the same room as Ann Beatty, the icy old nun, he was turned on. He felt an erection under his bathrobe. What he wanted was that Ann should leave, so that he could make love to Tricia again, right there in the kitchen. Maybe even on the oak table.

'Yes,' Timothy said, 'stay.'

Another moment of hesitation as Ann hovered at the table, neither fully standing nor sitting.

'You brought bagels?' Tricia said, spotting the bag. 'Have breakfast with us.'

Ann hesitated. 'All right,' she said finally, relieved that this young girl, despite the intrusion, was friendly after all. She folded back into her chair.

Seeing Timothy standing beside the coffee machine, helpless, Tricia said: 'Let me help you with that. You couldn't operate that machine if your life depended on it.'

'That's true,' Ann said. She smiled knowingly. 'That's exactly what—' She stopped herself.

'What?' Tricia asked.

There was a moment of uncomfortable silence.

Timothy finished Ann's sentence. 'That's exactly what my wife used to say. Ann has been here for many a breakfast and has observed my incompetence first hand.'

Ann said, 'I'm sorry. That was thoughtless.'

'No,' Tricia said. She pretended to make a pained smile. Or maybe, Timothy thought, it really was a pained smile. Katherine was wily, after all. 'It's okay. I understand.'

Tricia turned and began to make the coffee. Timothy sat down at the table across from Ann. There was nothing else to say, so they watched Tricia fit the paper filter into the machine and start measuring the beans.

Finally, Timothy said softly to Ann: 'I know this must seem a little strange.' He stared at the back of Tricia's soft thin white neck. 'But sometimes love appears in the damnedest places, at the damnedest times.'

Ann nodded.

Now Timothy was glad Ann was here, that he could begin the process of creating the story, of integrating Tricia into his life. He knew that once Ann left his house, the phone calls would begin, to other neighbors first, and then to mutual friends, old girlfriends of Katherine, tennis partners, church members, Palo Alto grandees. The headline would circulate: Timothy Van Bender Sleeps with Young Girl Just Weeks After Wife's Suicide.

Timothy said: 'I met Tricia at work. She's my secretary.'

Correction. This just in: Timothy Van Bender Sleeps With Young Secretary Weeks After Wife's Suicide.

'Really?' Ann said, but it sounded as if she did not want to hear too much more.

'Yes,' Timothy said. 'Funny how life works. One door closes and another opens.'

'I suppose,' Ann said.

Tricia joined them at the table with the plate of bagels. 'Let me get some cream cheese.' She laid the bagels on the table, and disappeared into the refrigerator.

'She seems to know her way around,' Ann said. It was equally a compliment and an accusation.

'We've spent a lot of time together,' Timothy said. 'Things are really good.' He smiled at Ann,

263

who – although it clearly pained her – smiled back.

Later that afternoon Tricia said, 'I think we should get married.'

They were in the living room, lying on opposite sides of the couch. He was watching golf on television, drinking a beer. She sat facing him, her legs in his lap, as she worked on the Sunday crossword puzzle.

He looked up at her when she said it. Her face was down, buried in the crossword. She had folded the paper in half to make a surface, and held a pencil in the air, ready to jab the point into the pulp.

He said, 'Really?'

'Well,' she said to the newspaper, 'I am your wife. It's just a matter of formalizing for the rest of the world what we already know.'

'But, Tricia,' he said, stressing the name, dripping it with honeyed sarcasm, because it always felt good and strange to call her that. 'We've only been dating for a week.'

She looked up at him. 'We probably had an affair before your wife died.' She paused and then added: 'That's what everyone will think, anyway.'

'But I didn't,' Timothy said evenly.

'If you say so.' She went back to her crossword and jotted an answer into the boxes. Thinking the conversation was over, he returned to the golf game on television.

'The point is,' Tricia said, 'it won't seem strange

to anyone if we get married. We really should. Not just for outward appearances, but for us. I mean, I love you.'

She rubbed her foot against his crotch, and there it was again, an erection. Timothy was now at an age when he counted his erections, noted them the way a meteorologist might scan the horizon and note nimbus clouds. In the last week he had experienced more erections than he had the entire six months before. God, she turned him on.

'Oh yeah?' he said. 'I love you, too, Katherine.'

She dropped the newspaper and pencil to the floor, and the pencil rolled under the couch. She scrambled toward him over the cushions. 'I thought we agreed,' she said, her breath hot and wet in his ear, 'that you wouldn't call me that anymore.'

'Okay, Tricia.'

She kissed his ear gently. 'If you marry me,' she said, 'I'll make it worth your while.'

'How will you do that?'

'Watch,' she said. She slid her face down his chest, unbuttoning his shirt as she went. She kissed his chest, licking his hair. She worked her way down to his pants buckle. She unfastened it, expertly, and kissed his soft doughy abdomen. She lifted the elastic band of his briefs, and tongued the skin beneath.

'Oh,' he said, 'I guess I really should propose.'

'You really should,' she agreed.

CHAPTER 32

The next week, Tricia quit working at Osiris without saying goodbye to the Kid. One day she simply did not appear at work, and Timothy off-handedly told him that Tricia had decided to 'move on.' From the look on his face, it seemed the Kid knew exactly where Tricia had moved on to – specifically, Timothy's house and bedroom.

Timothy called a temp agency and asked for a replacement secretary, who appeared the same day: an overweight Russian woman who smelled like cigarette smoke and cheese blintzes.

Meanwhile activity at Osiris ground to a halt. After Barclays liquidated the yen position, Citigroup did the same the following day. Now the entire yen trade had been closed out at a staggering loss of fifty million dollars. Over half of Osiris' capital had vaporized in less than a month.

All that was left at this point was to wind down the firm, to calculate the final losses, send the last financial results to investors, and return their remaining money. There was the small issue of the CFTC subpoena, and of Pinky Dewer's lawsuit.

Throwing in the towel, Timothy sent a check to Pinky for a bit less than half the amount Pinky had originally invested, lamely enclosing a handwritten note that apologized for the delay and for 'the unexpected loss of capital.' It was the best he could do. He hoped for a miracle, that Pinky would then drop the lawsuit against him personally, but – not surprisingly – the lawsuit remained and Pinky refused to take his calls. The loss of sixteen million dollars, Timothy understood, tends to make people prickly.

There remained thirty-four million dollars of cash in Osiris' various brokerage accounts. But soon, Timothy knew, that money would be returned to investors, and he would be left with nothing, except an expensive three-year lease on prime Palo Alto real estate, at least one lawsuit – possibly more – and a potential indictment on conspiracy and fraud charges.

And yet Timothy felt unburdened.

What was happening in his professional life was unpleasant but manageable. He could walk away from his career as a hedge fund manager. He never really enjoyed it anyway. For years, he had been able to make money, but he knew, secretly, that he was intellectually outgunned, in over his head – just lucky. When he'd started twenty years earlier, finance was a business about connections, about whom you knew, and who your friends were. To be successful required only that you had rich acquaintances and a pleasant manner, that you could call a Yale classmate on the phone, reminisce about the old days for a few minutes, and then ask for a five-million-dollar check. But, recently, the world had changed. The finance industry had opened its doors. Talent and intellect mattered. There were Indians now, people with strange exotic names, Chinese men who had never attended the Ivy League, and it wasn't uncommon to brush shoulders with men from Bangalore who held PhDs from schools Timothy had never heard of. The old world – of investing with your gut, of relying on the word of people you trusted, of cashing in on inside knowledge, of doing deals on a handshake – was being replaced by a world of spreadsheets and Monte Carlo simulations and black boxes and quants. It was time for men like Timothy to move on.

It didn't matter, anyway. Timothy's net worth was still tens of millions of dollars. His house in Palo Alto was worth three million dollars. He never needed to work again. Frank Arnheim was confident that Pinky Dewer's lawsuit was beatable, or at least could be quickly settled. Even the CFTC charges could be defeated, since the blow-up at Osiris was caused more by incompetence than by fraud – or at least that was the case that could legitimately be made, if only the Kid agreed to stay quiet.

So Timothy regarded his travails with equanimity. He thought of them as the price he was paying for getting Katherine back – a kind of

Conservation of Happiness principle. For every happiness in life there is an equal and opposite unhappiness. He had magically been given one more chance with Katherine. Ergo: his professional life would be destroyed. But it seemed like a fair price to pay for the woman he loved.

There was only one problem: the Kid.

He could make or break Timothy. If he said the right thing when he testified at the CFTC in Chicago, if he explained that Timothy had in fact followed all the rules, but had simply guessed wrong on the direction of the yen – an occupational hazard, after all – then Timothy would walk away unscathed. If, instead, he told the Commission that Timothy had ordered him to lie to investors and withhold financial statements, that he had issued blasé pronouncements about the state of Osiris while aware that it was losing money, he would seal Timothy's doom.

In the evening, after the Kid had left for the day, and after Natasha, the fat Russian receptionist, had departed, Timothy returned to his office. He removed the corporate check ledger from his desk drawer and wrote a check for fifty thousand dollars, payable to the Kid.

For Timothy, it was more than simply paying him off. He felt sorry for him. Jay Strauss had gotten a bad break, getting hooked up with Osiris. And despite the Kid's anger at having his career derailed, and despite his disgust with Timothy for sleeping with the young secretary (whom he himself had desired), the Kid was, in the end, a gentleman. He did, after all, agree to stick around after giving notice, and to help Timothy wind down Osiris gracefully. So Timothy owed the Kid something. If he happened to remember Timothy's generosity when testifying in Chicago, well, that would be all right, too.

Besides, this kind of generosity was easy. The fifty-thousand-dollar expense would come out of his investors' hides. It was always easy to be generous with OPM – other people's money.

Timothy decided to drive over to the Kid's house and give him the check. It would be a sign of respect to personally hand it to him rather than to mail it, to meet him on his own ground.

He looked up the Kid's address in his Rolodex. He lived in Menlo Park, a few minutes away.

The Kid lived in a leafy residential neighborhood behind the Safeway. It was a mix of small houses and low-density apartments – duplexes and quad-plexes – but the houses were primarily rented by Stanford students and professors.

Timothy pulled into a gravel driveway and stopped at the Kid's house. You can tell when a house is a rental: the grass is never mowed or properly watered. It was the same at the Kid's – brown grass, too long in places, and an old hose and sprinkle snaking around the front yard, looking like it hadn't moved in a while.

Timothy rang the doorbell. He heard the sound of music, unfamiliar rock music that had mercifully skipped his generation. The music went mute, and the Kid opened the front door. He was dressed in a T-shirt and jeans.

'Timothy,' he said. The Kid seemed surprised.

'Sorry to drop by unannounced,' Timothy said. 'I thought I'd surprise you. I have something for you.' He removed the check from his pocket. It was still folded neatly in half. He held it out between his middle and index finger.

'What's this?'

'A beautiful fruit plate. Can't you tell?' Then: 'Let's just say it's a Thank You, and an I'm Sorry.'

The Kid opened the check and looked at the amount. He raised an eyebrow. 'This is unexpected.'

'It's my pleasure.'

'Well, thank you.'

'Really,' Timothy said pointedly, 'my pleasure.'

Suddenly Timothy felt strange and uncomfortable. Why was the Kid blocking his entrance to the house? Why wasn't he inviting him in?

'This is nice of you,' the Kid said. 'I would normally invite you in, but . . .' His voice trailed off.

In the background, from the house, came the sound of a footstep and a floorboard creaking.

Then Timothy understood. 'Oh,' he said. The Kid had a guest. Probably a female guest. It was something Timothy had never considered. He felt like a dolt. 'I'm sorry.'

271

'No, it's just, uh . . .' The Kid looked over his shoulder, nervously.

'Okay,' Timothy said. 'Sorry to interrupt. I just wanted to give you that. To thank you.'

'I appreciate it,' the Kid said. He kept his arm across the doorway, blocking the entrance.

'All right, I'll see you tomorrow.'

'All right. Thanks.'

Before Timothy could say another word, the Kid nodded and closed the door.

When he arrived home, Tricia was in the kitchen, sautéing sliced onions in a skillet, cooking dinner.

'Hello, dear,' she said. 'Busy day at work?' It was a running joke, now that Osiris was winding down, and Timothy did even less work than usual – practically nothing.

He kissed her. 'The usual bullshit. Too many martinis at lunch.'

'How is Natasha, your new secretary? Are you going to replace me with her?'

'I already did.'

'I mean in the bedroom.'

'That's what *I* meant.'

'You're terrible.'

'She smells like blintzes. How is that possible?' He took off his suit jacket and folded it over the chair at the table.

'You're not going to leave that there, are you?' It was the same question Katherine had always

272

asked, since they moved into the house years ago. In the week since she had returned to him, he had gradually grown used to her being there, in the body of Tricia – so much that it started to seem natural. But then she would say something, an off-hand remark, like the comment about his jacket on the chair, or a complaint about uncapped toothpaste – and it would so obviously be Katherine's familiar words coming from Tricia's body – that it was like lightning over a strange volcanic landscape, a sudden flash in a previously dark sky, revealing the utter weirdness of it, the gray ash and charred tree stumps, the unearthliness, which until then had been hidden.

'Sorry,' he said. He took his jacket from his chair, was about to leave the room. He noticed something. 'What's that?'

She looked up. 'What?'

He pointed to her neck. 'That.'

Under her blouse, he could barely see it. Tricia was wearing the necklace he had given his wife at Big Sur, the fifteen-thousand-dollar diamond and sapphire pendant.

She touched it, pulled it out of her shirt for him to see. 'It's my anniversary present,' she said. 'You gave it to me.'

'Where'd you find it?'

'Where I left it. In my underwear drawer.' Then: 'What's wrong with you?'

He shook his head. 'Nothing.' Another flash of

lightning on that weird volcanic scenery. 'Sometimes it's strange. I know it's you, but it's not you.'

'But,' Tricia said, 'it *is* me.'

On Saturday afternoon they decided to go to the Menlo Circus Club, to play tennis and have drinks.

He managed to finish a single set before his knee started to ache. 'Come on, Gimpy,' Tricia said to him, as they met at mid-court. 'Your war wound acting up?'

'A little.'

'Too bad you're so old.'

'No kidding.'

'One more set? I feel great.'

So he played one more set, to entertain his young girlfriend and former wife.

Afterward, soundly beaten, he trudged off to the men's locker room to shower. They agreed to meet on the veranda for drinks in twenty minutes.

In the locker, Timothy limped into the shower, then dried and walked naked into the wash room. He stood in front of the mirrors above the sink basins, and began to comb his hair. When he looked up he saw Michael Stanton, ex-CEO of the medical device company, currently under indictment by the federal government – but still a member in good standing at the Circus Club – looking at Timothy's reflection.

'Timothy!' Michael Stanton said. 'Good to see you out and about. Play some tennis?'

Timothy felt silly, combing his hair, buck naked. 'Yes.'

'Who with?'

Like you don't know, Timothy thought. 'I have a new girlfriend, Michael,' Timothy said gamely.

'Good for you. I think I saw her walking around. A great-looking lady. Quite a bit younger.'

'Is she? I hadn't noticed.'

'Ha! Good for you. Say, why don't we get some drinks together on the veranda – you, me, your girlfriend, my wife.'

Timothy thought, Yes, Wife #2. But of course he could not remember her name.

'Susan,' Michael continued, as if reading Timothy's mind.

'That sounds terrific,' Timothy said, even though it did not sound terrific.

'All right,' Michael Stanton said. 'See you there in about ten.' Then, looking at the reflection of Timothy's penis in the mirror, he said: 'And don't forget to put on some pants.'

They sat on the veranda in the late afternoon sun, drinking daiquiris. Wife #2 pulled her chair close to Michael Stanton. The thing that surprised Timothy, as he looked at her, was that she was older than he remembered. Two months ago, before Katherine's death, she seemed scandalously young – the Stantons had been the cause célèbre at the Circus Club, not because of Michael's SEC indictment, his insider trading and possible ten-year jail term, but because of the unceremonious way he had dumped his older wife and traded down to a much younger model.

But now Timothy was shocked to see that Susan was in fact older than Tricia, that the new Mrs Stanton had the faintest trace of dark circles under her eyes, that lines were beginning to form at the corners of her mouth. And he realized, proudly, that it was official: he was sitting on the veranda with the most desirable woman that had ever stepped onto Circus Club grounds.

'So tell us, Timothy,' Wife #2 said. 'How did you both meet?'

Timothy was about to answer, to say something vague about Tricia being a business associate, but Tricia spoke first. 'We met at work.' She leaned over the table and said, in a stage whisper, 'I was his secretary.'

Wife #2 laughed. 'Isn't that funny? Us too. Well, actually, I was Michael's Investor Relations hack. But same thing.'

Timothy looked over the heads of the Stantons to the other club members sitting on the veranda. He noticed that they were whispering, looking with sidelong glances at Wife #2 and Tricia.

'The way we fell in love,' Michael Stanton said, 'is that I was on Cavuto, you know, on CNBC? And they had me waiting for about an hour under the hot lights before my segment. And I must have been melting, I'll tell you. I mean, sweating like you have never seen sweat before. So they were about to go live and Susan here—'

Oh yes, Timothy thought. *Susan. I must remember that.*

'—Susan said: "You are not putting him on national TV looking like a wet noodle. Either you dry him off or we walk."' Michael laughed and turned to Susan. 'Isn't that right?'

'You're my wet noodle,' she said.

'Thank you, sweetheart.'

'What a great story,' Timothy said.

'Tell you the truth,' Michael Stanton said, 'I'm glad to see you two together. I felt like a bit of a letch at first, coming here with Susan, since she's so much younger than me. But now it looks like I have some company.'

'Timothy and I plan to come here all the time,' Tricia said.

'I don't blame you,' Susan said. 'Isn't it unbelievable? Sometimes I just wake up and I have to pinch myself. I can't believe my good luck.' Timothy wasn't certain what she was referring to: the splendid club grounds? Michael Stanton's six-bedroom house in Atherton? His eight-figure bank account?

Tricia said, 'I'm glad to meet someone my age.'

'Oh, I don't know about that,' Susan said, flattered.

'Ladies,' Michael Stanton said, 'please. You're practically burying me and Timothy. We're still alive and kicking.' And then he said: 'I'd like to

277

propose a toast.' He raised his daiquiri glass. 'To second chances.'

'To second chances,' Tricia said.

'Hear hear,' Timothy said.

They drank.

They left the Circus Club at four o'clock in the afternoon and headed home. The club was located in a residential neighborhood of Atherton. It was secluded, cut off from the rest of the city by dead ends and one way streets. It was usually deserted; Timothy could drive for blocks without seeing another car.

So it was strange when Timothy pulled out of the club and saw a black Chevy Impala across the street from the club entrance, with its engine idling.

Timothy drove a few blocks, glancing at his rearview mirror. The black Impala followed closely behind.

He turned left on Valparaiso and looked in the mirror. The Chevy also turned left, and continued tailing him.

'Strange,' Timothy said.

'What?' Tricia asked.

'Nothing, I just . . .' He slid the BMW into the left lane and made a quick left turn. Like two horses on a carousel, the Impala hugged the BMW, staying close behind.

'Where are you going?' Tricia asked.

Timothy gunned the motor and raced past the car in front of him. He zoomed out of the residential neighborhood and made a quick right on Santa Cruz, a busy four-lane street.

The Impala sped up and followed.

'What the hell?' Timothy said. He raced the BMW down Santa Cruz.

Tricia grabbed the dashboard. 'Timothy, slow down!'

The cars sped down the street.

'That's it,' Timothy said. He jerked the steering wheel right and pulled into a strip-mall parking lot, then slammed on the brake. The BMW skidded to a stop in front of a tanning salon.

Timothy cut his ignition, threw open his door and jumped from the car. He turned to face the entrance of the parking lot and wait for the Impala.

The Chevy pulled into the parking lot. Its prow was low and wide, like a hammerhead. It rode slowly toward Timothy. Timothy saw the driver, a young man with long, dark, stringy hair, staring at him. The Impala and the long-haired man slowly drove past. The driver turned in his seat to continue looking at Timothy. What he did next was unmistakable: he put his index finger to his neck and slowly pulled it across his throat. He smiled at Timothy.

Then the Impala gunned its engine, its tires screeched, and it sped from the parking lot and disappeared down Santa Cruz.

'Did you see that?' Timothy called to Tricia. His heart was racing and he could feel that familiar cocktail, of fear laced with anger, course through him. He looked down to see his fists were clenched. 'Did you see what he did?' He bent down into the BMW to look at Tricia. 'Did you see that?' he asked again.

Tricia looked pale. 'Let's go home.'

'Do you know him?'

'No,' she said.

Timothy climbed into the BMW and started the engine.

'Did you see what he did? Like he wanted to kill me.'

'He was probably drunk,' Tricia said.

'He didn't look drunk.'

He turned to Tricia. 'What the hell was that about?'

She shook her head. 'I have no idea.'

When they arrived home, he expected to see the long-haired man and the Impala waiting in his driveway. But he was not there.

After a few hours, the sharp edges of the incident faded, and what at first seemed frightening quickly turned ridiculous: some drugged-out kid in a Chevy trying to scare one of the snobs at the Circus Club; Timothy racing around Menlo Park, screeching to a halt in front of a tanning salon; Timothy standing in the parking lot, his fists clenched, dressed in prissy tennis whites, waiting for the druggie – and hoping to do what exactly? Backhand him with a Wilson?

At dinner, he and Tricia laughed about it.

'All in all, I'd say that was a successful day,'

Timothy said. They were sitting in the dining room, with barbecued steaks and a half-finished bottle of Petit Sirah. 'Playing a full set of tennis with a woman half my age, protecting her from some druggie teenager. All I need now is a cape and red 'S' on my chest.'

'Superman, that was hardly a full set of tennis.'

'I played, didn't I?'

'You waddled.'

'Forget the tennis, then. I still saved you from a druggie teenager.'

'You did. My hero.' She finished her wine, put down the glass. 'You looked so silly, standing there.'

'I thought I was your hero.'

Under the table, she slid out of her shoe and stroked his pant leg with her foot. 'You are my hero,' she said. 'I couldn't believe how brave you were. The way you did sixty through Menlo Park. And then you ran out of the car to confront him. Fearless.'

'You know what they say? The best defense being a good offense—'

'Yes.'

'I needed to protect my woman.'

'You were awesome,' Tricia agreed.

Timothy's smile froze on his face. He looked her. 'What did you say?'

She seemed puzzled. 'Nothing. I said . . .' Her voice trailed off. She shook her head.

He reached under the table, grabbed her shin, pushed it away from his leg. 'What did you just say?' His smile was gone now.

Tricia stared at him, and she looked frightened. He insisted, 'Tell me what you said.'

'Timothy, what is wrong with you?'

Timothy stared at Tricia. It had been weeks since Katherine's return. It had been weeks since there had been any doubt in his mind that it was really her. But now, that word – that single, dumb word which Katherine would never have used, but which came so naturally to Tricia, the stupid secretary – made him wonder.

'Timothy, you're scaring me,' she said.

He stared at her, at the cool blue eyes, the dark hair swept back with an elegant tortoiseshell barrette. The old sexy outfits that Tricia had worn were gone, replaced by a new wardrobe – a Katherine-style wardrobe – muted cardigans and graceful pleats – clothes bought one afternoon in a whirlwind trip to Talbott's and Ann Taylor. But, under the clothes, was it still Tricia sitting across from him? He tried to look into her eyes, to see something devilish, and sly, and knowing. But her blue eyes were flat; they revealed nothing. And maybe, he thought, maybe that's all it is – nothing.

He said, 'Sorry.' He shook his head. 'Strange day. That's all.'

She shook her head and went back to cutting her steak. He noticed it was rare, which was how Katherine ate it, and that comforted him – the dark red blood in her plate.

*　　*　　*

282

That night, after they climbed into bed and turned off the lights, Timothy lay awake.

He heard Tricia snoring beside him. He realized that something had been bothering him. It was in the back of his mind, all day, unexamined, and he probably would have forgotten about it, were it not for the incident at dinner, when his wife said one wrong word.

It had happened the previous night, when she was wearing the diamond and sapphire necklace that he gave to her at Big Sur. He remembered the conversation: 'What is that?' he had asked. And she replied, 'It's my anniversary present.'

At the time, something about her words seemed wrong. At first he thought that it was simply his own discomfort at seeing the necklace he had bought for Katherine wind up on Tricia's body.

But now, lying in bed, he realized that it was something else entirely. How had she known the necklace was an anniversary present?

This woman sleeping beside him was not the original Katherine Van Bender. She was Katherine's backup – a duplicate copy. The backup had been made the day before they left for Big Sur. Katherine had said so in their conversation through the computer terminal. ('How was Big Sur?' she had typed. 'Did you score?')

So how, Timothy wondered, did she know that the necklace was an anniversary present? She could not have known. This woman beside him would have no memory of the trip to Big Sur, would have no memory of receiving the necklace. If she had found it in her jewelry box, she could not have known what it was.

He turned to her in the dark bed. 'Tricia,' he said softly.

She stopped snoring.

'Tricia,' he said again.

'Hmm?' She was half asleep.

'How did you know about the necklace? How did you know it was an anniversary present?'

'Hmm?' She still sounded sleepy. But it was dark, and Timothy couldn't be sure. Were her eyes wide open now? Was her mind whirring, racing to come up with an answer?

'You knew it was an anniversary present, but I gave it to you in Big Sur – after you were backed up. You couldn't have known.'

She said dreamily, 'Hmm.'

'So how did you know it was an anniversary present?'

She sighed. She stirred in the bed, and turned on her nightstand lamp. They both squinted in the sudden light. 'Because,' she said, now sounding both very awake and very annoyed, 'what else would it be? For God's sake, Timothy, do you think I'm a dope? Do you think I'm your dumb secretary? I've been married to you for twenty years. I know you like a book. I know how you think. I know your tricks. You bought me something big and expensive on our trip to Big Sur – so I'd forget

284

I was miserable. Wasn't that it? I bet you didn't even have the gift when we went there. I bet you bought it there, at the last minute. Am I right?'

He thought to himself, Yes, that is uncanny. You know me as if you are my wife. You know me too well.

'Am I right?' she asked again, angry now.

'You're right,' he said. He was surprised that his words came out sounding sheepish.

She huffed and sighed, reached for the night-stand and turned off the light. In the darkness, the body beside him turned away, pulling the blankets with her.

Yes, it is uncanny, he thought again. Maybe she is right. She knows me like a book.

He closed his eyes and tried to sleep, tried to keep the necklace out of his thoughts.

CHAPTER 33

On Monday morning he rose early.

He wanted to get to the office before eight-thirty, to prepare for a nine o'clock meeting with his lawyer, Frank Arnheim. They were to review his CFTC testimony and go over the documents that they would hand to the agency.

Timothy glanced at Tricia in bed. She was still asleep. Quietly, he put on his bathrobe and descended the stairs to the foyer. He decided he would start his day in a civilized fashion: read the newspaper, have a cup of coffee, and relax.

He peered through the peephole of the front door. The *San Jose Mercury News*, wrapped in a schoolbus-yellow plastic bag, waited in his driveway.

He opened the front door. The day was already warm and beautiful. The sun was bright, the sky cloudless. Timothy trundled down the stairs and across the flagstone path to the driveway. He bent down for the paper.

'Mr Van Bender!'

Timothy looked up. Detective Neiderhoffer walked toward him from the street. He carried two cups of coffee. Why had Timothy not seen his car?

'Detective . . .' Timothy said.

'Neiderhoffer,' Neiderhoffer said.

'Yes, I remember.'

Neiderhoffer walked up the driveway toward him. 'I was hoping I could catch you before work. You have a few minutes?'

'For what?'

'To chat.' He shrugged. 'You know, about your wife.' He held up the two coffees. 'I brought you some Joe. To make it worth your while.' They sat at the kitchen table, Timothy still in his bathrobe. The detective flipped though a small notepad.

'How have you been holding up?' Neiderhoffer asked.

'Fine.'

'Good, good. Because I know how hard it must be for you.' He stared at his pad intently. 'By the way, ever find out who your wife's last doctor was?'

'No.'

'Because she must have changed doctors, right?'

'Hmm,' Timothy said.

'That's a strange story. The day before she dies, your wife calls you and says she's very sick. But her regular doctor – Dr, um . . .' He flipped through his notes. 'Dr Charles – he hasn't seen your wife in a year, and the last time she visited him, she was in perfect health.'

'She must have switched doctors, like you said.'

'Yes, that's one explanation,' Neiderhoffer said.

For the first time, Timothy realized that Neiderhoffer was not there simply to check on him and bring him coffee. 'What's the other explanation?'

'Maybe she wasn't sick after all.'

Timothy said, 'But she told me she was.'

Neiderhoffer looked up at him. 'Yes, when she called you that morning. That mysterious but very illuminating phone call. The one where she told you she was about to commit suicide. Yes, I remember.' Neiderhoffer looked down at his pad and scribbled something. Almost as an after-thought, he asked: 'Would you mind if we subpoenaed the telephone company and looked at your phone records?'

'Go ahead.'

Neiderhoffer nodded, as if Timothy's answer pleased him. 'Okay, good.' He flipped through his pad, continued reading his notes. Neiderhoffer said, 'I finally went down to Big Sur. Beautiful place. Can you believe, I grew up in San Jose but never even visited? Isn't that funny? I guess it's true what they say, that you never notice the things that are most familiar to you.'

He waited for Timothy to say something.

'So,' Neiderhoffer said, 'I finally got down there. You know, just to make sure everything was copasetic.'

'Was it?'

'Sure. You went down to the Ventana Inn, had a – what is it? – a 'Sea Enzyme Organic Mask' with your wife, ate in the restaurant, got a massage from a man named Tony, stayed in the Lodge two nights. It all checks out.'

'Well, then.'

'Just a few things that stuck out. I showed your picture to the hotel staff. On Sunday, you pulled into the hotel reception area. A bellboy remembers you. You made quite an impression on him. Handed him a twenty, asked him to watch your car. You were very sweaty, he said, and out of breath. And, you were, um, alone. No wife in the car.'

'Oh that's silly. Katherine forgot her sunglasses at the hotel. She sent me back to look for them.'

Neiderhoffer scribbled something in his pad. 'Did you talk to anyone at the hotel about the sunglasses? The front desk?'

'No.'

Neiderhoffer nodded.

'And I had to piss,' Timothy said.

'Okay. We all have to piss on occasion. But you can understand why it seems . . . interesting.'

'No I can't. What exactly are you implying? That I murdered my wife, and then drove back to the hotel in an empty car and made a fuss? Why would I do that?'

'Relax, Mr Van Bender, no one said anything about murder. This is just a missing persons case. Take it easy.'

'Fine,' Timothy said. He sipped his coffee and noticed his hand was shaking. He put the cup down before Neiderhoffer could see.

'The other thing,' Neiderhoffer said, 'is the necklace.'

'What necklace?' But of course Timothy knew exactly which necklace Neiderhoffer spoke of.

'The sales lady at, what was it? – let's see, Michael Sherman Jewelry Design, distinctly remembers you. Apparently you made quite an impression there, too. Walked into the store, bought a fifteen-thousand-dollar piece of jewelry for your wife after shopping for sixty seconds. Your wife wasn't with you, of course.'

'She was in the restaurant.'

'Right, it was a surprise. That's what the woman said. Apparently you were very memorable. The woman at the store couldn't stop talking about you. Fifteen thousand dollars in two minutes. Diamonds and sapphires. You stood out. Like you wanted to be remembered.'

'What does that mean?'

'It doesn't necessarily mean anything,' Neiderhoffer said. 'But it could mean that you wanted to show everyone how much you loved your wife. Fifteen thousand dollars' worth. That's probably a lot of money, even for someone like you.'

'I loved my wife very much,' Timothy said. He was angry now. He wanted to glare at Neiderhoffer, to make eye contact, to stare him down, to let him see who was in charge.

He stared, but Neiderhoffer did not stare back. The detective's attention was drawn to something else – something behind Timothy.

Timothy turned to follow his glance. Behind him, in the doorway of the kitchen, stood Tricia. She was dressed in a gray skirt and white blouse. Around her neck she wore the diamond and sapphire necklace.

CHAPTER 34

'Good morning,' Neiderhoffer said pleasantly, as if it was the most natural thing in the world that a twenty-something-year-old girl was sleeping in a middle-aged widower's house, weeks after his wife's death, wearing the dead wife's jewelry.

'Hi,' Tricia said. She gave Timothy an uncertain look. Who was this man in their house? She walked to Timothy and kissed him on the lips.

Timothy turned away from the kiss. 'Tricia Fountain,' Timothy said, 'this is Detective Neiderhoffer. He's investigating my wife Katherine's disappearance.'

She sat down. 'I thought your wife was dead.'

'She is,' Timothy said. He realized that he sounded a bit too insistent about this point. So, more gently, he said: 'But I guess it's still an open case.'

'Just a formality,' Neiderhoffer said.

'I see,' Tricia said.

Neiderhoffer studied her. 'You must be . . .' He let his voice trail off.

'I worked with Timothy.'

'Really?'

'His secretary. But not anymore.'

Neiderhoffer nodded. 'I see.'

Timothy expected more – further probing, further testing by Neiderhoffer. But Neiderhoffer shut down. He closed his pad, rose from the table, and slipped his notepad into his jacket pocket. 'Well, I'm sorry for the intrusion. I know you need to be getting to work.'

'Yes,' Timothy said. 'Sure.'

Neiderhoffer started toward the front door. Timothy followed close behind, leaving Tricia in the kitchen.

'Nice to meet you, Ms Fountain,' Neiderhoffer called over his shoulder. Timothy kept walking, hoping that by barreling ahead, he might speed Neiderhoffer's exit, too. 'I look forward to speaking to you again.'

In the foyer, Timothy opened the front door. He smiled grimly at Neiderhoffer. 'I guess this doesn't look very good, does it?'

'Which part?' Neiderhoffer asked. 'The girlfriend sleeping over just weeks after your wife's death? Or the part where she's wearing the necklace you bought your wife? It is the same necklace, isn't it?'

Timothy nodded.

'I suppose it could be worse,' Neiderhoffer said. 'There could be blood all over your house, for example.' His eyes darted around the foyer floor, as if to look for just such a clue. He pantomimed wiping sweat from his brow, and said, 'Phew.' He laughed.

Timothy laughed, too.

'Well,' Neiderhoffer said, 'I wouldn't worry about it. In this line of work, you see a lot of things that don't look good at first glance. Usually they mean absolutely nothing.'

'Okay,' Timothy said. He shook Neiderhoffer's hand. 'Thanks.'

Neiderhoffer walked out the door, started down the front steps. Timothy was about to shut the door, when the detective called to him.

'Mr Van Bender?'

Timothy stopped the door, held it open.

'It is sort of early to have a new girlfriend, though, isn't it? What's it been? Four weeks?'

'Five.'

'Early, right? Unless you were having an affair before your wife committed suicide.'

Timothy did not answer.

Neiderhoffer persisted. 'So were you? Having an affair?'

Timothy thought about his response. What did Neiderhoffer know? Was he testing him? Wouldn't it appear worse to admit that he had been cheating on his wife before her death? Wouldn't that suddenly become a motive for killing her, to get her out of the picture without a messy divorce? Or maybe Neiderhoffer thought he killed her without premeditation, in a violent argument about infidelity.

'No,' Timothy said. 'I was not having an affair. Good day, detective.' He shut the door.

CHAPTER 35

Back in the kitchen, Timothy said, 'Jesus Christ, Tricia. Did you have to wear that necklace?'

She laughed. 'You are obsessed with this damn necklace. Here.' She reached behind her neck, unclasped it, and slapped it down on the kitchen table. 'Take it.'

'That's not my point.'

'What does he think? That you killed me?'

'No, he thinks that I killed my wife. You, he thinks I've been screwing in my office for the past six months.'

'Well, have you?'

'No, Katherine.'

'Tricia,' she corrected.

'Tricia.' He walked over to the sliding glass doors, looked out into the back yard. A rabbit scampered across the grass. 'The thing is, it doesn't look right. None of this looks right. You living here with me, so soon after the suicide.'

'But I'm your wife.'

'I know that, and you know that. But who's going to believe it? To the rest of the world, you're my twenty-three-year-old secretary. I didn't think that part through. I should have chosen someone else. Someone older.'

'Somehow that seems unlikely,' Tricia said.

Of course she was right. She knew him too well, even better – sometimes – than he knew himself. He would only have chosen Tricia. He knew he would choose her the moment Dr Ho explained the procedure. And Katherine, now inside Tricia's body, knew it, too.

Tricia said, 'Why don't you just bribe him? Don't you always bribe police officers that give you trouble?'

Timothy knew what she was referring to: the incident, years ago, when they were driving to the opera in San Francisco, and he was pulled over for doing seventy on Highway 101, and he flashed two hundred-dollar bills along with his driver's license to the poor working stiff CHP officer who had been demoted to speed trap duty. That had outraged Katherine, offended her sense of fairness and propriety.

'It's a little different,' Timothy said. 'Speeding and murder.'

'Will you stop being melodramatic? You didn't murder anyone. I committed suicide.'

'But there's no body. The only evidence is the phone call you made to me. And it's only my word.'

'Well, your word has to be worth *something*, right?'

Timothy turned to look at her. Was that a dig, a little jibe?

She continued: 'Anyway, the whole thing is absurd. You had no motive for murdering me. You could have just gotten a divorce. We had a prenuptial. Just show him the agreement. It's only one page long.'

Another jibe? Timothy didn't care anymore. He probably deserved it. He had been a terrible husband to her. It was amazing, really, that she had stayed with him for all those years. He sighed. 'Maybe you're right.'

'Which leads me to what I really want to talk about,' Tricia said. She rose from the table and joined Timothy at the patio doors. She stood behind him, put her hands on his shoulders and began to massage his tense muscles.

'That feels good,' he said.

'Maybe this isn't a good time to bring it up. But . . . we should get married.'

He turned around to face her. 'Again, marriage. Why is that so important to you, Tricia?'

'Because,' she said gently, 'I'm not Tricia. I'm your wife, Katherine. And because I love you. And because it's strange to be someone else, and to *not* be married to you. And I know you don't understand it, because you can't. But try to imagine: you look in the mirror and see someone else's face. Imagine what that's like. I just feel . . .' Her voice trailed off as she searched for the word. 'Helpless. Like I'm drifting. And I want to go back to how things were. I want to be married to you. At least I can have that.'

'That's fine,' he said. He was still thinking about Neiderhoffer. The detective would subpoena his phone records. That would at least establish that Katherine had called the morning of her death. Maybe there was nothing to worry about after all.

'We don't need a big ceremony,' she said. 'We can go down to San Jose city hall. It'll take ten minutes. We can do it as soon as we get a death certificate.'

'Okay. You're right. That's fine.' He thought about it. Maybe marrying Tricia would look good, would establish to Neiderhoffer that he loved the young woman, and was not simply having a fling with her. 'I'm meeting with Frank Arnheim this morning. He can throw something together.'

Tricia looked hurt. 'What? Who's Frank Arnheim?'

'My lawyer. We'll just use the old document. Put your name in instead. Once we get a death certificate for Katherine—'

'What old document? What are you talking about?' She was still smiling, but now it was a hurt and brittle smile.

'The agreement. The prenuptial. Oh, come on, you're not going to get upset again, are you?'

She shook her head in disbelief. 'I've been married to you for twenty years. You want a fucking prenuptial agreement?'

'Tricia, you know—'

'I know what?' she snapped. 'I know that you are the biggest . . . *shit* I've ever met. That's what I know.'

She turned and walked out of the kitchen. In the doorway, she stopped. She returned to the kitchen table, grabbed her necklace, stuffed it in her pocket. 'I'll take that,' she said, and stormed out.

CHAPTER 36

B ecause of Neiderhoffer, Timothy was late for his eight-thirty meeting.

He pulled out of his driveway at eight-thirty-five and raced up Waverly into downtown Palo Alto. It was a minute-and-a-half commute. He pulled into the underground parking lot of the Bank of America building, grabbed a ticket from the time-stamp machine, and descended two floors to park in the area marked 'Monthly.'

He climbed out of his car and tapped his remote-control key chain. The BMW alarm chirped. Timothy walked up the steep grade toward the elevators. His heels clicked against the concrete, echoing through the low-ceilinged space. Even though it was eighty degrees outside, the garage was cool and dark, and quiet.

Timothy walked, thinking about Tricia, her insisting on marriage, about his upcoming meeting with Frank Arnheim, about his testimony to the CFTC.

Timothy heard another set of footsteps behind his. They approached rapidly. He turned around.

It was the stringy-haired man, the driver of the

Impala that had chased him through Menlo Park the day before. He was heading toward Timothy with a strange smile on his face.

Timothy stopped. He felt a jolt of adrenaline, his heart race, his testicles shrink into cold pebbles.

'Hey—' Timothy said. It was a tepid word – a half-greeting and half warning. His voice was hoarse, his mouth dry.

The young man continued walking toward him with the strange smile on his face. His heels clicked briskly on the ground. Timothy looked down to see steel-toed jackboots.

'Hey,' Timothy said, louder now. At that moment he had a crystalline realization: that he was helpless. During his entire life he had always been in control, using his wealth and his name and his upbringing to command the society around him, to decide what would happen next, to him and to others. But in that instant, as the long-haired man walked toward him in the parking garage, with a sick smile and a taut body promising cruelty, Timothy understood that his own power was ephemeral; it was an illusion, a confidence game; it depended solely on everyone else's agreeing to it, and it vanished the moment it was confronted with something cold and hard – with threat and violence.

Timothy thought about what to say. Words had always saved him. He always figured out what to say at the last moment. This would be the same.

The words would come to him, sudden and surprising, a gift from heaven.

The long-haired man walked toward him. Now, up close – ten feet away – he didn't seem like a druggie teenager. He seemed older. He had a long, gaunt face, and sunken eyes. His hair was flat, stringy. He had more serious matters to attend to than hygiene.

He walked to Timothy, and Timothy expected the man to say something, since conflict always began with words, but there were no words. The man simply swung his fist with all his might into Timothy's abdomen. Timothy bent over, grabbing his stomach. He had never been punched before. His mouth opened in a silent 'Oh' – half pain, half shock. The long-haired man grabbed Timothy's Hermes tie and yanked it downward. Timothy fell to the gray concrete. He held out his hands to break the fall, but his chin still struck the ground hard, and he felt something cold on his face and knew it was blood.

'If you don't stop fucking my girlfriend,' the man said, 'I'm going to kill you.'

'Your girlfriend?' For an instant Timothy was relieved. He had no idea what this man was talking about. So it was all a misunderstanding, after all. He would simply explain there had been a mistake . . .

The man said, 'If I see you with Tricia again, next time I won't use my fist.' He produced a switchblade from his jeans pocket and snapped it open. He waved it in Timothy's direction and then turned and walked off. Timothy lay on the ground, listening to the jackboot footsteps grow distant. Then the footsteps broke into a run and disappeared.

Timothy climbed to his hands and knees. A Jaguar pulled around the corner, with its headlights on. The driver saw Timothy on the ground and stopped. The Jaguar door was thrown open and a middle-aged man got out. He wore a fine dark business suit and an expensive red Ferragamo tie. 'Hey, buddy, are you all right?' The businessman leaned over Timothy, who was sitting up now, clutching his stomach. 'Are you okay?'

Timothy nodded.

But the businessman looked helpless. We all are, Timothy thought. Our money and power mean nothing to these men of violence. We are helpless.

Timothy made his way to his office on the thirty-second floor. People in the elevator regarded him curiously. He realized he must have been a sight: his shirt billowing from his pants, his tie loose and disheveled, his chin bleeding. He was a mere step away from the homeless men that visited the Bank of America plaza each afternoon trolling for quarters. Timothy was surprised no one stopped him and escorted him from the building.

He reached the Osiris offices and Natasha, the fat Russian receptionist, greeted him. 'Timothy! What happened to you?'

'I was mugged.'

'Should I call the police?'

Timothy shook his head. He wanted no more interaction with the police today.

The Kid walked into the reception area. 'Timothy, Frank Arnheim is here for your eight thirty. He's been waiting —' The Kid stopped when he saw Timothy. 'My God, what happened to you?'

'Nothing,' Timothy said. 'Just a little altercation.'

'With who?'

'Would you believe an angry investor?'

'Do you want some ice?'

'No.' Timothy waved him off. 'No, I'm fine. I'm going to clean myself up. Tell Frank I'm going to have to postpone the meeting. We'll do it tomorrow.'

'Okay.'

Timothy went to the men's bathroom. He looked in the mirror. His chin wasn't as bad as he had feared. Just a scrape. He wouldn't need stitches. The long-haired man was only trying to scare him.

Timothy splashed cold water on his face, then dabbed his chin with paper towels. Yes, the man was just trying to scare him.

CHAPTER 37

That evening, at home, Tricia forgot about the morning's argument as soon as she saw the dried blood on Timothy's face. She led him upstairs to the bedroom and told him to lie down on the bed. She sat beside him. He recounted the events that had happened in the parking garage.

'He knew you,' Timothy said. 'You must know him.'

'But I don't.'

'Well Tricia did. He must have been that boyfriend. She mentioned him a couple times.' He tried to remember. There had been some vague talk of a boyfriend, and he recalled Tricia saying that she drove with a boy from Los Angeles when she moved north.

But the boyfriend she described sharing a car with was an unambitious, unthreatening, pot-smoking slacker – a bit different from the man in the parking garage. And except for that casual mention, she never spoke of him again. It certainly didn't seem like Tricia was involved with someone.

And yet . . . he recalled that drunken evening

when he had followed her from the BBC back to her apartment, and they entered the door with the upside-down letter D. Hadn't she behaved oddly then? Didn't she seem afraid, as if someone else might be in the apartment, and might find them? Could Tricia have been living with such a dangerous man even back then, and not told Timothy? It seemed hard to believe.

'Apparently Tricia, my innocent secretary, had a few secrets,' he said.

She stroked the caked blood on his chin. 'I don't think we should criticize people for having secrets.'

They had sex then, which surprised him. Katherine had always been a sex-before-bed kind of woman. The sex was much better now, with Tricia's body, but the timing and activities themselves had not changed: before sleep, and please-face-and-kiss-me-while-you-do-it.

So it was a pleasant surprise that she initiated. He lay back, his abdomen sore from the punch, and she caressed him, and kissed him, and removed his tie and shirt, and then his pants. She kissed his chest, and then his stomach, softly. 'Does this hurt?' she asked.

'No.'

She lowered her head and kissed his thighs gently. She put her fingers beneath the elastic band of his briefs, and pulled them down to his knees. Then she bent over and began to perform fellatio – and that was something strange, something that

Katherine hardly ever did. The first time Katherine did it they were in her parents' house, visiting Cambridge a few months after their wedding. They were staying in the old room that Katherine used to sleep in as a girl, and it must have done something to her – made her excited, to do something forbidden with her new husband, in the bed where she grew up, under the same roof as her parents.

Now Tricia was using her lips and mouth, licking him, rubbing her dark silky hair against his skin, and – despite the ache in his belly – it felt good, and he couldn't control himself. It was over in a minute, and then she lay down in the bed beside him, and kissed him, and he tasted himself on her lips.

'Do you remember,' he said, 'the first time you did that?'

Tricia smiled.

He said, 'It seems like yesterday.'

She touched a finger to his nose. It was a gesture that could have meant anything: agreement, happiness, playful naughtiness. It was not, it occurred to him, what Katherine would have done. Katherine would have been matter-of-fact about it, would have recounted the details of that first experience, would have enjoyed dissecting it, explaining exactly how she felt at each moment. Katherine was a diarist, a woman who noted her two pieces of wheat toast and jam, who was aware of every detail in her life.

He tried sitting up in bed, pushing off his elbows, but his stomach ached, so he flopped back down and merely lifted his neck to look at her. 'Do you remember?' he asked. His tone had changed, and it was clear he was challenging her now, quizzing her. 'It seems like something you would remember. Where were we the first time you did that to me?'

Tricia kept her face blank. She did not look nervous or upset. She shook her head and said, simply, 'I don't remember.'

'We were in your parents' house. Do you remember where?'

She smiled. It was either the smile of a loving wife, or the smile of a poker player ready to bluff. 'Of course. We were in my bedroom. The bed where I slept as a little girl. The bed where I grew up.'

Which was true, Timothy thought, suddenly relieved.

She leaned over him, and kissed him softly on the lips. 'Are you going crazy on me?'

'No,' he said, 'sorry.'

'Do you know who I am?'

'Yes,' he said.

'Who am I?' She kissed him again. 'Tell me.'

'You're Katherine.'

'Yes,' she agreed, and kissed his lips again, softly. 'I'm your wife. I'm the woman you were married to, and the woman who wants to marry you again. Do you understand that?'

'Yes,' he said.

★   ★   ★

That night, he dreamed.

He dreamed of Katherine climbing the switchback at Big Sur, her fingers sliding along the thick chain on the edge of the path. He dreamed of her body, splayed face down on the rocks below, her long blonde hair fanned and floating in an inch of water, her legs broken and akimbo. He dreamed of Dr Ho, and his tiny spectacles, and the red line they left in his brow, and he dreamed of the man from the parking garage, with the stringy hair and the gleaming knife and the steel-toed boots. He dreamed of Katherine in her parents' house, of lying with her on her childhood bed, of Katherine leaning over him, performing oral sex, of his fingers stroking her hair, brushing wisps from her face so he could look into her eyes.

He woke to the sound of footsteps.

The bedroom was dark. His first thought was of the man with the long hair and switchblade, of his threats to kill Timothy if he continued to fuck Tricia. Timothy whispered, 'Tricia?'

He reached his arm to her side of the bed, to reassure himself that she was all right. But the bed was empty. Timothy looked at his nightstand. The digital clock, with comforting amber numbers, said 2.33 a.m. He flipped on the bedside light. Tricia was gone.

He tried to sit up. He was surprised by the pain in his abdomen, and then he remembered the punch he had received that afternoon. He touched his face and felt the scab on his chin.

He tried again to get up, more carefully now, sliding his feet to the floor, and then slowly pushing himself to a sitting position using his hands. He rose from the bed.

He thought about Tricia, and wondered where she was, and if she was all right. He wanted to call out her name. But perhaps that was unwise. Perhaps the long-haired man was there, in the house. Could he have broken in, somehow, through the patio door, or the den window? Did he know where Timothy lived?

Timothy walked out of the bedroom and peered into the hall. It was dark. He could see nothing. But he did not turn on the light. He knew the hallway better than any intruder could, and the darkness would be his advantage. He stepped into the hall. The floorboard creaked. He stopped, remained motionless, and listened for noise. Was there someone else in the house?

He saw a dim glow at the end of the hallway, a line of light under a doorframe. It was the door to the attic. He began to walk carefully toward it, through the dark, toe-first, the way he was taught as a child that the Indians walked through the forest, sliding their moccasin feet under branches and leaves to surprise their enemies. He slid his finger against the wall as he walked, to maintain a straight path through the blackness, and he felt the bumps and bubbles of the cool plaster beneath his skin.

He approached the attic. Even in the dark he

knew where the doorknob would be, and he grasped it and turned it quietly. He pulled open the door and was surprised that it did not squeak.

There was a light shining in the attic.

He climbed the attic stairs slowly. He expected to see the steel-toed boots first, as he ascended, and then the dirty jeans, and finally the switchblade at the ready, near the man's waist.

On the third step, the floorboard creaked again, and Timothy stopped. He listened. There was a sound of paper rustling. He climbed to the fourth step, faster now, and then the fifth, and he no longer cared about remaining silent; he simply wanted to confront whoever was in the attic, and to end his feeling of dread.

He reached the top of the stairs. At the far end of the attic, Tricia sat on the floor, her back to him, with a pile of Katherine's journals beside her. She was flipping the pages, reading intently, and then flipping more. It was as if she was looking for some passage in particular.

'What are you doing?' he asked.

If she was surprised by his presence, she did not show it. She continued flipping the pages with her back turned to him. 'Writing my journal,' she said calmly.

'Writing?' he asked. 'Or reading?' He climbed the final step now, and began to walk toward her. 'Trying to brush up on all the details?'

She turned to him. He was surprised that she had tears in her eyes and streaking her cheeks.

311

'I came up here to write. But now I'm just reading. Looking at old entries. From years ago.' She laughed, a quiet, self-pitying laugh.

'Who are you?' he asked. 'Are you Katherine? Or are you Tricia?'

'Oh God,' she said, shaking her head, sniffling. 'Not again.'

'What are you doing here, reading her diaries at two o'clock in the morning?'

'I told you. I was writing. In *my* diaries. They're mine, Timothy. *Mine.* Don't you understand? Don't you believe me? Why did you put them up here, anyway? Did you think I wouldn't find them? Are you trying to take everything from me?'

Her emotion surprised him. This was the sort of hysterical overreaction that was typical of Katherine: turning the tables on him, using verbal jujitsu to direct his own anger back at him.

'I put them away,' he said, 'after Katherine . . . after you died. I forgot about them.'

'Did you read them?'

'No,' he lied.

She sniffled again, wiped the tears from her eyes. 'I just wanted to write about today. About how you got hurt. And I started thinking, and reading, you know, old entries. I almost never do that. I've been writing these damn journals for twenty years, and I hardly ever read a word of what I've written. But tonight, I guess with everything that's been going on, I just wanted to read some of the old pages. I wanted to reassure myself that I am . . . me. God,

Timothy, you don't understand what it's like. Sometimes I feel like I'm going crazy. Imagine waking up in someone else's body. And if that isn't bad enough, imagine that your own husband doesn't believe it's you.'

'I believe it's you,' he said. And at that moment, staring at the tears on Tricia's cheeks, he did.

'Then why do you constantly question me? Who do you think I am?'

He didn't answer.

'Do you think this whole thing is – what? – an elaborate con? That I'm a twenty-three-year-old secretary trying to fool you? In order to do what? Fuck you, Timothy? Do you think I need to go through all that just to fuck you? Looking like this?'

'I said I believe you,' he said.

'Then stop already. Stop questioning me.'

'Come to bed,' he said. He reached his hand down and offered it to her. She took it, and he helped her from the floor. His stomach ached when he pulled her up, but he didn't want her to know and so kept his face still.

She stepped toward him and fell into his arms, and she hugged him tightly and rubbed her tears into his shoulder.

'I love you,' she said. 'I do.'

'Then come back to bed,' he said, and led her back downstairs.

CHAPTER 38

The next day, he met Frank Arnheim for breakfast at Buck's, a coffee shop in Woodside.

'Here's the situation,' Frank explained to Timothy. 'You might go to jail.'

Timothy was eating an egg-white omelet with cheddar cheese. He put down his fork. This was not what he expected to hear. He was meeting Frank to review the testimony he would give to the CFTC about Osiris' collapse. He was scheduled to fly to Chicago in less than two weeks.

'For two hundred and fifty dollars an hour, that's the best you can do?'

'A lot of important people lost a lot of money on Osiris. From the CFTC's perspective, someone's got to pay.'

'I don't mind someone paying,' Timothy said. 'I just mind the someone being me.' The thought of jail had never occurred to him.

'Well, that's my point. Yesterday, while you were being beaten up in the parking garage, I spent some time with your assistant, Jay Strauss.'

'Good kid, Jay,' Timothy said.

'No,' Frank said. 'I don't think so.'

'Really?' Timothy was surprised.

'Oh, yeah,' Frank said. 'Absolutely. When he testifies in Chicago, he's going to destroy you.'

'The Kid? I mean Jay? Are you sure?'

'You must have done something to really piss him off. Let me ask you something. How much does he know? Did you ever ask him to lie? Did you ever ask him to tell investors something that was untrue?'

'No.' Timothy thought about it. He did tell the Kid to lie to Pinky. 'Yes.' Then: 'Maybe. I don't know.'

'Put yourself in Jay's shoes. He's a scared twenty-four-year-old kid. He's worried about the rest of his life. Meanwhile, the government doesn't care about him. He's a nothing. They want you. They can make an example of you. They can teach everyone a nice little lesson about how powerful and all-knowing the CFTC is. See where I'm going with this?'

'They're going to make a deal with the Kid.'

'Maybe they already have, for all we know. They tell him: give us Van Bender and you can walk away. You can keep working in the industry, no public censure, nothing on your record. In fact, I'll give you five to one that he makes up stuff about you, exaggerates the things you said, makes you seem much worse than you are.'

'That's hard to do.'

'I know.' Frank bit into his toast, ripped it in

half with his teeth. 'My point is, you have to assume the worst.'

'So what can I do?'

'You could always kill him.' Frank laughed. 'Just kidding, of course.'

'Of course.'

'I think you need to have a talk with him. See where he stands. Once you feel him out, we can decide what to do.'

Before he could feel out the Kid, to see if he would betray him, Timothy had another betrayal to think about. He returned to his office and called his wife on the telephone.

'What are you doing now?' he asked nonchalantly.

'Just cleaning up around the house.'

'You have lunch plans?'

'I was going to meet Ann Beatty at noon. But I can cancel.'

'No,' he said. 'You should meet her. It's important that Tricia gets to know people around the neighborhood. I'll stick around here.'

'You sure?'

'Yes,' he said.

When he hung up, he knew what he was going to do. At noon, when Tricia left the house for lunch, Timothy went home.

He no longer believed her. It wasn't merely the episode the previous night, in which he found her studying Katherine's diaries in the attic at two o'clock in the morning. It was a series of strange incidents: her using the word *awesome*, knowing that the necklace was an anniversary present, forgetting that first sexual experience in her childhood bedroom, bringing up marriage but rejecting a prenuptial agreement . . .

Now, in the daylight, without a drop of alcohol in him, without the buzz of sexual desire clouding his judgment, he thought maybe he had been a fool. Maybe the woman sharing the house with him, the woman inhabiting Tricia's young body – maybe it was simply Tricia after all. How long ago had she started planning this game? Did she take a job at Timothy's firm knowing all along that she would try to marry him? Or did the plan come to her when she learned of Katherine's suicide?

She had known that, as Tricia, she might be able to seduce him, but that he would never trust her completely, and she would never be able to get her hands on his money. But as Katherine, his wife of twenty years, the woman he loved and missed, the woman he trusted, it could be different. That was the reason for the rush to marriage, and the anger over the prenuptial agreement.

It was brilliant. The story was convincing, but only because he wanted to be convinced. He wanted his wife back. He wanted a second chance. At the same time, he desired Tricia. And in a fit of genius, she made it all possible – to have another chance with his wife, while simultaneously possessing a beautiful twenty-three-year-old girl. The plan itself required almost nothing – a rented office on Sand Hill Road, some cheap computers stuffed into racks, a Chinese actor playing a scientist – and he had fallen for it. Because he *wanted* to fall for it. Because he was weak. And because he missed his wife. And because Tricia was beautiful.

What gave it away were the diaries, of course. It was a stroke of luck for Tricia that Katherine had kept such detailed journals. How had Tricia known? Timothy must have mentioned it to her, as he did to others – a flip remark about his wife's bizarre obsession with recording the details of her life. He couldn't remember telling Tricia about the diaries, but it was certainly possible.

And when Tricia found the diaries in the attic, she made the most of them, studying them, like a legal student poring over case law before the bar exam, learning the citations, memorizing the important facts.

Perhaps she had even entered his house to read them, before coming back as Katherine? It was possible. And then, once she had the opportunity, she studied them every day, learning more about Katherine and her life, until, finally, she could *become* Katherine.

But the simulation was only as good as the material she had to work with. And that was the problem with her plan: she only knew the things recorded in the diaries.

The sex gave it away. Katherine recorded how

many pieces of toast she ate for breakfast, but about sexual matters she was very private. That was why Tricia 'remembered' certain details about Katherine's life – the time they received a speeding ticket and Timothy tried to bribe the police officer – but not other details – not sexual details, for example, like the first time she fellated him in her childhood bedroom. Tricia didn't know about it because Katherine didn't write about it.

Now Timothy needed to make sure. He needed to read the diaries for himself, to prove that his theory was correct, that Tricia could only recount incidents that had been written about, and not others.

He arrived home at five minutes past noon. Tricia's car was gone from the driveway. He knocked and rang the doorbell, to make sure no one would answer. He wanted time to study the diaries on his own, without interruption.

He turned the key and entered the house. In the foyer, he called out, 'Tricia?'

The house was empty.

He went immediately to the staircase and climbed to the second floor, then opened the attic door at the end of the hall. The air inside was warm and humid. He turned on the lights, and climbed the staircase. It smelled musty. At the far end of the space he saw the journals, piled neatly where Tricia had left them the night before.

He looked at his watch. He decided he had about an hour before Tricia would return from lunch.

And so for the third time in his life, he sat down on the floor, and he began to read his wife's diaries.

He was right, of course.

The incident about the bribe and speeding ticket was there, as he knew it would be:

> 'When the police officer pulled us over, Timothy smiled at him and tried to bribe him. He did it in his usual charming way, so that it hardly seemed like a bribe. It was, of course, typical of him. Why does he feel that he is above all rules, that he can get away with anything, that the laws of the universe do not apply to him? I suppose it gives the people who work for him a kind of comfort – that this man is so clearly in charge, and able to navigate the world without impediment. But, truthfully, it disgusts me.'

The passage was familiar, because he had read it years before – the first time he sneaked around the house to read her journals. There it was, the word 'disgusts' underlined twice, the second line harder than the first, the pen pushing through the vellum.

Now, he needed to confirm his theory about the sex. He would search the diary for a mention of the sex in her childhood bedroom. He was sure that he would not find it.

He tried to think back: when had she done that? It was years ago, when they were first married . . . in 1979. They had traveled back east to visit her parents. He scanned the pile of journals on the floor, with the years handwritten on the fabric binding: 1977, 1978 . . . there. 1979.

He lifted the volume and began to flip through. It didn't take long to find it. It was November. Yes, they were visiting her parents for Thanksgiving. Reading her description of those days, the memories came back to him: their arrival at Logan; Mr Sutter shaking Timothy's hand and calling him 'Son,' the cold wind snapping in their faces when they stepped out of the airport; Katherine showing him upstairs in her Cambridge house, to her old bedroom. It happened the first night there:

'November 20, 1979. I'm in Cambridge, back home with Timothy. I showed him around Mom and Dad's. It is strange to have the man I married sleeping in the tiny bed where I used to sleep as a girl, before I even knew about men, or sex, or marriage. He is snoring now, under my pink covers. We just had sex. How strange.'

That was it. Six words about sex. But she did not describe the act in detail, did not note that it was the first time she had fellated him; did not remark upon what it felt like, or what she thought.

Which was why, Timothy understood, Tricia did

not know about it. She couldn't, because it was not in the journal.

He continued reading the journals, and lost track of time. He could not stop himself. Once he began, he needed to continue, to follow the arc of her story, from her girlish excitement when he proposed to her, to her realization that Timothy was not who she thought he was, to her ultimate loneliness and despair. It happened gradually over the course of volumes, interspersed between details about what she wore and what she ate. It was a story told in static still-lifes, like a cartoon book with hundreds of individual sketches that, when you flipped the pages, revealed a smooth motion from one side of the page to another.

He read about her depression when she miscarried, her excitement when she finally carried to six months – and then her despair when she miscarried again, that final time.

He read about her growing realization that he was selfish, and egotistical, and did not consider her feelings.

But what Timothy did not read was anything about his affairs. At first, it was remarkable to him. He kept reading the pages, waiting for the shoe to drop, to finally see the passage where she described her fears that he was cheating, to read about himself as an unfaithful cad.

It took him some time to realize that he would never read such a passage. He would not read it for the same reason he would not read about explicit sexual details: because it embarrassed her to write about them. And so the angry words about his affairs were mysteriously missing from those pages. Posterity would never learn about his philandering.

And that led him to a Plan, a way to learn for certain exactly who Tricia was – a way he could be sure.

He scanned the pile and found the journal from 1996. That was the year in which Timothy cheated on her for the final time. It was the year he traveled to Palm Beach and visited Mack Gladwell, the cocaine-snorting record producer, and had gone home with the cocktail waitress who then called Katherine.

Of course it was an incident neither of them ever forgot. But he was sure that it would not appear in her journal. He opened the 1996 volume and read the days leading up to his trip to Palm Beach. He found the pages.

On April 30 she wrote, 'Timothy left for Palm Beach today, and will return on Friday.'

Then on Friday, May 3, her entry was three words long, 'Timothy returned today.'

On May 4 she wrote: 'Breakfast: toast and jam.'

On May 5, she wrote, 'Breakfast: soft boiled egg.'

The journal entries continued in that laconic fashion for an entire week. Finally, on May 11, she wrote, 'He came back.'

It was all he needed to read. No mention of

Mack Gladwell, of the phone call from the waitress, or of Katherine kicking Timothy out of the house for a week and making him stay in the Hyatt. Now Timothy knew how to test Tricia one final time, to know for certain if she was lying to him. He closed the journal with a solid thump and replaced it on the pile. He straightened the edge of the bindings so that the books appeared the way he found them.

In the house down below, he heard keys tinkling and the front door opening. He walked calmly out of the attic and went downstairs to greet Tricia.

CHAPTER 39

He did not confront her immediately.

It was more than simply wanting to revel in his secret knowledge. He didn't want the illusion to come to an end. He had enjoyed believing the yarn, that Katherine had returned to him, that somehow a scientist had backed up her brain like so many computer files, and then had restored it into a young girl's body.

Now, following her around the house as she described her lunch with Ann Beatty, he realized that the last few weeks, with Tricia playing the part of his wife, had been the happiest in his life. He now had everything he wanted. He had a second chance with the woman he loved. He slept each night with a young, beautiful girl. It was a fantasy. Which was why, he understood, he had believed it. And why he did not want the fantasy to come to an end.

They sat together on the patio as she told him about her lunch.

He said suddenly, 'Would you like some wine?'

Tricia cocked her head. 'A bit early in the day, isn't it? Even for you?'

'It's such a beautiful afternoon,' he said, waving his hand across the back yard.

'All right, then.' She smiled.

And so he went down to the wine cellar and picked out a fine chardonnay, a 1998 Whitehall Lane, returned to the patio with it, and said, 'Momentous days call for great wines.'

'What makes this a momentous day?'

'You'll see,' he said.

He uncorked the bottle and poured them each a glass of wine, and then sat in the wicker chair and pulled it alongside hers, so that their knees touched. He reached out and stroked her knee, and underneath her linen pants he felt her flesh, shapely and taut, and he knew that he would miss it.

'I think Ann really likes me,' Tricia said. 'She likes the idea of taking a young girl under her wing. It makes her feel young, I guess. It's hard, not letting her know that it's me. There are so many times I want to say, 'You already told me that, Ann.' Or I want to blurt out: 'Ann, it's me, Katherine!'

'Really?' Timothy said. He stroked her thigh. He wondered: should he have sex with her, one last time, before he revealed to her that he knew about her game? 'It must be hard.'

'If you only knew,' Tricia said.

'Maybe I do know.'

Tricia looked at him, as if to say, What a strange thing to say. Then she said, 'Okay, Timothy, what's going on now? Are you having another breakdown?'

'If that's what you call it.' He gripped her leg, tighter now. It was not exactly threatening, but it could become so, quickly. He felt a strange sensation, a combination of anger and sexual excitement, as if he wanted to fuck her and then knock her head into the patio flagstone.

'What's going on?' she said.

'It was so perfect,' he said. 'So perfect. Just give people what they want, right? Me, I wanted my wife, and I wanted you. So you made it possible for me to have both. All in one package.'

'Oh God, no,' she said. Timothy noticed that she said it with a sad smile, as if she really were Katherine, and could not believe that her husband was doubting her again.

'You can stop now, Tricia,' he said. 'Just stop.'

'I'm getting a little sick of this,' Tricia said. The smile was still there, but it was brittle, on the cusp of anger.

With his left hand he took a swig of wine. 'What was the plan, Tricia? That I would marry you?'

'You *are* going to marry me. I'm your wife.'

'That's what this is all about, right? Money.'

'Timothy, I'm your wife. I'm Katherine.'

'Stop already!' He slammed his wine glass down on the table. The stem shattered and glass tinkled onto the patio. A puddle of chardonnay spread over the table, slowly, like honey. Tricia tried to pull back, but he continued gripping her leg, hard, pinning her to the chair. The wine poured off the edge of the table, into her lap, and onto his hand.

'Timothy. Get a grip on yourself.'

'Oh, I have a grip,' he said, squeezing her leg. 'You all want to screw with me. First the Kid wants to send me to jail, and now you want my money. Do you want it so badly that you would sink to this? You must be insane.'

'Let go of me!'

He did not. His hand squeezed her thigh, and she tried kicking her leg away from him, but his grip was relentless. He knew that he was bruising her.

'Tell me something, *Katherine*. Answer one question for me. Answer correctly and you win a prize. And if you don't answer, you'll lose.'

'Timothy . . .'

'Are you ready . . . *Katherine*? Here's the question. Tell me about the time I cheated on you. Tell me, *Katherine*, how you found out. Tell me what happened.'

Tricia shook her head.

'Do you know, *Katherine*? It wasn't in her diary, was it? Tricky, right?'

'Timothy, listen to me.'

'Think think think,' he said, quickly, like a ratchet releasing one sawtoothed gear at a time. 'Think think think. You always manage to come up with convincing answers. But this one's impossible. You can't even guess, can you?'

She shook her head in disgust.

'Go ahead, Katherine. Or Tricia. Or whoever.

Pretend to be angry at me. That doesn't help. I'm not buying it. Listen, all you need to do is answer one question. One simple question. When did I cheat on you? How did you find out? Tell me what happened and then I'll believe you.'

She tried to grab his hand and remove it from her wet leg. He kept hold. She said, through clenched teeth, 'I am your wife, Katherine, you stupid son of a bitch. I am your wife. Believe me.'

'I don't. I don't believe you. Because you don't even know the story! It wasn't in the diary, so you don't know.'

'I am your wife!' With her left hand, she swung and slapped Timothy across the cheek. He was surprised, didn't see it coming; her finger brushed the jelly of his eyeball. He pulled back, released her leg, clenched his hand over his eye socket.

'Oh God, I'm sorry,' she said. 'Are you okay?' She stood up, and the back of her legs shoved her chair so that the wicker seat fell backward onto the flagstone patio.

He stood up too, his left hand still gripping his eye. With his right hand he grabbed Tricia's blouse, and pulled her close to him. He put his face an inch from hers and held her tight, so she could not escape.

'Tell me the story,' he whispered. 'I cheated on you. I admit it. I fucked another woman. God, I fucked her good. You must know all about it, since you're my wife. So tell me. Tell me how I cheated on you. Can you?'

Her eyes looked pleading. 'Timothy, I love you,' she said.

'I fucked her, Katherine. Tell me all about it. Tell me how you found out I fucked her.'

'Timothy . . .' Her voice was soft, full of pain, as if his words were tearing her heart.

'You can't tell me, because you don't know.'

She repeated softly, 'Timothy, I love you.'

'Tell me!' he spat. 'I fucked another woman. Tell me who. Tell me where.'

She was about to cry. Her lip quivered. She opened her mouth, but only soft breath came out. She looked shocked, hurt, lost. For the first time, he realized with satisfaction, she did not know what to say.

'Tell me!'

'Palm Beach,' she whispered.

'What?'

'Palm Beach. You were visiting Mack Gladwell.' She started talking faster, rattling off her words. 'You screwed some woman, and then she called me while you were flying home. She told me you had sex. I kicked you out of the house for a week.'

He shook his head.

'You stayed at the Hyatt. Does that make you happy? Making me say it out loud? She knew about the mole on your thigh. I should have left you then.'

'No . . . it's not possible . . .'

'I should have left you, but I couldn't. Because I love you.'

330

'No . . .' he said.

'Why don't you believe? Why can't you believe that . . . it's me? Why can't you accept this? It's a gift.' Her voice lowered to a whisper. 'A gift. We've been given a gift. Accept it.'

She kissed him, then stepped back and looked at his face. His eye was red and tearing; the cut on his chin had opened and started to bleed.

'Accept it,' she whispered again. 'It's a gift.'

He kissed her passionately, and he pulled her tightly to him, and he realized that it *was* Katherine, that it had to be her, that she was back, and that he would never let go of her again.

CHAPTER 40

They spent the afternoon in bed, first making love, and then sleeping, until the phone rang and woke him up.

He reached to the nightstand and picked up the receiver, checking the clock. It was four o'clock in the afternoon.

'Hello?' he said.

No one spoke. He heard the sound of breathing, and then two series of clicks, like two sets of knuckles being cracked.

'Hello?' Timothy said. 'Who is this?'

Tricia stirred in the bed beside him and turned to look at him. 'Who is it?' she said groggily.

The caller must have heard her voice. 'Is that her?' the caller said. 'Is that Tricia?' He spoke with the soft and breathy voice of an angel.

'You know,' Timothy said, 'that I have Caller ID. I will report you to the police.'

'I don't think so,' the caller said, simply. 'Remember what I told you? About what I'm going to do to you?' He waited, as if Timothy might want to volunteer an answer. When Timothy didn't, he said, 'I'm going to kill you. You've been warned.'

The line went dead. Timothy reached over and hung up the phone.

'Who was that?' Tricia asked.

'Your – Tricia's ex-boyfriend, I guess. The guy that beat me up.'

'What did he say?'

'That he wants to kill me.'

'Let's call the police.'

Before he could reply, the phone rang again. Tricia sat up in bed. 'Don't answer it.'

It rang again.

'I'm not going to live in fear,' Timothy said. He sat up in bed and snatched the phone from its cradle. 'Now listen to me,' he said to the caller, 'you cock-sucking son of a bitch. You know what I'm going to do to you? Huh? I'm going to kill you. I'm going to track you down, and hunt you like a dog. Then I'm going to kill you. You like that idea?'

The line was silent for a moment and then someone spoke. 'Uh, Mr Van Bender?' It certainly wasn't the long-haired man in the Impala. But the voice was familiar.

'Yes?'

'This is Ned Neiderhoffer. Is everything okay?'

'Detective. I'm so sorry.'

'That how you guys in the world of high finance talk to each other? "Buy a hundred shares of IBM, or I'll kill you like a dog." '

Timothy sighed. 'Actually, it's a bit more serious than that. I've received . . . threats.'

'What kind of threats?'

'You know, death. Yesterday a guy roughed me up a little in the parking garage at work, and threatened to kill me.'

'Did you report it?'

'No.'

'You want me to send someone over? Maybe if you tell us who the guy is, we can pick him up and have a talk.'

The last thing Timothy wanted was more detectives coming to the house, asking him questions. Because, ultimately, he would need to explain that the long-haired man was Tricia's ex-boyfriend. Which would lead the police to ask Tricia questions. Which would be a problem, since Tricia would not be able to answer questions, since she was no longer . . . Tricia. Which could finally lead to uncomfortable questions like: what happened to Tricia? Oh nothing, Timothy would say. I just drugged her and then overwrote her brain.

'No, that's okay,' Timothy said. 'It's nothing really, probably just a prank.'

Neiderhoffer said, 'Let me know if you change your mind.'

'I will. Now what can I do for you?'

Neiderhoffer said, 'I have a quick question.'

'Shoot.'

'When your wife called you that morning, the morning before she . . . disappeared, did she explicitly tell you where she was?'

'No.'

'See, I'm looking at my notes, and you mentioned she was near the ocean. How'd you know that?'

'I could hear it. I heard waves in the background.'

'Okay,' Neiderhoffer said. 'That makes sense.'

'That's it?'

'That's it. I'm just preparing some final paper-work and I want to make sure I have everything right. Thanks, Mr Van Bender.'

'No problem.'

'Let me know if you change your mind and you want me to send some police over.'

'Okay.'

He hung up the phone.

Tricia asked: 'What did he want?'

'I think he wanted to send a message,' Timothy said. 'That he hasn't forgotten about me.'

CHAPTER 41

The next day, Timothy walked into Osiris' office on the twenty-third floor. He greeted Natasha with a smile. 'Hello, Natasha, how are you this morning?'

Her rotund body filled the entire space behind the reception desk. Times had certainly changed since the days when a sexy Tricia greeted visitors, and Osiris was one of the hottest funds in the financial universe. Now Osiris was being shut down, its manager was under investigation, and its receptionist smelled like blintzes. 'Fine, Timothy. Thank you.'

'The Kid around?' Timothy was going to act on Frank Arnheim's advice: he would feel the Kid out and see exactly where he stood regarding the upcoming CFTC testimony.

'In his office.'

Timothy walked down the hall to the Kid's office. The door was closed. Timothy pushed it open without knocking.

The Kid was at his desk, with the phone cradled in his neck. He looked up at Timothy, surprised. 'I have to go,' he said softly into the phone. 'He's here.' The person on the other end of the line said something. Then the Kid smiled, as if at a funny joke. 'Yes, okay,' he said. He nodded. 'Me too. Bye.' He hung up.

Timothy cocked an eyebrow. 'Hey, Kid, that sounds like love talk. You got a new girlfriend?'

The Kid shrugged. 'Not really.'

'You have a minute? We need to talk. Meet me in my office in five. I have to take a whiz.'

After emptying his bladder, Timothy returned to his office. The Kid was already there, sitting across the desk, waiting.

Timothy circled his desk and sat down. 'So, how's it going today?' He tried to sound upbeat, chipper, without a care in the world. As if the thought of spending ten years in prison was the farthest thing from his mind. 'You have a new job lined up yet? When's your final day here? Friday, right?'

The Kid nodded. 'Yeah, Friday. I think I'm going to take some time off after Osiris. You know, just unwind for a while.'

'Great idea,' Timothy said. 'Me too.' For maybe a decade or so, in a medium-security facility. 'Kid, the reason I wanted to talk to you—'

The Kid interrupted. 'Timothy, before you start, there's something I need to tell you.'

Timothy sat back in his chair, pressed his lips closed.

'I need to give this back to you.' The Kid held

out the check for fifty thousand dollars which Timothy had given to him. 'My lawyer says it might not be a great idea.'

'Your lawyer? You mean Frank Arnheim?'

'No . . . I have my own lawyer now. From Brobeck. I think it's probably the best thing for both of us.'

Timothy thought: Not for both of us. For you.

The Kid stretched his arm further toward Timothy, so that the check was only inches from his face. Timothy stared at it, refused to take it. The Kid lowered his arm. He placed the check on Timothy's desk, laying it like a flower on a gravestone.

Timothy looked at the check for a long moment, then back at the Kid. 'Let me ask you something,' Timothy said. 'What exactly are you going to say to the CFTC when you testify?'

The Kid shook his head. 'Nothing. Just the truth.'

Timothy smiled. 'And what is the truth, exactly?'

The Kid kept a poker face. He didn't look happy; he didn't look scared; he didn't look angry. He just looked . . . like a kid.

'Is there something you don't want me to say, Timothy?'

Timothy regarded the Kid carefully. Was this a trap? Could the Kid possibly be tape recording him? He wanted to lean over the desk and pat down the Kid's suit jacket to feel for a wire. Which of course would be crazy. Or would it?

'No,' Timothy said. 'It's important you just tell the truth. Always tell the truth. That's an important business lesson I've always tried to teach you.'

He smiled and winked at the Kid. The wink could have meant anything. But in this case, Timothy stood up behind his desk, and it was clear that the wink meant the conversation was over.

CHAPTER 42

Driving home from work, Timothy used his cell phone to call Frank Arnheim.

'The Kid's going to screw me,' Timothy said.

'That's the impression I had, too,' Frank said. 'What did he say?'

'That he's going to tell the truth.'

'That doesn't sound good,' Frank said. Then: 'There's something else we need to talk about.'

'Tell me.'

'I've had a few conversations with John Allen from Shearman and Sterling. That's Pinky Dewer's lawyer. He's handling the lawsuit against you – you know, the twenty million dollars against you personally?'

'Yes, I vaguely remember that one.'

'I think they have a case.'

'Really?'

'I'm not saying that it's a shoo-in. But your actions did cause Pinky's deal to fall through, and he can legitimately ding you for the damages. That's more than twenty million dollars. Do you have that much?'

'Yeah, behind the couch, in nickels.'

'I bring it up because I think you should settle.'

'And offer what?'

'I don't know. A nice round number.'

'Zero?'

'Not that kind of round number. Maybe two or three.'

'Million?'

'I'm just throwing it out there. Now, as far as the CFTC goes, we can try to plead for mercy. You know, admit guilt, offer to make restitution to your clients, and agree never to work in the securities industry again. You could possibly avoid jail time.'

'Restitution? Frank, my clients collectively lost fifty million dollars.'

'Well, it beats prison.'

Timothy wasn't so sure. Being penniless and being incarcerated seemed about equal. At least in the slammer, if you stamp enough license plates, you can afford a pack of smokes. 'I don't know,' Timothy said.

'Something to think about. We have three weeks before your testimony.'

'So that's your high-powered legal strategy? Don't fight; admit guilt. That's the collective output from the finest legal minds at Perkins Coie?'

'Something like that.' Timothy sped down the street. Up ahead he saw his house. He turned into the driveway.

Frank continued, 'Look on the bright side. It can't get much worse.'

'Oh, I don't know about that,' Timothy said, as he saw the police cruiser parked in front of his garage.

'Detective Neiderhoffer, what a pleasant surprise,' Timothy said as he entered the kitchen.

Neiderhoffer was standing, with his notepad at the ready. Tricia sat at the table with a pained smile.

Neiderhoffer said, 'I was just asking Tricia how you two met. Very romantic story.'

'Yes.'

'Do you have a few minutes, Mr Van Bender?'

'Of course.' Timothy put down his briefcase, pulled up a chair. 'If I didn't know any better, I'd think you were suspicious of me.'

'Missing wife, new girlfriend,' Neiderhoffer said. 'That kind of thing.'

'Not missing. Dead.'

'But no body. So we can't find a cause of death. That's where the stupid people always screw up. You know, after they shoot someone, they put the gun in the victim's hand, but in the left hand, when the victim is a righty. Or they drown the victim in the bathtub, but then drop the body in the chlorinated swimming pool. Or they hit someone in the head with a hammer, and then use gasoline to burn down the house. So then we have a suspicious fire, and a smashed skull. But if I was a smart person – a Yale graduate, with a mind for numbers and finance – I would eliminate the problem altogether. Just make the body

342

disappear, and say it was a suicide. Mies van der Rohe School of Foul Play. Less is more.'

'You work on a lot of murders, here in Palo Alto?'

'One or two.' He smiled. 'Between all the eggs and shaving cream cases each Halloween.'

'I promise you, Mr Neiderhoffer. I did not kill my wife.'

Neiderhoffer squinted at him, as if weighing the value of just such a promise. Finally, he said: 'I spoke to Ann Beatty, right down the street from here. A good friend of your wife's, right?'

'Not my biggest fan.'

'She mentioned that. She also mentioned that, about a year ago, your wife talked to her about getting a divorce. Ms Beatty even recommended her own lawyer. I saw her house; I guess that lawyer must be pretty good. She seems to think that your prenuptial wasn't enforceable, since it was signed just a few days before your wedding. Did you know that?'

'No.' Timothy glared at Tricia.

'I didn't think so.'

'I think maybe,' Timothy said pleasantly, 'I ought to end this conversation.'

'Sure. It's up to you.' He closed his pad and smiled. 'No problem.'

Timothy stood, holding out his hand. Neiderhoffer shook.

'You mind if I ask one more question?' Neiderhoffer said.

Timothy smiled pleasantly. Always one more question.

Neiderhoffer continued. 'There was something that bothered me about your wife's phone call, the one she made from the beach. I mean, that's the critical part of the story, right? She tells you she's going to commit suicide. You're the only one she tells. No note. No body.'

'I told you. You can check the phone records.'

'I did,' Neiderhoffer said. 'Lo and behold, there is a phone call to your home on Tuesday morning, right when you said there'd be. So that checks out.'

Timothy thought about this. He knew the detective was not simply going to tell him that everything 'checked out.' There was a catch. What was Neiderhoffer going to spring on him?

Neiderhoffer said, 'Then I realized what's bothering me. She's standing on the beach, making a phone call? From what phone? No pay phones up there.'

'It was her cell phone,' Timothy said. Now his mind raced ahead, as if in a maze, trying each path, then reversing and trying another. Why was the cell phone important?

'Right, that's what the phone company logs say. The call to your house that morning was placed on a cell phone – your wife's. Just like you claimed.'

'So there's no problem.'

Neiderhoffer nodded. But when he spoke, the words didn't sound like agreement. 'You know what's funny about that phone call? It's the only evidence we have that your wife was still alive when you woke up that morning.'

'I'm not following you.'

'Where's her phone?'

Timothy said, 'What?' but he immediately understood.

'No cell phone in her car. No cell phone in the rocks down below. She wasn't wearing clothes when she jumped, so there were no pockets to put it in. If she drove to Big Sur, and called you from the beach, and killed herself . . . you'd sort of expect to find the phone nearby. Know what I mean?'

'I guess.'

'Because that phone call is the only thing proving you were ninety miles away from your wife the moment she died. Without that phone call, who's to say she even came home with you that weekend? The bellboy didn't see her in your car. No one saw her in Palo Alto Sunday or Monday night. You claim you drove home with her, but what if you drove home alone, after you buried her in a forest near Big Sur? Did you notice all those big empty forests down there?'

'No.'

'They're beautiful,' Neiderhoffer said. He paused, as if he was conjuring an image of the beautiful forests. Then he snapped back into the room. 'So what if Monday morning you're standing right here in this house, and you use her cell phone to call your own number. That way you

345

establish she's alive when you wake up in Palo Alto. That would have been pretty clever. Don't you think?'

Timothy felt sick. 'But you can find out. The phone company knows your location when you make a call.'

'Nowadays. On the new digital phones. If you owned a CDMA phone, or a GMS phone, or TDMA phone. If you had bought a new cell phone in the last five years, there would be no problem. We wouldn't even be sitting here. But, there we go, another weird coincidence. You guys both drive the latest cars, and you have the latest televisions, and the newest gizmos. But your wife's cell phone is four years old – old-fashioned analog. No location recorded. You could place a call from anywhere, and no one would know. But you weren't aware of that, were you, Mr Van Bender?'

'No.'

'There you go. I guess you're off the hook, so to speak.'

Timothy shook his head.

'Is there anything,' Neiderhoffer said, 'that you want to tell me? Now might be a good time.'

The detective stared at Timothy with a warm, open expression.

'I did not kill my wife.'

'Okay, Mr Van Bender.' He nodded to Tricia. 'Ms Fountain. You both have a good day.' He turned and left.

⋆ ⋆ ⋆

After he watched Neiderhoffer pull out of the driveway, Timothy returned to Tricia in the kitchen. 'When were you going to tell me that you talked to Ann about a divorce attorney?'

Tricia shook her head frantically. 'No, Timothy, I didn't – I wasn't serious. It was just talk – one day I saw Ann, and I was upset and depressed – I don't remember why – and she encouraged me . . . you know how she is – but I told her no, I wasn't interested.'

'Why didn't you tell me?'

'Because,' Tricia said, 'there was nothing to tell. Where was I going? You think I want to end up like Ann, alone in a big house in Palo Alto, with a cat and menopause to keep me company? I wasn't really going to divorce you.'

'Did you meet with a lawyer?'

She shook her head, vaguely.

'Did you?'

'Once. Just once. It was just a ten-minute meeting. It was nothing. It happened before I got sick. Months before. I just wanted to . . . to see . . .'

'About the prenuptial agreement?'

'You can't blame me.'

'I can't blame you? Don't you understand? Now they have a motive. They think I killed you.'

'Well, we can tell them. It's simple. You didn't do it. I can prove who I really am.'

Timothy laughed. He pulled a chair, swung it around and then sat backwards in it, facing her.

He ran his hands through his hair. 'You've got to be kidding. First of all, assuming they believe that you're my wife – assuming that we get Dr Ho to explain what's going on, which does not exactly seem likely to me – but even assuming we do – then what do we tell them about Tricia? That we gave her a lobotomy without her consent? You see? Either I killed you, or I did something horrible to her. There's no winning.'

Tricia reached out her hand and touched his shoulder. 'You're overreacting. You didn't kill Katherine. And you didn't kill Tricia. That's the reality. Remember that. There's no evidence that you did either thing. It's all circumstantial. He's just fishing, because things look strange to him, and he can't piece it together. But what do they have? Nothing.'

'Then where's your cell phone?'

Tricia said, 'I don't know.'

'You went to Big Sur that morning, and you stood on the rocks, and you called me with a cell phone. What did you do with it?'

'We've been through this. It wasn't me that day. I'm the backup. I have no idea what happened that day. Maybe I threw the phone in the ocean.'

'Well, think about it. Imagine that you're about to kill yourself. Would you take a moment to throw your phone in the ocean?'

'I don't know. Maybe.'

Timothy shook his head. 'I'm going to get fucked. And if I get fucked, you're going to get fucked, too.' He meant it as a let's-bear-down-and-beat-this-thing-together motivational speech, but it came out sounding like a threat. 'What I mean is, we need to figure something out. We need a plan. I don't want to keep playing defense.'

CHAPTER 43

They drove to the Arestradero Preserve in Portola Valley to hike through the foothills, away from distractions – away from police officers and lawyers and death threats. Timothy needed to clear his mind and think.

Things were out of control. Tricia's coked-up boyfriend was trying to kill him, Pinky Dewer was suing him, the Kid was betraying him, the government was threatening him with jail, and now the police thought he had murdered his wife. For forty-seven years, Timothy Van Bender had been in command of his life. He was never the smartest man he knew, or the most ambitious, or the most handsome. But he was successful. And that success bred confidence – gave him a regal bearing and easy-going comportment – which in turn comforted the people around him, and bred still more success.

But now, bad things were happening – a chain of ugly luck – and there was no end in sight. The thing that prevents success, Timothy realized, is needing it. You can always recognize a desperate man: the haunted eyes and brittle smile. No matter how hard he tries to seem casual, the desperate man is one

350

step away from ruin, and everyone knows it. To these haunted souls, success never comes.

Timothy tried to pinpoint the moment his slide began: going back to Tricia's apartment? His gamble on the yen? Holding Pinky's money? They were symptoms of a tepid kind of risk-taking, a desperate man's gambles – too little, too late – and so of course they could not succeed.

The only recent success in his life was getting Katherine back – and he had achieved that by being bold, by taking a huge risk: by drugging Tricia, and dragging her body to a laboratory, and then performing a medical experiment upon her. It was crazy, of course, and no one would believe it, but it had worked. And now he needed a similarly bold plan, a radical change of course. He could not sit back and let the Kid send him to prison, or give all of his money to his investors as restitution, or live in fear of a coke-head punk, or worry about the police pinning a murder on him.

He needed a way out. And, hiking in the preserve, with the September sun beating down on his scalp and hot dust in the air, he knew what he had to do.

They climbed Meadowlark Trail to the highest point in the park. Tricia walked slowly, to allow him to keep up. But his knee ached, and his abdomen hurt, and it was impossible to keep pace with his young wife.

Finally, they reached the summit. It was the view

351

that they had always loved: the grassland, rolling out below them, the San Mateo Bridge slicing through the blue bay, the white salt ponds that looked like pools of cream in the water.

'Look at me,' he said. His shirt was soaked with sweat. He was short of breath. Tricia, twenty years younger, hardly seemed winded. Her forehead glistened with perspiration, but she seemed vibrant, strong.

'You're out of shape. That's all.'

'I'm getting old,' he said.

'Who's feeling sorry for himself today?'

'I'm not feeling sorry for myself,' he said. 'I feel defeated. Like I've lost a chess game. All I want to do is knock the pieces off the board and start again.'

'What are you talking about?'

'I can't win. If the Kid testifies, I'm finished. I might go to jail. At a minimum, I lose everything. And I don't see an end to it. I don't see an end to Neiderhoffer digging around. I don't see an end to the lawsuits. I don't see an end to some punk terrorizing us. I need a way out.'

She squinted at him through the sun. 'That doesn't sound like the man I married. That doesn't sound like Timothy Van Bender.'

'That's what I'm trying to say. There is no way out for Timothy Van Bender. Timothy Van Bender is trapped. That's why I don't want to be Timothy Van Bender.'

★   ★   ★

He called Dr Ho's cell phone and, after a brief conversation, they agreed to meet at the office on Sand Hill Road at nine o'clock the following morning. Tricia and Timothy drove there together.

Dr Ho led them into the waiting room. 'Hello, Katherine,' he said to Tricia. He nodded to Timothy. 'Mr Van Bender.'

Tricia grabbed Dr Ho and hugged him. 'Dr Ho, thank you. Thank you so much.'

The little Chinese man's eyes barely peeked over Tricia's shoulder. He looked surprised. 'It's quite all right,' he said, into the fabric of her shirt. He extracted himself from the hug. 'Come,' he said. 'Let's go into my office.'

He led them into the tiny closet that was his office. The space was almost completely occupied by his old metal desk. On the floor, piles of papers and stacks of manila folders covered the carpet. Timothy and Tricia stepped over them carefully and slid into the tight chairs in front of his desk.

'Excuse the mess, as usual,' Ho said.

He found a folder on his desk and opened it. He scanned the contents. 'So,' he said, 'how has everything been, Katherine? Is it the way we discussed?'

Tricia nodded. 'It was strange at first. Getting used to it. The tastes are different. And the smells. But otherwise, I feel . . . like me. I feel healthy. And you know what else? I feel happy now. Much happier than before. Honestly, Dr Ho, what you've done is wonderful. I can't ever thank you enough.'

Ho seemed pleased. 'Good, good.' He closed the folder, looked up at Timothy. 'But of course, that's not the reason why you're here.'

'No,' Timothy said.

'Mr Van Bender, you want me to perform the backup procedure on you?'

'That's right.'

'Yes. After we spoke last night, I thought a great deal about our conversation. I'm afraid I can't help you.'

Timothy was surprised. 'But I thought—'

'Yes, I'm sorry, Mr Van Bender. I'm a doctor. This is a medical procedure. It's not a get-away plan. I haven't spent twenty years of my life and millions of my investors' dollars to help you commit bank fraud.'

'I'm not doing it to commit fraud,' Timothy said.

'Then why are you doing it?'

To get a second chance, Timothy thought. To knock the chess pieces off the board and play again. 'Because,' Timothy said, 'I have no other choice.'

Dr Ho clasped his hands together on his desk primly. 'Mr Van Bender, I agreed to help your wife because she was sick. She was going to die. You . . .' He gestured to Timothy. 'You're fine. There's nothing physically wrong with you. I can't simply give you a new identity. That's not what this is about.' He thought about it. 'It's not right.'

'It's not right?' Timothy asked. 'It's not *right?* Are you out of your mind? Nothing you've done in this office is right. Ask my secretary, whose brain you erased, if that was right.'

'I kept a copy of it,' Ho said, 'so that, when the time comes, I can restore her—'

'That's great, Doctor. That must be a great comfort to her. That she's been stored in a computer file somewhere. You're a real fucking humanitarian.' Timothy stood up and leaned over his desk. Ho slinked down in his chair. 'You listen to me, Ho. You and me are in this together. You helped my wife, and that's great. I appreciate it. But you did it for your own selfish reasons – whatever they are – to show investors you have a business, or to get some cash in the door, or maybe just to make sure everything works right. Maybe you weren't even sure, and Katherine was your guinea pig. You know what? That's fine. It did work, and that's great. But we are accomplices in a crime. Do you understand that, Frankenstein? We stole someone's body. We erased somebody's brain. Think about it. That will not look good to your investors. And it will not look good to the police. Should they find out.'

'Are you threatening me, Mr Van Bender?'

'Yes,' Timothy said, 'absolutely.' He bent down and lowered his face to Ho's. He looked at Ho's little wire-frame spectacles, pressing the skin of his nose. 'In fact, let me make it very clear. If you don't help me, I'm going to take you down with me.'

Timothy kept his face just inches from Ho's. He stared at the man, at his small, fine features, his smooth skin. He waited.

Ho said, 'Well I suppose I could help you one more time.'

Timothy agreed to pay Dr Ho a hundred and fifty thousand dollars by wiring funds into the same Citibank account that Katherine had used a month earlier. Dr Ho's instructions to Timothy were similar to the ones the doctor had issued before: Timothy would need to find a 'vessel' – a body into which Timothy could be restored after the backup procedure was done. And there was one other complication that Timothy had not considered.

'You'll need to commit suicide, of course,' Ho said to him.

Timothy was surprised by this.

'It's the same thing I told your wife. It's unacceptable to have two extant copies of the same person,' Ho said. 'More than the ethical issues it raises, it creates complications. Complications are unacceptable. Ideally, we would terminate one branch as soon as the backup and restore process is completed.'

'Terminate one branch?' Timothy asked.

'Kill you. But I will not participate in your death in any way. That's up to you.'

'I see.'

Ho said, 'I want you to be prepared for how difficult it will be. Because you will still be you.

Once you have been backed up, you – Timothy Van Bender – will be living a life independent of the copy you've made. Do you understand what I am saying?'

Timothy did. He wondered how he would do it, and if he would be able.

'But remember,' Ho said, 'your backup will be living its own life, independent of your initial branch. That should give you comfort.'

The plan was elegant and beautiful. He could solve all of his problems with one bold action. Was the original Timothy Van Bender suspected of murdering his wife? That problem would be solved, since Timothy Van Bender would commit suicide.

Did the original Timothy Van Bender face a ruined reputation and endless legal problems? Was he being terrorized by a malevolent drug addict? Those problems would be solved, since Timothy Van Bender would vanish from the face of the earth.

The plan required him to choose a 'vessel.' He needed to choose someone young, of course. He needed to choose someone healthy. He needed to choose someone who, if not wealthy, could rapidly become wealthy, without raising any suspicions. He needed someone, in short, who could assume the enjoyable aspects of Timothy Van Bender's life, but none of the burdens. There really was only one choice.

★   ★   ★

'Hey, Kid,' Timothy said into his cell phone, as he and Tricia drove home from Dr Ho's office. 'I'm just checking in. I know Friday's your last day in the office.'

The Kid's voice sounded far away. 'Yeah, Friday, right. I want to say that I'm sorry about the way things are ending. I hope there are no hard feelings.'

'Absolutely not,' Timothy said. 'In fact, I was thinking: maybe next week, after you've had a chance to unwind a little, we can all get together for drinks. You know, me, you, and Tricia. Sort of like old times. How does that sound?'

The Kid sounded surprised. 'That sounds great.'

'Good,' Timothy said. 'All right Kid, I'll see you tomorrow in the office.'

All that remained was the money.

It was well and good to come back as the Kid, unencumbered by murder indictments or fraud charges or a gimpy knee, but it wouldn't be fun to live off eighty grand a year in a four-plex behind the Safeway.

The Kid would need cash, at least a few million dollars' worth – enough to allow Timothy to enjoy the lifestyle to which he was accustomed.

The next day at work, Timothy shut the door to his office and called his lawyer, Frank Arnheim.

'Frank,' Timothy said, 'I have a legal question for you. Let's say I knew I was going to die, and I wanted to leave liquid assets to someone and avoid probate. What's the fastest way to do that?'

'You care about taxes?'

'No.'

'You have two options,' Frank said. 'A revocable living trust is one. That'll take you some time to set up. It's faster to just go to a bank and open a Payable On Death account. You name the beneficiary when you establish the account. Then, when you die, the beneficiary just walks into the bank with a death certificate and some form of identification, and the money is his.' Frank paused. 'Why? You planning on going somewhere?'

'No,' Timothy said.

'You're not going to do anything stupid, are you?'

'No,' Timothy said.

He set up the POD account at Union Bank that afternoon and within an hour began the process of liquidating his assets and transferring cash into the account. He sold his stock portfolio, which was about six million dollars, and then liquidated his IRA (another four hundred thousand). There was not enough time to take out a second mortgage on the Palo Alto house – a process that would have taken several weeks to close – or to move money from the Van Bender trusts into the POD account. Those assets would need to pass through probate, which was unfortunate, because there they would be slowed by the inevitable lawsuits that would hit Timothy's estate after his suicide. But Timothy figured that, after taxes, the Kid would wind up with an immediate windfall of about four million dollars, which would be a good start, and which Timothy could live comfortably off for the year or two it would take for the rest of his assets to pass into Tricia's hands.

He couldn't marry Tricia, because there was no final proof of Katherine's death. Without a death certificate, the best he could do was change his will, and to leave the remaining assets to his former secretary. That process took exactly one hour on Friday afternoon. They drove to the office of Jack Decker, Esq., the Van Bender family lawyer in San Jose, drew up a new will document, and had it notarized and witnessed by two of the law firm's secretaries.

When they left the office, Tricia hugged him and said, 'Soon this will all be over.'

The entire process of transferring Timothy Van Bender's wealth to his new vessel took seventy-two hours.

CHAPTER 44

Timothy Van Bender scheduled his own death for the evening of Wednesday, September 29.

He would asphyxiate himself in his Palo Alto garage by running a garden hose from his BMW tailpipe into the car.

It was important that Tricia and the Kid – both beneficiaries of his death – not be present during the suicide. It was important also that they have an iron-clad alibi, and that they be somewhere far away from Timothy's garage when he died.

The Plan, then, was this. On Wednesday evening, Timothy would invite the Kid over for dinner. He would spike the Kid's drink with valium – the strategy that had proven successful with Tricia weeks earlier. When the Kid passed out, Timothy and Tricia would drive the Kid to Dr Ho's office. There, Ho would perform the backup procedure, digitizing the contents of Timothy's brain, and then restore it into the Kid.

Next, the Kid – now inhabited by Timothy – would drive, with Tricia, to SFO airport, where they would board the red-eye to New York, which departed at 10 p.m. The process of buying tickets, showing IDs, and boarding the plane would establish Tricia and the Kid's alibi. In the meantime, at exactly ten o'clock, as the flight was taking off, Timothy Van Bender – the original Timothy Van Bender – would end his life in the dark garage of his 1930s Tudor.

The only problem with the Plan, Timothy knew, would be the final few minutes. Would he be able to drive back to his house and end his own life? He would, after all, still be Timothy Van Bender, still the same man, in the same aging body, with the same will to live. The other Timothy Van Bender, his backup, would be checking into a flight at SFO with Tricia. Wouldn't he want to go along?

But the more he thought about it, the more he believed he could do it. It was simply a question of will. And one thing he had was will – not smarts, just a blind confidence in his own ability to get out of any mess. Yes, he could do it. He had done harder things than that. Besides, with a little Scotch and a few valiums, how hard could it be?

CHAPTER 45

On Tuesday evening – the night before he was to die – Timothy Van Bender made love to his wife.

It would be the last time he would do so using his old body. In less than a day, he would become the Kid – a twenty-something MBA hotshot with his whole life ahead of him, with sturdy knees and a full head of hair, with low cholesterol and high testosterone. Timothy felt like a boy the night before Christmas, when the promise of the next day's gifts seemed infinite, so much sweeter than the gifts themselves ever proved to be.

They made love differently. In the weeks since Katherine had returned as Tricia, their love-making was passionate and frenzied, and he devoured her new body, wanted to have it, to grab onto her and not let go. It was the passion of a man who didn't want to lose his wife again.

But that evening, during their final night together, it was different. Their lovemaking was slow and lingering, as if each of them wanted to remember what it felt like, his old body, with the graying chest hair and soft stomach; and she kissed each part of him, slowly and thoughtfully, and he lay back and tried to be still, to record it somewhere in his mind – so he would always have it, no matter who he was.

Afterwards, she lay quietly on his chest, listening to his heart. 'I'm going to miss this Timothy Van Bender,' she said. And it sounded strange, that the twenty-three-year-old Tricia was wistful in a way that only comes from age.

'We'll still be together,' he said.

'I wonder what it will be like. I'll feel silly, being with such a young man. Like those ridiculous women you read about, the old Hollywood stars that date young boys.'

'You sound like an old lady. Look at you. You're only twenty-three.'

She held up her arm, stared at her skin. 'I suppose. Sometimes I forget.'

He said, 'Everything's going to be fine.' How many times in his life had he said that, without believing it? But tonight it was important to believe it, to keep going forward, to execute the Plan. It was important that he believe, too.

They lay together, silent. She nuzzled her head under his chin. He smelled Katherine's mint shampoo, and even though it smelled foreign on Tricia's scalp, it brought back a rush of familiar memories: of summers on the veranda at the Circus Club; of sweaty kisses at mid-court, after a tennis match; of dancing on the club's ballroom floor.

She asked: 'Do you remember our first date? In New York?'

'Our first date?' he said. He tried to recall it. 'How can I forget? The way we walked through Midtown, and we were so overcome by passion that we couldn't wait, and so we made love in the Port Authority restroom? I remember how that homeless man kept trying to barge into the stall, to shoot up, but we just ignored him . . .'

She pretended to slap him on the cheek, but her fingertips stopped midway, and it turned into a caress. 'Stop it,' she said. 'You're terrible.'

He smiled. More gently: 'What about our first date?'

'We went to a museum. It was the Met, I think.'

He remembered now: the young Katherine, still attending Smith College, confident and beautiful, striding through the marble-floored exhibition, holding his hand . . .

'We were looking at a painting. By Ducreux. It was the portrait of the Count of Bougainville.'

Even before she completed the sentence, he had a sinking feeling. This was not a wife's loving reminiscence. This was a lawyer's opening argument.

She continued: 'Except I called it Bow-Gan-Villa. I had never heard the proper French pronunciation. Remember?'

'Yes.'

'And you laughed and corrected me loudly, in front of all those people. And you said: "That sounds like a great Italian restaurant. We should

365

go there.'" She mimicked his voice, made it sound deep and stupid, like a loutish football player.

She paused, turned to him in the bed. She was waiting for him to say something, but he wasn't sure what to offer. So instead he said, softly, 'Yes.'

'That hurt my feelings. I still remember it, to this day. It was really symbolic, I think. I mean, I probably should have known.'

And even though he understood exactly where the conversation was leading, and even though he didn't want to go there, he could not think of a reasonable way to stop it. He said: 'Known what?'

'That you weren't a nice man. But I was too young. And not at all confident in myself, you know? If that day in the museum had happened later – if we'd dated when I was forty instead of twenty – I probably would have just walked away, right then and there, and never given you a second thought.'

It was typical Katherine, to inject melodrama into what had been a gentle, quiet evening. But she was right. Back then, he had not been a nice man. 'Katherine . . . I don't know what to say.'

'Nothing,' she said. 'There's nothing to say. I'm not mad.' She added: 'Anymore.'

'It happened twenty years ago. I was young, too. I'm not the same person I was. Things are different now.'

'Are they?'

He laughed. It was an involuntary reflex, because her question seemed preposterous. The evidence was lying in bed with them. His wife was inhabiting his secretary's body. He was about to transfer his mind into yet another body. His career was in ruins. He was under suspicion of capital murder.

'Yes, I'd say things are pretty different now.'

'No,' she said. 'I don't mean this.' She gestured at Tricia's – now her own – body. 'I mean . . .' She paused, turned away from him. She repositioned herself in bed, sat up, and turned to him. Tricia's gorgeous twenty-three-year-old's breasts were inches from him, and her posture – arm extended, body turned slightly – highlighted her smooth, well-defined abdomen. But despite this, Timothy felt nothing sexual. He felt – he realized – cowed. It was a feeling he often had when Katherine went on the attack. And the best strategy was to let the blows rain down, to absorb them. They would pass. And besides, as usual, he deserved them.

She continued: 'I mean, now we have a second chance. Now we get to do it all over again. But will anything be different?'

'Everything will be different.'

'How can it be, if we're the same people we were?'

'But we're not,' he said. 'We're not the same people.' He thought about it. More gently now: 'I'm not the same person. I mean, it's been twenty years, for godsakes. You think I haven't learned anything in twenty years? You think I'm the same person I was? I'm not. I've learned, Katherine.'

'Tricia.'

'Katherine,' he insisted. 'I've learned. I've changed.'

'We'll see.'

She stared at him for a long moment, as if searching for physical evidence that he had, in fact, changed. Then she called off the search and lay down on the bed. She repeated to the ceiling: 'We'll see.'

She reached over to the nightstand lamp and turned off the light. They lay in darkness, neither speaking.

Finally, he said into the darkness: 'I'm sorry for every mean thing I ever said to you, Katherine. I'm sorry for every time I hurt you.' Which was, in fact, true.

He waited for a reply. None came.

So he tried one more tack. 'I love you,' he said.

To this, she did reply. 'I love you too, Timothy. I always will love you. Remember that.'

Which was comforting enough. So he fell asleep.

CHAPTER 46

On Wednesday night, the Kid came over for dinner.

It surprised Timothy that he had agreed to come. He thought the Kid's lawyer would warn him to stay away from Timothy, or that he would be suspicious of his motives, or even that the Kid hated him too much to spend an entire evening at the Van Bender house.

But the Kid was surprisingly gracious. 'I would love to come,' he had said when Timothy had called two nights earlier. 'I would love to see you and Tricia.'

So he showed up on Wednesday night at their doorstep, with a bottle of 1997 Côtes du Rhône – Timothy would need to improve the Kid's taste in wine when he had the opportunity – and smiled at Tricia, who answered the door wearing an elegant black cocktail dress.

'Wow, look at you,' the Kid said. 'You got dressed up.' From his tone, it sounded like he expected Tricia to be wearing spandex and glitter.

Tricia hugged the Kid. 'Hi, Jay,' she said.

Timothy joined them in the doorway. The Kid

handed him the bottle of wine and stepped into the house. 'I didn't know what kind to get. I hope you like this.'

Timothy looked at the label. 'It looks great,' he said. 'I'll serve it tonight.' He shook the Kid's hand. 'Good to see you, Jay.'

He led the Kid into the living room to sit with Tricia on the couch. Timothy said, 'Let me get some drinks. Jay, what would you like? You want to join me and have Scotch on the rocks?'

'That sounds great.'

Timothy turned the corner and walked into the recessed bar area. In the living room, he heard Tricia ask about what Jay was up to these days – had he found a new job, was he interviewing, was he still living in the apartment? Timothy opened a new bottle of twenty-one-year-old Dalmore. He threw some ice in two tumblers and filled both glasses halfway with Scotch. From his pocket, he removed three blue valium tablets and dropped them into Jay's drink, then stirred the drink with his finger and waited for the tablets to dissolve.

He returned to the living room and handed the Kid the laced drink. 'Here you go,' Timothy said. 'To Mr Dalmore, aged twenty-one years.' He raised his glass.

Jay stood from the couch and tapped his glass to Timothy's. 'To old friends,' he said.

'Who are you calling old?' Timothy protested.

At which they all laughed.

★   ★   ★

They ate in the dining room, seated around the glossy ebony table, with the chandelier dimmed low and braided candlesticks flickering on the table between them. Jay had finished his first Scotch and was now on his second – which meant that he was in the process of drinking valiums number four and five. Except for an occasional slur of the word 'Timothy,' which came out 'Timthee,' he didn't seem particularly inebriated; Timothy chalked it up to Jay's young body and hearty constitution – something that Timothy would soon be taking advantage of, perhaps while polishing off some good Cabernet the following night.

They ate steaks with arugula and parmesan shavings, and corn on the cob. It was a dinner that Timothy had chosen, as the last in his old body. The Kid wolfed down his steak.

'I just think it's great,' the Kid said, 'that you two are happy together. I have to admit, Timothy. I was a little jealous at first . . .' He pointed his fork at Timothy, who sat across the table. 'But I see that you are both in love, and that is great.'

'Thank you, Jay,' Tricia said. 'That's nice to hear.'

'Yeah,' Timothy said. 'It is.'

'Yeah,' Jay said, 'I mean, love is hard to find.' He took a swig of Scotch, then put down the glass, too hard. 'Whoo. I feel good.'

'You okay there, Kid?' Timothy asked.

'Oh yeah. I feel fine. Really fine. Maybe I better slow down on the Scotch for a while.'

The candlelight created flickering shadows under the Kid's eyes, made him seem haggard. Timothy noticed the Kid's forehead glistened with sweat.

'Sure,' Timothy said. 'This will be your last glass. Just finish it so it doesn't go to waste.'

'Okay,' the Kid said. 'Bottoms up.' He downed the Scotch. 'Ahh.'

'Good work,' Timothy said.

'I feel a bit tired,' the Kid said. 'You mind if I lie down?'

'Go right ahead. The couch is over there.'

Tricia and Timothy stood and helped the Kid to the couch. He sat down and collapsed back into the cushions. 'God, I'm sorry,' the Kid said. 'I don't know what's gotten into me. Maybe if I just rest for a minute . . .'

The Kid closed his eyes.

'Kid?' Timothy said.

The Kid was asleep. His mouth dropped open and he started to snore.

Tricia poked him. 'Jay?'

The Kid was out cold.

'All right,' Timothy said. 'Let's go.'

CHAPTER 47

They dragged the Kid to the garage and loaded him into the back seat of the BMW. The first problem was that the back seat was only five feet wide, while the Kid was six foot two. Timothy pushed the Kid's shoes up into the rear windshield in order to fit the body in the car.

'Tim-thee?' the Kid said, dreamily.

'Yeah, Kid. You had a little too much to drink. Me and Tricia are going to take you home.'

'Thanks, Tim-thee.'

Timothy searched the Kid's pocket for his car keys. 'Here,' he said, tossing them to Tricia. He glanced at his watch. 'We're late.' The backup-and-restore cycle would take a few hours, and he needed to catch the ten o'clock red-eye to New York.

Tricia said, 'We'll be okay. Drive slowly.'

Timothy pulled the BMW out of the garage. Tricia followed in the Kid's Jetta. They headed toward Sand Hill Road.

As Timothy drove, he looked in his rear-view mirror to make sure Tricia was keeping pace. Again, he glanced at his watch. He stepped on the gas. The speedometer needle touched forty-five miles per hour.

He looked again in the mirror. Tricia and the Jetta were falling behind him; she was refusing to speed up to maintain pace.

Timothy realized he was a bit drunk from his own glass of Scotch. It was affecting his judgment. Even without valiums in it, Dalmore packed a punch. He lightened up on the accelerator and watched the needle fall back to forty.

But it was too late. The red and blue police lights appeared behind him, with bright high beams and three quick honks of an electronic siren.

'Damn it,' Timothy said.

Timothy pulled the BMW to the side of the road. He was on Sand Hill now, just a mile from Dr Ho's. If only he had been a bit more careful . . .

Timothy looked in the rear-view mirror. The police high beams reflected off it and highlighted a rectangle of yellow light around Timothy's eyes. He squinted. He saw Tricia and the Jetta continue driving past him. She turned to look at him as she passed.

The police officer got out of his cruiser and walked, heels crunching gravel, to Timothy's window. 'License and registration, please.'

Timothy smiled gamely. He tried to keep his mouth closed, to prevent the tell-tale odor of Scotch from leaving his car. He leaned over, popped the glove compartment. He took out the registration and handed it to the police officer.

'License please?'

Timothy reached into his pocket and pulled out his wallet. His fingers flipped through a thick stack of hundred-dollar bills. He thought about it, weighed the probabilities. Cash had worked that night at the opera, years ago, when he was caught speeding on highway 101.

His index finger rested on the dirty, oddly consoling texture of the bills. He recalled the conversation with his wife in bed the previous night, when he had promised her that he had changed. The old Timothy would have grabbed the thick wad of hundreds, waved it at the cop, comforted by the knowledge that money always let him buy his way out of trouble. But what would the new Timothy do? He was half surprised to see his own index finger leave the bills and skip to the wallet pocket where he kept his license. He watched himself remove it and hand it to the police officer, then he shut the wallet tightly, with the hundreds trapped inside.

'He all right?' the officer asked. It took a moment for Timothy to realize he was talking about the Kid, who lay sprawled across the back seat of the car, snoring. His feet were stuffed into the back window.

'He had a little too much to drink,' Timothy said. 'I'm designated driver tonight. Just trying to get him home safe. Right down the road.'

'You been drinking?' the officer asked.

Timothy thought about this. It must have been obvious to the policeman – the smell on his breath.

Maybe he was slurring his words. 'A lot less than him,' Timothy said. 'Just trying to do the right thing and make sure he doesn't get himself killed.'

The policeman looked at Timothy's driver's license, then at Timothy. He handed the license back.

Timothy took it and glanced at the photograph. It had been taken only two years ago, but he was surprised by how young he appeared. He looked at himself in the rear-view mirror. There were bags under his eyes, and his skin was pale in the police high beams. His hair was grayer now. He looked tired.

'Okay,' the policeman said. 'Take him to his home. When you get there, sit down for an hour or two, until you can drive safely. If I see you on the way back, you're going to spend the night with me.'

'Okay, Officer.'

When he arrived at the 3600 Sand Hill Road office complex, the parking lot was deserted except for Tricia, sitting in the Kid's Jetta, waiting for him.

He pulled into the space beside her and got out of the car.

'You made it,' she said. 'Any problem?'

'Nothing I couldn't talk my way out of,' he said. 'Help me get him out of the car.' They pulled the Kid out of the BMW, feet first, and sat him gently on the pavement. Each grabbed an arm, and lifted him to his feet.

'You okay, Kid?' Timothy said.

The Kid moaned.

'Okay,' Timothy said. 'Let's go.'

They carried him up three flights of stairs to Ho's office. When they knocked on the door, the doctor answered immediately. 'You're late,' he said, and looked at his watch.

'Sorry, Doc.' Timothy and Ho carried the Kid down the corridor, into Laboratory #1, and stretched him out on the floor. Timothy was out of breath.

Dr Ho walked to his computer terminal and typed something. In the back of the room, the hundreds of computer fans hummed.

'All right,' Dr Ho said. He walked to the laboratory island in the center of the room, lifted a hypodermic needle, held it up to the light, tapped it. 'Are you ready, Mr Van Bender? This is a sedative. It will help you sleep during the backup procedure. The procedure itself will be painless.'

'Where do we do it?' Timothy asked.

Ho gestured to the door at the back of the room marked 'Keep Out.' It led to Laboratory #2.

'Can I see the equipment?' Timothy asked.

'Sorry, Mr Van Bender,' Dr Ho said. 'These are the rules. No one sees the lab or the equipment. Not even the patients on whom I perform the procedure. Your wife wasn't awake, either.'

Tricia said, 'That's true, Timothy.'

Timothy regarded the doctor suspiciously.

Ho said, 'It's up to you, Mr Van Bender. We can do the procedure, or not.'

Timothy thought about it. Was there even a choice? He couldn't continue living as Timothy Van Bender. He had gotten this far. Now, all he needed was to exert his will. That was all that was required: sheer will. 'Okay,' Timothy said.

Dr Ho approached with the needle. 'Are you ready?'

Timothy turned to Tricia. 'I love you, Katherine.'

She kissed him. 'I love you, too.' Then, brightly: 'Nothing to worry about. I'll see you when you wake up . . . Jay.'

He smiled. He would need to get used to that. When he woke up, he would be Jay Strauss, the Kid. At least, one of him would be. The one that was destined to continue living. 'Okay,' he said. 'Let's go.'

He rolled up his shirt sleeve and held out his arm. The doctor wrapped a rubber tourniquet around his forearm. 'Make a fist, please.' Ho rubbed the vein in his arm. Timothy turned to look at Tricia and felt the needle go in, and then the warmth of the injection.

'There,' Ho said. 'You'll start to feel very relaxed now.'

Timothy did.

'Come,' Ho said. 'Have a seat.' The doctor led him to a plastic chair near the computer monitor. Timothy sat down. He was going to ask for a glass of water. But before the words could come out, he went to sleep.

CHAPTER 48

When he woke, he was seated in the same chair. Ho was standing over him, saying, 'Mr Van Bender? Mr Van Bender?'

Timothy's eyes fluttered open. He was still groggy from the sedative. He knew something momentous was happening, but couldn't quite remember what. He looked around the room, at the racks of computers – hundreds of them – and at the plasma computer monitor in front of him, filled with an endless string of binary digits scrolling off the screen.

'It's done, Mr Van Bender. The backup procedure was a success. An identical copy was restored into the new vesscl.'

Timothy remembered now. The Kid. He was to become the Kid. He looked down at his clothes, and at his body. He was wearing the same chinos and a white button-down shirt that he had worn to dinner. He looked at his arm – the graying hair on his forearm poked out from his sleeve.

'But I'm still—'

'You are Timothy Van Bender. The Timothy Van Bender whose line will not continue.'

Timothy looked around the room. Rows of computers hummed. 'Where's Katherine? Where's—'

'They left for the airport. They said it was important for them to catch a plane. They said you'd know what that meant, and that you would understand.'

Now it was coming back to him. He was the unfortunate Timothy Van Bender. There was another one, the lucky one, who was driving to San Francisco Airport with his wife. Timothy looked at his watch. It was five minutes before ten o'clock. Tricia and the Kid – or rather, Katherine and Timothy – would be boarding their flight soon, and would be taking off on the red-eye for New York.

'Do you remember what you have to do now, Mr Van Bender?'

Ho peered at him through his tiny spectacles. He looked sad, as if he regretted this part of the Plan.

'I know,' Timothy said. 'I need to end this line.'

'The sooner you do it,' Ho said, 'the easier it will be. Remember, you are alive somewhere else at this moment, living in another body, driving in a car with your wife.'

'I know,' Timothy said.

'I'm going to give you something,' Ho said. 'A sedative. It won't put you to sleep, but it should make things . . . easier.' He produced another hypodermic needle and held it, needle side up, near his face.

Timothy was groggy already, and so didn't protest. Ho took his arm and rolled up his sleeve. Again Timothy felt a pinch, and then heat, as the injection spurted into his vein.

'Can you get up?' Ho asked.

Timothy tried. He pushed up from the seat and stood, shaky, off-balance.

'You know what you have to do now, Mr Van Bender?'

Timothy nodded. He knew. He looked around the room one last time – at the computers, at the monitor, at the door marked Keep Out. He knew he would never return here. 'I know,' he said.

He stumbled out of the lab.

He drove back on Sand Hill, toward Palo Alto. He half expected to see red and blue police lights behind him, to be pulled over by the same officer and have to explain that, in addition to a Scotch, he was now under the influence of a mild intravenous sedative. But the lights never appeared and so he continued driving, careful to keep the speedometer needle at thirty-five.

He glanced at the clock in the dashboard. It was ten minutes past ten o'clock. At that moment, the Kid – or rather, the other Timothy Van Bender – was flying on an airplane with Tricia Fountain, who was, in fact, his wife Katherine. It boggled his mind. He felt dizzy. Maybe it was the drug Ho gave him. He found it hard to concentrate, to focus on the events of the evening. There was something bothering him, some doubt gnawing at his gut – and it took him a moment to realize that it was, in fact, fear. He was afraid of what he had to do next.

He understood what Ho meant when he said that the sooner he did it, the easier it would be. Every minute he spent alive, in his old body, made him grow further apart from the other Timothy Van Bender. If he ended it now – by driving into a telephone pole at sixty miles an hour, say, or by pulling into his garage and letting his BMW engine idle – he would exist independently only for a few minutes. He could comfort himself by knowing that his existence as a being that was separate from the other Timothy Van Bender was limited – limited only to a car ride down Sand Hill Road – a ride that was essentially meaningless, a ride he had taken a thousand times before.

But the longer he waited, the more distance would open up between himself and the other Timothy – the Kid Timothy. He would have more experiences, like the smell of jasmine rolling down the foothills and pouring through the car vents, and more thoughts, like the one he was having now. It was as if they had been standing beside each other – he and the other Timothy – and then the earth opened and a chasm split the ground between them, and grew wider, and carried them further apart, into their own worlds. The longer he waited, the further away he would be carried, the more he would live independently. The longer he waited, the harder it would be.

He was going to head home, and just do it – just pull into the garage, and close the garage door behind him, and let the car run, and fall peacefully asleep – but then he rolled down his window and he smelled the warm night air, and he decided, what the hell, why not have one more drink?

So he stopped in downtown Palo Alto, across from the train station, and parked alongside the Old Tavern. It was a place he liked to go because they kept it dark, and they let you smoke, and it smelled like cigars.

He left the BMW without locking it, figuring that, if it was stolen, then so be it, and he walked ten feet from his car into the tavern.

It was Wednesday-night dead, with a smattering of people – some college students, and a few businessmen in tight, itchy suits, looking around for girls that were not there. Timothy walked to the bar and ordered a Scotch. One more for the road. The very long road.

'Here you go, buddy,' the bartender said. He was an old man, balding, with a goiter on his head. He slid a glass of neat Scotch to Timothy. Timothy took a seat.

There was a sudden increase in crowd noise – some kids behind him were laughing too hard at a joke, and clapping their hands in drunken approval. Timothy tried to ignore it and concentrate instead on what was important – his Scotch. He picked it up and took a sip, and it warmed his throat and tasted astringent, and he thought, My last Scotch. That is good.

He did not doubt that he would be able to do it, to finish the Plan that he had set in motion days ago. He knew that he – sitting alone in a bar – was the only loose end, the only thing standing between Timothy Van Bender and success. Within hours, the lucky Timothy Van Bender would arrive in New York with Tricia Fountain, and he knew exactly where they would go next – because it was where *he* would go – to the Four Seasons on 57th Street in Manhattan, and they would check in, and maybe head to the bar for a nightcap, and then, finally, go up to bed, and fall asleep in the cold clean sheets, in each other's arms. A week or two later, when the excitement in Palo Alto died down, Jay Strauss would return to the Bay Area, and would head straight for the Union Bank on University Avenue, and would withdraw four million dollars from the POD account, and then begin his new life. He would not be haunted by the federal government, or by lawsuits from angry investors, or by a Palo Alto policeman trying to pin a murder on him, or by Tricia's old boyfriend with steel-toed boots.

He would simply live his life, alongside the wife he had known for twenty years and, together, they would have their second chance.

He finished his Scotch and put the glass down on the bar. He felt good now, and tired, and a bit dizzy. The bartender said, 'Another?' and Timothy shook his head no. He would end things here, with the last taste on his lips a good one, and an easy warmth in his belly.

The bartender nodded, and handed him a check. He took out his wallet and put a hundred-dollar bill on the bar. Why not? he thought.

He stood from the bar, and was about to leave, when he heard a voice behind him.

'Timothy Van Bender?'

The voice was familiar – a raspy, sloppy-drunk voice – and Timothy turned around to see who it was. It took him a moment to place the face: the mop of blond-gray hair, in no particular style, the two-day stubble, the bags under the eyes, and the pasty skin of someone who spent too much time awake, in dark smoky bars like this one. 'Timothy Van Bender? It *is* you.'

It was Mack Gladwell, former Exeter classmate and former blue-blood, but now simply a record-producer of dubious ability, and a coke-addict of great ability. The last time Timothy had seen Mack was in Palm Beach, three years ago, when Mack had taken Timothy for that night on the town 'Gladwell Style.'

'Hi, Mack,' Timothy said.

'How's it hanging, big man?' Mack stuck a cigarette in his mouth and then slapped Timothy on the back. 'I see you have your wallet tonight.'

He pointed to the billfold Timothy was holding. 'You're not going to leave it at some lady's house, are you?'

Mack laughed uproariously. His laugh started dry and raspy but turned quickly into a cough. He coughed cigarette smoke from his nostrils.

'You remember that?' Mack asked. 'Palm Beach? What was that? A few years ago?'

'Three years.'

'You were so fucked. Remember that? The girl called your wife. What are the fucking chances of that? You leave your wallet in some slut's house and she tracks you down and calls your wife! That is the goddamn funniest thing I ever heard!' Mack laughed.

'Yeah,' Timothy said, 'that was pretty funny.'

'But she was good going down, right?' He laughed again. The laugh turned into another cough. It took him a moment to recover. Then, suddenly: 'So how've you been?'

'Not bad. Yourself?'

'Not bad. Still doing the music thing.' He waved his hands vaguely, either to describe his career or to brush cigarette smoke from his eyes.

'Why are you in town?'

'Oh, you know. Here's where the money is nowadays. Trying to raise a few bucks.'

Timothy tried to picture Mack in a room full of Sand Hill Road venture capitalists, pitching them an Internet record label. It seemed preposterous.

Timothy put a hand on Mack's shoulder. It felt

386

hot and sweaty. He said, 'I should get going, Mack. Good to see you.'

'Yeah, you too.'

Timothy turned to leave.

'Hey, Timothy?'

Timothy stopped. 'Yes?'

'How was your surprise party?'

Timothy shook his head. 'Sorry?'

'They use my bit? Where I told that story about the wallet? I didn't know if they would actually use it, because maybe it would bring back bad memories. But it was pretty funny, so I thought what the hell – I'll tell the story, and let the chips fall.'

Timothy squinted at Mack. 'Mack, what are you talking about?'

'Your surprise party. Didn't they throw you a party a few months back? For your forty-seventh?'

Timothy shook his head. 'No. No party.'

'How about that?' Mack said. 'Son of a bitch. Well, some young girl came down to Florida to interview me. You know, the whole bit – video camera, microphone. She was from the company that was putting together a videotape for your party. They were going to make a funny tape, all your friends telling funny stories about you. I guess she knew you and me went to school together. She asked me what were some of the most memorable stories we had together. You know which one I told her, right?'

'The one where I left my wallet.'

'Right,' Mack said, 'in the slut's house. And she called your wife, who made you stay in a hotel! Now that's some funny shit!' He laughed again, and then started coughing.

'What did she look like?'

'Who?'

'The girl that interviewed you. For the video-tape.'

'Oh, hell, she was hot. Good-looking girl.'

'What did she look like?' Timothy asked again, insistent now.

'Well she had dark hair, glasses . . .'

'Blue eyes?'

'Yeah, sure, I guess.'

'What was her name?'

'Hell if I remember,' Mack said. 'I just want to fuck them, not listen to their life story.'

Timothy felt dizzy. He grabbed the bar to keep from falling. His knees went weak.

Tricia had interviewed Mack Gladwell months before. She didn't need Katherine's journals. She had researched his entire life, knew important details, had them ready.

'Are you okay?' Mack Gladwell said. 'You don't look so good.' Mack leaned closer.

Timothy shoved him away.

'Hey man, relax!' Mack said.

Timothy stumbled out of the tavern into the warm night air that smelled like jasmine and rosemary.

★   ★   ★

Now he did a neat forty miles per hour on Sand Hill Road, back to Dr Ho's. Let the cops follow, he thought. The headlights of the oncoming cars left streaks across his field of vision like jet contrails. What kind of drug had Ho given him? He tried to marshal together all the known facts, but each time he focused on one thing, the rest of the facts marched away from him. He couldn't concentrate. When had he met Tricia? She had applied for the job six months ago. He tried to think back, to recall the story she had told him. UCLA graduate? Los Angeles native? He had checked no references, didn't even verify that she had graduated from college. Was it possible that Tricia Fountain was not a ditzy secretary, but was, rather, a cunning grifter? Had she planned this entire con from the beginning, since before they met?

No, it was the Kid. Of course, the Kid. He was the brains behind it. He had the analytical mind, could see all the angles. He was smarter than Timothy; Timothy always knew it. And it was the Kid that had introduced Tricia to Osiris. He claimed to have met her at the Stanford Coffee House one afternoon, and suggested she apply for the vacant position of secretary. Now the Kid was just days away from walking into Union Bank and claiming Timothy's four million dollars. A nice payday, for an acting job.

Timothy tried to think back. The initial yen bet – hadn't that been the Kid's idea? And he knew how Timothy would react to the first string of losses: with a gambler's bravado and a stupid person's confidence. What was the plan? To keep Timothy off-balance, to drive him further into desperation, to entice him with Tricia – who was always so available, too available, Timothy now realized. Why would a twenty-something-year-old girl want an old man like him? He had fooled himself all this time.

But he couldn't quite figure it out. He knew the broad strokes of the con now: Tricia was not Katherine – of course not. How could he be so stupid? Tricia was just Tricia. They had planned it all in meticulous detail, even flown across the country to interview Timothy's old acquaintances, to get the story right. She had been a convincing Katherine, but she was not Katherine.

Which made Dr Ho what? Was he even a doctor? Of course not. He was in on the con, one more bit player, a little Asian man playing mad scientist.

They had come *this* close. They almost convinced him: that Tricia was Katherine, that his wife had been sick, and then was backed up into Tricia's body; that another version of Timothy had been restored into the Kid's body. It was ridiculous, of course. But he had believed it. They had known Timothy was a technophobe, that he would fall for the computer hocus pocus. They had come *this* close to convincing Timothy to go home and asphyxiate himself in his garage, so that Tricia and the Kid could take his money. This close.

Timothy pulled his car into the 3600 office complex on Sand Hill. He reached under his seat and popped the trunk. He threw open the door, ran to the back of the car, grabbed a tire iron from the trunk. He slammed it shut and headed for Ho's office. Now he would get some answers.

He ran up the three flights of stairs with his shoes scuffing concrete in mad rhythm. His knee spasmed. He ran faster, circling the staircase, one hand on the L-shaped tire iron, the other on the banister, hoisting his body upward in tight spirals.

He came to Suite 301. The door was closed. He was out of breath and dizzy, from either the Scotch or Ho's drug. He lifted his good leg and slammed his shoe into cheap plywood. The door burst open.

Timothy rushed inside. The room was dark, deserted. There were shadows against the wall, empty chairs that waited for patients that never came, never would come. Across the room, the reception desk sat empty.

'Ho!' Timothy shouted. 'Where are you?'

He did not wait for an answer, but slipped through the shadows, to the rear door that led to the hall. He grabbed the knob, wrenched it open.

'Ho!'

The corridor lights were off – dimmed to a feeble glow, barely enough to let janitors vacuum.

Where was that little man? He couldn't have vacated the office already. Timothy had just left . . . how long had it been? He glanced at his watch. Less than an hour ago. No, Ho was still there, holed up in his office, perhaps cowering under his desk.

'I know you're here, Ho!' Timothy yelled.

He limped down the hall, dragging the tire iron against the carpet, until he came to Ho's private office. He tried the knob. Locked.

'Dr Ho?' Timothy lowered his voice, trying to sound calm, reasonable. 'I know you're in there, Doctor. Please open the door. I really just want to talk to you. I think there's been a misunderstanding.' He knocked softly. 'Doctor?'

He waited for an answer. There was none.

So much for being reasonable. He raised the tire iron over his head and swung it into the door. On the arc down, the tip cracked against the fluorescent light case on the ceiling, knocking the beveled plastic cover. The sharp edge of the cover spun down, nicked Timothy's cheek, landed at his feet. Blood dripped from the gash on his face. The tire iron landed in the flimsy door and tore a furrow down the entire length, as if a splintery zipper had opened in the wood.

'Doctor?' Timothy said. His voice was still calm, despite the tire iron and the broken door and the blood dripping copiously from his cheek. He pulled the tire iron from the wood and kicked the door. His heel crashed through it, but the door stayed in its frame. Timothy stood ridiculously for a moment, one foot still in the hall, one foot in

Ho's office, like a ghost stuck midway while passing through a wall.

'Ho?' Timothy said. His mouth was pressed up against the intact wood of the door. He could smell his own hot breath, the strange stink of Scotch and spit and blood. He turned the tire iron around and used the grip side to smash the door, tearing open a larger hole. He peered through the split, tried to see Ho. But the office was dark.

Timothy reached through the hole and felt for the knob on the other side. He crooked his elbow, found the lock, turned it. He extricated himself from the door, entered, and flipped on the lights.

He looked around Ho's office. No doctor. The familiar furniture was still there: a steel desk occupying most of the tiny room, a bookshelf, cheap paneling on the walls. But the paper piles, which had previously covered every inch of floor space – in little stacks sorted in a way only Ho understood – were gone. No manila folders. No medical records. No trace of Katherine Van Bender's charts. No proof that she had ever seen a man named Dr Ho.

Timothy glanced at the wall behind Ho's desk. The doctor's framed medical certificates, which had once reassured Timothy about the doctor's credentials, were now conspicuously missing. Two nails, barely visible, poked out from the walls, like little thorns in Timothy's heart.

He walked to Ho's desk. He knew it would be bare, but checked anyway, pulling open drawer after drawer, wrenching them from their tracks. Empty. No papers. No documents. Just dust and paperclips and a few forlorn pens.

'You son of a bitch,' Timothy said quietly, to the empty room. He turned and left the office. He proceeded down the hall to Lab #1.

He stopped at the door and took a breath. There was an outside chance Ho was still there. Maybe the doctor had been cleaning his office – removing all traces of himself and his elaborate con – when he heard Timothy coming, and so he hid in the lab. Maybe he was there right now, just feet from where Timothy stood, behind this very door, hiding, his mind racing, trying to think of a way out, trying to string together another elaborate explanation, a series of reassuring words. And why not? Why should Ho not try? The man had fooled Timothy for this long. He had woven an elaborate, ridiculous story which Timothy had not only accepted, but had accepted eagerly. Why would Ho change plans now, in mid course? If Timothy rushed into the lab and found the doctor cowering, the little man would surely spin yet another yarn, one more story to convince Timothy he could have everything he wanted – everything – if he would just listen . . .

Now the anger bubbled up in Timothy. He wanted to kill Ho, or whatever the man's real name was. He had come *this* close to convincing Timothy to end his own life. Ho and the Kid and Tricia had planned a meticulous con, at the same time devilish and absurd. They had used Katherine, manipulated Timothy, prodded his every weakness, exploited his own personality flaws against him . . .

Timothy reached for the door. He was ready for more tire-iron remodeling work. He wanted to swing the iron with all his might into the wood. He wanted to feel the door crack beneath his fury. He wanted splinters to fly, the door to give, one solid kick to send it erupting back into the room, terrifying Ho as Timothy burst forth like an avenging angel—

Timothy turned the door knob. He was disappointed when the laboratory door opened easily. He felt himself deflate, the anger seep from him.

'Dr Ho?' he said quietly.

The room was frigid, pumped full of chilled air. The sound of computer fans filled the space. The racks of machines blinked rows of lifeless lights, like a phalanx of automatons – mute, brainless, unaware. Just dumb lights. Just props.

'Doctor?' Timothy said. But now he wondered if perhaps Ho was gone after all. Maybe Timothy had missed him. Maybe they had passed in the parking lot downstairs, but in Timothy's drug-addled state, he had failed to notice.

Timothy tried to find fury one more time. He wanted to destroy Ho, to beat him senseless, to kill the man. But Ho was hiding, maybe not even present. So Timothy decided to destroy the next best thing. He took two quick strides to the computer racks and swung his tire iron. He yelled – an inarticulate howl of anger, an animal-like scream. His cry echoed off the concrete floors and ceilings. He expected his swing to be met with soft give and brittle plastic. But the iron slammed into the metal rack and clanged, shooting a vibrating jolt of pain up his arm. He swung again, more carefully now, into a beige computer. He yelled: 'Fuck you, Ho!' The computer cracked like an egg. He hit it again. 'Fuck you!' And again.

Timothy had a rhythm going: lifting his tire iron, bringing it down on a plastic computer, cracking it open, then lifting it again.

'Fuck you! Fuck you! Fuck you!' Timothy yelled. He grabbed a computer rack and shook the metal with all his might. It was bolted to the floor, but the metal hinges began to give, and he shook more, harder, and then the rack was loose, and he shoved it, so that it fell into the next rack like a domino. Cables ripped out of sockets, and computers fell from the rack to the floor.

Timothy stomped to the last row of computers, swung at what seemed like the heart of the thing – a black metal box in the center, arrayed with blinking lights, snaked with cables. When he swung, he hoped for more – some pyrotechnics – or at least sparks and smoke. But his tire iron thumped into the metal box as if it was the hood of a car. There was a clang of steel, and then the lights in the box simply died without protest. No sparks. No smoke.

Timothy left the computers and went to the back

396

of the room, to the metal door marked 'Keep Out.' Could Ho be hiding in the second lab? Could this be his final refuge?

He stood at the threshold of Lab #2, the room where Ho had assured him that magic happened – where brains were transferred, minds backed up, personalities digitized and encoded and stored. It was the room that contained the arcane equipment, the technology so secret that no one was allowed to see it, not even the subjects of the medical procedure themselves.

As he stood at the door with his hand on the knob, a vision came to Timothy, of the door swinging open and Timothy entering . . . an empty room. Just cement floors and high ceilings. No machines, no computers, no high-technology brain transfer equipment. Just empty space, rented at eleven dollars a square foot, triple net. The cost of the con. Empty office space on Sand Hill. Nothing more. How stupid had he been?

'Are you in there, Ho?' Timothy called through the door.

He tried the knob, but it was locked. He took the tire iron, raised it over his head, and brought it crashing down on the laboratory door. Unlike the other doors, this one was metal, and it deflected the blow. Timothy swung again. The door was denting at the point he hammered, but it remained sturdily in the frame.

'Let me in, Ho!' Timothy yelled, pounding the metal with his tire iron. 'Let me in!'

He pounded the metal door, again and again, at the same point, hoping to puncture it, to find a weakness, to work his way inside. But the door met each blow firmly, gave nothing but the smallest dent.

'Ho!' Timothy screamed, louder still. 'Let – me – in!'

He wound up for one final blow, brought the tire iron over his head, stretched back, and then slammed it into the door.

The iron clanged. The door stayed closed.

'God damn you, Ho,' Timothy said. But he said it softly. He was deflated. Spent.

He threw down the tire iron. It clattered to the concrete.

Timothy turned and left the office.

He wasn't sure what to do next, so he drove home. He had been set up by Tricia and the Kid. They had hired Ho, had established him on Sand Hill Road, had bankrolled him like some kind of simu-lacra of venture capitalists, had bought fake computers and rented empty office space. Now they – like the Chinese man playing Dr Ho – were surely gone, maybe to New York, but maybe to somewhere else, farther away. The Kid and Tricia would return eventually, to Palo Alto, to collect Timothy's money, but it was unlikely Timothy would be around to greet them.

He would be in prison, probably, for murdering his wife, or for committing financial fraud.

Timothy would rant to the police and to the judge about how he had been set up, about how he had believed his wife Katherine had come back to him, inside the body of his secretary Tricia, and they would roll their eyes and think that he was angling for an insanity defense.

Perhaps the police would return to Sand Hill Road at Timothy's urging, and find that the space Ho had previously occupied was empty. Maybe even the computers would be gone by then, and the man playing the brilliant Chinese doctor would be whisked off to a safe location where he could enjoy his cut of the four million dollars.

Timothy wanted to sit down and think, to figure everything out, but his mind was buzzing from alcohol and drugs.

He drove the BMW up the quiet Palo Alto streets. The dashboard clock said midnight. The houses on Waverly Drive were dark and shut down for the night. People wouldn't venture out until the next morning, when the sun rose and it was time to make money again.

He pulled into his driveway and the gravel crackled beneath his tires. He walked up the flagstone path, through the sound of summer crickets, past the ornamental grasses swaying in a gentle breeze, and past the gnarled apricot tree. At his front door, he stopped. The door was slightly ajar – not firmly closed in the frame. He pushed it gently, and it creaked open.

For a moment, he thought that Tricia's long-haired

druggie boyfriend would be in the house, waiting for him with a switchblade. Was the long-haired boy part of Tricia's plan, too? Was he also an actor hired to play a part, to carefully ratchet up the stress that Timothy felt, to convince him that there was only one way out of his predicament – to be backed up and then restored into someone else's body? Or was he a loose end, a random mistake, a real boyfriend who intruded on Tricia's careful plan and forced a quick improvisation?

Timothy walked into the foyer and turned on the light. The hall was empty.

Perhaps there was no one in the house. Perhaps he had raced out of the house earlier that evening and forgotten to close the door firmly. He had been drunk, after all, and excited to put his own plan into effect, to bring the sedated Kid over to Ho's and begin his transformation.

But there was something wrong. Timothy looked at the black side table near the entrance. It was empty. The abstract white modern sculpture that Katherine had purchased at Big Sur had been there earlier in the evening, but now was gone.

Timothy shut the front door behind himself and locked it. At the end of the hallway a light shone. He followed the hallway, toward the light, into the kitchen.

On the floor, in a pool of blood, lay Tricia, curled on her side in her elegant black cocktail dress. On the ground next to her was the white sculpture, matted with hair and blood. Timothy looked closely at her. The back of her head was dark and wet, and through her clotted hair he saw specks of gray.

Timothy backed up a step. The dizziness that had never left him all evening grabbed hold of him and swung him around the room as if on a string. He stumbled backward, grabbing the kitchen table for support.

This made no sense. Tricia Fountain had set him up, was part of the plot to destroy him. Why was she on his kitchen floor, murdered?

He grabbed his head and tried to think, as if squeezing his forehead would keep the random bits from escaping – the images of the Kid drugged on his couch, and of Timothy and Tricia making love, and of Katherine lying face-down in the tide at Big Sur, with her long hair floating in water, fanned around her head.

At first he didn't hear her, and thought it was just the buzzing in his skull, but then she said something again. Timothy looked down, and Tricia's eyes were open, staring glassily, and her lips were moving, and she was saying something, whispering.

He bent down next to her, and his knees planted themselves in her blood, and he felt it soak through his pants and begin to spread up the fabric to his thigh.

'What?' he said.

She whispered something again, and he couldn't hear her. It was all breath, just the dry sound of lips clicking open and closed.

He leaned closer. 'Timothy,' she said. 'I'm so sorry.'

'Who did this?' he asked. He put his hand on her exposed shoulder, just above the scoop-top of the black satin dress, and he touched her soft skin, the skin he had just caressed the night before, and he was surprised by how cold it felt.

'I'm so sorry,' she whispered again.

'Tricia—' he said again.

She smiled, a tiny half-smile. 'Not . . . Tricia . . .'

'Stop,' Timothy said. 'Stop already.'

'I love you, Gimpy.'

'Who did this to you?'

'Jay. And . . .'

But then her jaw slackened and she stopped breathing. Her glassy eyes stared, lifeless, at the blood-covered floor.

Timothy stood up. His pants were stained with her blood now, and he walked across the kitchen, tracking bloody footprints across the floor. He went to the phone and picked it up from the cradle. He was going to dial 911– to have the police come and help, but then he realized that the moment the police arrived and saw his girl-friend brained to death on the kitchen floor, Timothy's freedom would come to an end. He replaced the telephone receiver. He saw that he had left bloody fingerprints on the handset, but it no longer mattered. There would be no escape.

He sat down in a chair, the same chair that he had used each night for a dozen years when he and his wife ate dinner together, and tried to think, to cut through the haze in his brain, to figure it all out.

If Tricia was here, dead on his floor, then she was not flying to New York with Jay Strauss. Which could mean only one thing: that she was expendable to the Kid, that the Kid had betrayed her and killed her. It was another loose end tied up elegantly by the Kid's mathematical mind: more money for him, one less person who knew the truth, one more murder to pin on Timothy Van Bender.

Timothy looked at Tricia's lithe body. Even with her terrible injury, she was still beautiful, and he couldn't help admiring her long, lean legs, shapely under her cocktail dress and splayed across a pool of her own blood.

Part of him felt sorry for her, that she had been taken in by the Kid, that she had trusted him and then been betrayed by him. She was just a young girl. In another place and time, she – like all young girls who are betrayed by men – would have learned from the experience, and grown stronger. But not this time. She would get no second chance to learn life's heartless lesson.

CHAPTER 49

He would turn himself in to the police, he decided, or perhaps go through with his original plan of sitting in the idling BMW with the garage door closed, but first there was one more bit of business he needed to attend to. It was unlikely that he would find him, but Timothy wanted to make sure, to see if the Kid had gotten sloppy and decided to stay around town after all.

He walked out of his kitchen and into his living room, tracking blood as he went, and headed for the alcove that contained his bar. He found the bottle of Dalmore and poured himself a glass and tossed it back. Thank you, Mr Dalmore. Now he was ready.

He got into the BMW and drove back through Palo Alto, crossed the Caltrain tracks, and headed into Menlo Park. The twenty-four-hour Safeway was open, and he passed the bright florescent parking lot, which was surprisingly busy with teens and college kids stocking up on beer and snack food.

He pulled the BMW down the long driveway that ended in the four-plex he had visited only weeks before. From the right top apartment unit, music blasted out of open balcony doors, and cheap linen curtains, lit from inside, fluttered across the patio. There was laughter, the sound of kids – young people whose only care, Timothy knew, was what might happen tomorrow. What I would give, Timothy thought, to be one of those kids, mindless of the future, devoid of a past . . .

The Kid's apartment was directly below the apartment that held the loud party. Timothy walked up the three steps and rang the Kid's doorbell. He wasn't expecting an answer, and he didn't get one.

He knocked, softly at first, and then harder. He gave a quick glance over his shoulder, to make sure that no one from the party upstairs was passing by. He turned the doorknob. The door was unlocked.

He entered Jay's apartment and shut the door. The sound of the music from upstairs was muted now by cheap drywall and shag carpet. The lights were on.

'Jay?' Timothy called out, gently. 'Kid?'

Timothy looked around. The apartment looked messy and half-emptied, as if someone had raced through it, grabbing some objects and putting them in a suitcase, tossing other objects aside. Timothy walked down a short hall and peeked into a bathroom. The toothbrush stand was wet with white paste residue, but there was no brush. Packed. Gone.

Timothy looked at it again. Two of the slots in

the toothbrush holder were wet. Perhaps there had been two brushes there, not long ago.

Timothy thought back to the time he had showed up unannounced at the Kid's apartment, with a bribe in hand, and the Kid had not let him in. Timothy had thought, vaguely, that there was a woman in the apartment, but it didn't seem important at the time.

Now he looked around the bathroom, and he saw telltale traces of a woman everywhere – the wide-gripped female disposable razor in the shower, even the feminine mint shampoo that seemed vaguely familiar to him.

Timothy walked down the remainder of the hall, into the bedroom, and here it was even more obvious: two places in the bed, unmade, two sets of indentations in two sets of pillows.

It was clear that Jay had skipped town, and he had taken a woman with him, but Timothy had been wrong about who it was. It wasn't Tricia. It was Jay's girlfriend, whoever that was – the woman who was about to enjoy Timothy's money with her newly rich young boyfriend.

Timothy shook his head. None of it really made sense. Such an elaborate charade, simply to take Timothy's money and ruin his life. It was as if someone hated him, as if someone loathed him more than anyone else in the world, as if the point of the hoax wasn't merely to take his cash, but also to humiliate him and betray him and hurt him and make him feel a burning pain.

And as he thought about this, something occurred to him.

That someone really did hate him. That someone who had been close to him had betrayed him. It was someone smart – someone much smarter than he – someone who could plan for years in advance, someone who could go through all the possibilities, see the permutations ahead of time and have a solution for every complication.

It was someone who knew him – knew exactly how he would react to each poke and prod, someone who knew his shortcomings: his over-confidence, his blindness, his ego. It was someone who knew Timothy better than anyone else knew him, better even than he knew himself.

And now he understood why the shampoo in the shower seemed so familiar. It was the same shampoo that Katherine used.

And now he remembered what Neiderhoffer had said, the afternoon he had accused Timothy of murder. There was something that bothered Neiderhoffer, and now, standing in the middle of the Kid's deserted apartment, it bothered Timothy too. If Katherine had called him from Big Sur and committed suicide there, then where was her cell phone? Why had they not found it on the cliff, where she committed suicide? Why did they not find it in that neat pile of clothes that she had removed before jumping? Why had they not found it in the rocks below? Why had it vanished on the day of her death, along with her body?

He didn't know why he felt so certain, but he saw the next thirty seconds of his life clearly, as if he sat in the audience of a play, but was reading the script two pages ahead; he knew exactly what would happen next. He reached into his pocket, took out his own cell phone, flipped open the clamshell. Of course he knew what would happen.

He dialed her cell phone number.

How many times had he dialed it in the past? As he was racing to and from his office; as he was driving home to her, or away from her; as he was lying about where he was going or where he had been, or about how hard he was working or about how much he missed her and couldn't wait to get home. He had dialed the number a thousand times, and each time it had meant nothing to him; but now, it was the most important seven digits he had ever dialed, and he pressed them with his finger shaking as it tapped the keys.

It took a moment for the call to be placed, for the radio signal to find an antenna, and for a computer to begin billing his account, and for another radio signal to go out searching for her phone, to wake it from electronic slumber and make it jingle.

The moment was pregnant and quiet, and at first nothing happened, but then something did.

From the Kid's living room came a pleasant electronic jingle, a phone ringing – *her* cell phone ringing. He followed the sound, keeping his own phone open and pressed to his ear. He found it on the edge of the Kid's coffee table, under a news-paper – the old black analog Motorola she never wanted to part with, and he realized that even that was part of her plan, to keep her old phone, the kind of old-fashioned phone that could make calls that were impossible to locate and trace. How many years ago had she started planning this?

He felt sick now, and thought he needed to sit down, but instead he vomited. The warm fluid – all alcohol and bile – splashed the Kid's floor.

He wiped his mouth with the back of his hand. He shut his cell phone and slid it into his pocket, and after a moment her black Motorola stopped ringing, too.

He sat down on the Kid's couch and wondered if he would vomit again. Nothing made sense. The only thing he knew with certainty was that he had been betrayed by the woman he loved most in the world.

But why the elaborate hoax? Why the tales of body switching and brain backups and Chinese doctors and suicide and sultry secretaries? Why not just divorce him and try to get the prenuptial agreement thrown out in court? Could she really hate him that much?

And as he sat on the couch, thinking about it, with the taste of vomit on his lips and Tricia's blood soaking his pants, he realized that, yes, she hated him that much.

CHAPTER 50

Four hours after a gardener, curious about a front door that was ajar, entered the Van Bender house and found the young girl's body, Detective Neiderhoffer arrived at Wells, on the Big Sur coast.

He pulled his Honda Civic off the dirt road called Mule Canyon, onto a dusty overlook facing the Pacific, and parked next to a police cruiser labeled 'The Town of Wells Police.' The stencil on the cruiser door – a weird diction Neiderhoffer had not seen before – suggested the cruiser held the entire Town of Wells police force. He realized after a moment that, in fact, it did.

A detective wearing a tan twill short-sleeve shirt and brown slacks sat on the hood of the cruiser, his eyes closed, his face tilted to the sun. Neiderhoffer got out of his car and approached.

'Detective Billings?'

The detective opened his eyes and looked annoyed. 'Yeah.'

'Ned Neiderhoffer. Palo Alto.'

Billings nodded.

'You find him?' Neiderhoffer asked.

The detective pointed. Nestled in a patch of bramble was Timothy Van Bender's black BMW. The car had been driven off the flat overlook, and its hood had jacked down into a ditch so that its trunk was raised a few inches in the air.

Neiderhoffer walked across to the BMW. The sun was high and bright, but a cold wind snapped off the Pacific. The wind made him nervous about the edge of the overlook. Only a skinny black link chain – knee-high, more a suggestion than a command – kept sightseers and shutterbugs from plummeting off the edge. Neiderhoffer kept his distance as he walked, an arm casually outstretched so that he might grab the chain link if a sudden gust knocked him sideways. He tried peering over the edge. He was a hundred feet up, maybe more. Below were a pile of rocks, jutting out of the water like ten-foot teeth. Waves broke hard against them, and the rocks vanished for a moment, and then reappeared as the sea washed out.

'Careful now,' Billings called. He yelled to be heard over the wind and surf.

Neiderhoffer glanced over his shoulder at the detective in order to give him a dirty look, but Billings had gone back to tanning, facing the sun, his eyes closed.

Neiderhoffer went to the BMW. He hoped to see Timothy Van Bender in the front seat, with brains splattered on the side windows and a gun in his hand. But the car was empty. The interior was intact, the black leather spotless. No suicide note.

He returned to the edge of the overlook and held onto the chain, bent over the edge, peered down. Rocks and ocean. Surf splashing violently. Loud waves. Much louder than he expected. No body. No clothes. No shoes.

'Careful!'

A hand grabbed Neiderhoffer around the waist. Billings was standing behind him. Because of the ocean sound, Neiderhoffer hadn't heard him approach.

'You know how many people we lose over this cliff, every year?' Billings asked. His mouth was close to Neiderhoffer's ear, and Neiderhoffer could feel his breath.

'How many?'

'None. No one ever comes up here.'

Neiderhoffer extracted himself from Billings' touch. He looked again over the edge of the cliff. 'No corpse down below?'

'A little hard to get to. We need to bring a boat around from the other side of the cove. We're working on it.'

Neiderhoffer scanned the water for a boat. There was none.

Billings said: 'But we're never gonna find one.'

Neiderhoffer turned. 'What's that?'

'The body. We're never gonna find it. There's a tough rip because of the cove. Anything that lands down there gets smashed up pretty good, then pulled out to sea. He's probably floating past Tijuana right now.'

'Maybe.'

'And then, you know, you don't last very long. Shark food.'

Neiderhoffer looked down at the rocks, searching for some trace of Timothy Van Bender.

'I mean, if you're asking me,' Billings said, 'he's dead. You don't survive that jump.'

'Maybe,' Neiderhoffer said again.

'It's kind of poetic, isn't it?' Billings said.

Neiderhoffer thought he was talking about the beauty of the sea down below. There was something awesome and fear-inspiring about it. It was poetic, yes.

But Billings continued: 'A man drives a couple hours just to commit suicide in the same exact spot as his wife. That's real love, isn't it? To follow your wife to the end – the very end. I know I wouldn't do that for *my* wife.' Billings thought about it. 'Well I might follow her, just to give her a little push, in case she changed her mind. But I wouldn't jump in after her.'

Neiderhoffer smiled.

Billings asked: 'How much do you have to love a woman to do that?'

'Well,' Neiderhoffer said. He was about to explain that Billings had it all wrong, that Timothy Van Bender had actually killed his wife, perhaps by pushing her from this very spot.

'Now that's love,' Billings said. 'You don't see that very often.'

Neiderhoffer pressed his lips closed, decided not

413

to speak after all. Looking down at the rocks below, the crashing waves, the foamed ocean, he wasn't sure what to think. Maybe it was love. Maybe you could hate someone enough to kill them, but still love them at the same time. Marriage was a funny thing. It made people mad.

'I don't know,' Neiderhoffer said.

He turned and headed back to his car to start writing his report.

CHAPTER 51

Palo Alto Daily News, October 1, 1999

Suspect Kills Companion, Then Self

In one of the most gruesome crimes in Palo Alto history, former hedge fund manager Timothy Van Bender murdered his secretary with a blow to the head and then killed himself by drowning himself in the sea on Wednesday night, police say.

A gardener found the female victim, Tricia Fountain, 23, dead in Van Bender's stately Waverly Drive mansion. She was killed by severe trauma to the back of her head. 'The evidence points to Timothy Van Bender being responsible for the murder,' Detective Alexander Neiderhoffer told the *Daily News* by telephone. Timothy Van Bender, 47, was under suspicion for murdering his wife, Katherine Van Bender, in August, but the police had not formally charged him with a crime. Timothy Van Bender maintained that his wife's death was a suicide.

Long-time Palo Alto resident Timothy Van Bender was for many years a successful manager of his own hedge fund, a vehicle designed for wealthy investors. But recently, according to CFTC documents released yesterday, Van Bender's fund, Osiris, had fallen on hard times and Van Bender was accused of stealing millions of dollars from his investors.

'I just can't believe it,' neighbor Ann Beatty, who lived a few houses away from the murder scene, said. 'I knew Katherine Van Bender for years. And I even met the young woman that they found murdered. She was a lovely girl. The whole thing is a tragedy.'

An autopsy is being performed on Ms Fountain. Results will be released later today. Mr Van Bender's body has not yet been recovered, but the Coast Guard is conducting a thorough search, according to the Palo Alto Police Department.

'We believe that Timothy Van Bender killed his wife, and his lover, and then himself,' Detective Neiderhoffer said. 'He was responsible for the death of two people, and the theft of millions of dollars that had been entrusted to him. When Mr Van Bender decided he couldn't escape, he ended his own life, thus drawing to a close a horrifying story.'

CHAPTER 52

VENTURE-GRAM
Daily email update for venture capital professionals
Funding News for October 14, 1999

New funding has been reported for secretive startup Amber Corporation, based in Palo Alto, CA. Sources report to Venture-Gram that Amber raised a third round of capital totaling over 30 million dollars. The round gives the company a post-money valuation of over 120 million dollars, sources say. The company's founder, Dr Clarence Ho, reportedly impressed the investor group with a demonstration of what some sources call 'astounding technology.' The investor group includes Kleiner Perkins, Sutter Hill, and Sequoia. The exact nature of the company's technology is unclear, but former employees have reported that the company focuses on brain/machine interfaces.

CHAPTER 53

The bar at the Four Seasons Hotel in Manhattan, with its cold marble and high ceilings and dim lights, was filling slowly with a typical Monday evening crowd.

Wall Streeters in Armani suits were led, with their pretty young female companions, to tables along the walls. There was time for one quick drink before the cab ride down to the Village where dinner reservations waited.

At the front of the room, a piano player tinkled jazz standards. Nearby, in the corner, a table was occupied by one couple that stood out from the crowd. They too were a mixed-age couple, but the roles were reversed; it was a young, attractive man, and an older middle-aged woman.

The woman was Katherine Van Bender and the man was Jay Strauss, the Kid.

They looked into each other's eyes and smiled. He reached across the table and took her hands in his. Wordlessly, he squeezed them.

A waitress appeared with a tray, carrying drinks. She put a Cosmopolitan down in front of Katherine. 'For the lady, a Cosmopolitan.' She laid the other drink in front of Jay. 'And for the gentleman, a Dalmore Scotch, neat. Is there anything else I can get you?'

The Kid shook his head. The waitress smiled and left.

Katherine raised her glass. 'To us.'

The Kid lifted his glass. 'To Mr Dalmore, aged twenty-one years.'

They drank to that.

AFTERWARD

Musée National du Château et des Trianons,
Versailles – nine months later

At first, he didn't notice her enter the room. He was staring at a painting, an eighteenth-century portrait of a young man in a powdered wig, with a pen nib raised delicately in the air, as if the subject of the painting were considering a mischievous poke into the eyeball of the portraitist, to keep the sitting lively.

The girl who entered the exhibition was young, closer to twenty than to thirty, and pretty, with long blonde hair to her shoulders. She wore a yellow sun dress. She held a sweaty copy of Fodor's France under her arm. She sidled next to the man, and he noticed her for the first time. She stood, hip cocked, observing the portrait. Although she tried to hide it, too much about her yelled American: the department-store map of Paris sticking out of the Fodor's, the tennis shoes, the fanny pack.

The girl stared at the portrait for a long minute, then fumbled with the museum guide. She turned the page, looking for something, but was unable to find it. She frowned, puzzled.

She turned to the man standing next to her. '*Pardon*,' she said, in passable French. '*Parlez-vous anglais?*'

Timothy Van Bender regarded the young girl carefully. There was no way this was a trap. She was too young, too befuddled. And, besides, it was unlikely anyone would recognize him. He had changed his appearance too much since his 'suicide' and escape from the United States: grown a beard, wore his hair long, traded Brooks Brothers suits for flannel shirts and cargo pants.

He looked around the room and made certain no one else was listening. 'Yes,' he said. 'I do.'

She smiled in relief. Timothy noticed that she had quite a pretty smile.

'Is this the Joseph Ducreux room?' she asked.

'One of them,' Timothy said. 'Yes.'

Something about the girl was familiar. He stared at her, tried to place it. It took a moment, and then he understood: she reminded him of Katherine, twenty years earlier. She was young, awkward, trying her best. Just a bit outclassed. But attractive. Terribly attractive.

The girl pointed at the portrait in front of them. She pointed like an American, one index finger outstretched. 'Is this . . .' She looked down again at the museum guide, turned it left, then right, tried to gain her bearings.

'Here.' Timothy gently took the guide from her.

He reoriented it, so that on the page the wall holding the Count of Bougainville portrait was at the top. 'This way,' he said. 'You're looking at this.'

The girl took the guide from him and held it in front of her. She nodded. Now it made sense. 'Thanks.' She read from the guide. 'The Count of Bow-Gin-Villa?'

Timothy froze. For a moment, he thought the impossible had occurred: that Katherine Sutter, the woman he had married, had somehow transported herself into the body of this young American tourist. But, no, it could not be. Timothy had learned — at the cost of everything he had ever had — that there was no such thing as body switching, no such thing as identity transfers. No. This girl standing beside him was not his wife Katherine. This girl was just a pretty tourist, stumbling over the same pronunciation that Katherine had, two decades before. It was coincidence, and nothing more.

The girl was looking at him. She was waiting for him to answer.

'Actually,' Timothy said, and he felt a laugh form at the base of his throat. 'Your pronunciation—'

He stopped suddenly.

The girl raised an eyebrow expectantly, and her face was open, receptive — as if she anticipated a correction, a reproof — maybe a friendly lesson in French. But the man had halted mid-sentence, as if something had suddenly occurred to him.

The young girl looked at the man. It was as if

he had been stricken, mid-word, with paralysis. He was frozen, mouth open, a smile stillborn on his lips, his head angled strangely.

Finally he smiled and said, matter-of-factly: 'Your pronunciation is perfect.'